# COMMUNITY, COLLABORATION, AND COLLEGIALITY IN SCHOOL REFORM

SUNY Series, Restructuring and School Change
H. Dickson Corbett and Betty Lou Whitford, Editors

# COMMUNITY, COLLABORATION, AND COLLEGIALITY IN SCHOOL REFORM

## An Odyssey Toward Connections

NINA G. DORSCH

State University
of New York
Press

Published by
State University of New York Press, Albany

© 1998   State University of New York

Production by Susan Geraghty
Marketing by Patrick Durocher

Printed in the United States of America

For information, address State University of New York
Press, State University Plaza, Albany, N.Y., 12246

Library of Congress Cataloging-in-Publication Data

Dorsch, Nina G.
     Community, collaboration, and collegiality in school reform : an
odyssey toward connection / by Nina G. Dorsch.
         p.     cm. — (SUNY series, restructuring and school change)
     Includes bibliographical references and index.
     ISBN 0-7914-3597-0 (hc). — ISBN 0-7914-3598-9 (pbk.)
     1. School management and organization—United States.
2. Educational change—United States. 3. Group work in education-
-United States. I. Title. II. Series.
LB2805.D67 1998
371.2′00973—dc21
                                                                        97-9047
                                                                        CIP

10  9  8  7  6  5  4  3  2  1

# CONTENTS

# ACKNOWLEDGMENTS

Many people made this book possible, and all deserve more thanks than these acknowledgments offer. First and foremost, I wish to thank my family: Don, Chris, and Evelyn. Their expressions of support have been innumerable, and I have appreciated all of them.

I also extend my gratitude to my mentors and friends at Miami University and Northern Illinois University: Ann Haley-Oliphant, Judy Rogers, Marcia Baxter-Magolda, Judy Pickle, Chris Sorensen, Connie Goode, and, above all, Frances Fowler. They constantly and consistently demonstrate their commitment to community, collaboration, and collegiality.

Most of all, I wish to thank those whose identities are concealed by pseudonyms but whose importance to this book is self-evident. I feel honored to have had the opportunity to know and learn with Dan Centers, Sheryl Hart, Bernie Lyons, and Tim Schwartz. Their generosity in sharing their odyssey was extraordinary. So it is to Dan, Sheryl, Bernie, and Tim—and to all who undertake an odyssey toward connection—that this book is dedicated.

# WELCOME TO
# CONNECTIONS:
# AN INTRODUCTION

Welcome to Connections! Your child is about to embark on a journey that few have taken before.

—*Connections Newsletter*, 1993

Change is a journey, not a blueprint.

—Michael Fullan, *Innovation, Reform, and Restructuring Strategies*

As the clarion call for school reform issued by *A Nation at Risk* (1983) has reverberated over the years, multiple strands of research have examined the attendant and continuing waves of reform and restructuring. One current, cutting across the waves like a riptide, courses through studies of such diverse initiatives as site-based management, inclusion, and interdisciplinary curriculum. All of these innovations associate their successful implementation with at least one of a trio of terms—community, collaboration, and collegiality.

Linked by alliteration and as descriptors connotative of a quality of relationship, these three terms seem at times to be used interchangeably. Yet each of the "three Cs" imparts a different shade of meaning. And all three shadings are necessary to define the contours of a relationship seen as integral to the success of so many reform efforts.

Community suggests bonds of "shared values, purposes, and commitments" (Sergiovanni, 1992, p. 46) that become the defining center for any reform initiatives. Dewey (1916/1966) also points to shared interests and goals in his standard of community: "How numerous and varied are the interests which are consciously shared?" (p. 83). With this understanding, the work of building community becomes that of achieving goal consensus, often through the development of an articulated statement of vision to

1

which all members of the school community would subscribe. Collaboration involves supplanting the traditional norms of isolation and autonomy, creating opportunities for interaction among educators. Provisions for shared planning time and staff development, for example, permeate plans designed to promote collaboration among teachers. While such arrangements foster increased teacher interaction, they are critiqued as most often generating only a surface collaboration that Andy Hargreaves (1993) labels "contrived collegiality." Collaborative structures *do* provide the *opportunity* for collegiality; but more than opportunity is necessary to collegiality.

That "something more" distinctive to a collegial relationship is elusive in both definition and implementation. For Judith Warren Little (1990), it is interdependence. For Susan Rosenholtz (1989), it involves "a stable, evolving, reciprocal relationship" (p. 67). For Joseph Kahne (1994), the collegial relationship is marked by a dynamic, ongoing, deliberative process of democratic communication. These principles of interdependence, reciprocity, and democratic communication find a unifying voice in a discussion of community by Robert Bellah et al. (1985): "A community is a group of people who are socially interdependent, who participate together in discussions and decision-making, and who share certain practices that both define the community and are nurtured by it" (p. 333). It is *this* sense of community, collaboration, and collegiality that I believe is at the heart of the relationship deemed essential to many reform efforts.

A collegial community, then, is characterized by a reciprocal relationship between the community and its individual members—each must promote the growth of the other. Notwithstanding this very Deweyan rejection of the dualism of individual and community, reconciling the traditional individualism of school cultures with the collegial community implicit in many educational reforms is not an easy task. As Little (1990) noted, "Tenacious habits of mind and deed make the achievement of strong collegial relations a remarkable achievement; not the rule, but the rare, often fragile, exception" (p. 167).

Such an exception may occur when teachers are engaged in work of sufficient complexity that a collegial relationship is essential. Huberman (1993) suggests that innovation may provide the catalyst that allows the usual cultural norms of teacher isolation, autonomy, and mutual noninterference to be suspended. In the concrete help colleagues can offer when their professional contexts overlap in the work of implementing reforms, there lies an incentive for individual teacher artisans to join together in collegial communities.

Yet the relationship between innovation and collegial communities is not unidirectional. Collegial communities also create a collaborative environment that supports a high level of innovation, high levels of enthusiasm and energy, and support for professional growth and learning (McLaughlin, 1993). Nor are the dimensions of community, collaboration, and collegiality tied together in a one-way linear path. Just as collaborative opportunities do not assure collegiality, acknowledging interdependence does not guarantee opportunities to work together for mutual benefit. These complexities render problematic attempts to neatly package implementation of those reforms which, by their very nature, demand a collaborative, collegial community among their implementors.

Further complicating the implementation of such reforms is the dynamism and unpredictability of the change process itself. Despite the abundance of reform recommendations, mandates, and initiatives, "School organizations have not been fertile ground for innovations suggested either from within or without . . . Proposals for curricular, instructional, or technological improvements have struggled and, in too many cases, gone by the wayside" (Joyce, Wolf, & Calhoun, 1993, p. 4). Furthermore, implementation studies suggest that the reform process is more often incremental and fragmented than total and systemic. In most schools and districts, many partially implemented innovations and pilot programs operate at any given time, while pervasive, systemic changes are rare.

Not only is change incremental and fragmented, it is also context-bound. As Milbrey McLaughlin (1991) reexamined the findings of the Rand Change Agent Study, she concluded that a process of mutual adaptation influenced the outcomes of innovations across implementing schools. Local implementation choices occurred within and through a local context of capacity, will, expertise, organizational routines, and resources. Moreover, within each local context, multiple and sometimes competing or conflicting environments existed. A complex web of communities within schools as well as structural conditions of teacher isolation and independence served to mediate a school's priorities and perspectives on change (Little & McLaughlin, 1993). Context matters, and understanding a complex dynamic like collegial community requires a lens that can focus light on local environments.

Fullan (1993) believes the first among the lessons of change is that local will and capacity cannot be mandated. The complex goals of change require new skills, creative thinking, and commitment. These elements cannot be coerced. Furthermore, the idiosyncrasies of local context preclude one-size-fits-all formulas for implementing innovations. Given these lessons, some policymakers have looked beyond mandates to incentives to encourage schools to undertake change.

In Ohio, both mandates and incentives served to advance educational reform and innovations agendas. Among the provisions of the Omnibus Education Reform Act of 1989 were mandates for a performance-based accreditation system, open enrollment policies, business advisory councils, and student proficiency testing. More than issuing mandates, the legislation also created the Commission on Education Improvement, which was empowered and funded to distribute incentives for innovation. As part of its duties, the commission was to select and evaluate pilot projects initiated by school districts and/or universities. Grants were made available to local districts through regional teacher training centers and venture capital grants.

Concurrently, the Ohio Department of Education's Division of Special Education developed an action plan for reform in the area of special education. This plan, entitled *Ohio Speaks: Working Together to Shape the Future of Special Education* (1990), identified eight goals and the strategies for their implementation. Along with mandates for new rules and regulations governing special education in Ohio, the plan issued incentives in the form of requests for proposals. Waiving regulations and allowing school districts to develop and implement pilot programs of collaboration between regular and special education, these requests for proposals encouraged innovation in the form of model programs of inclusion.

Thus Ohio responded to the clarion call for reform issued at the national level by creating mandates and incentives designed to encourage schools to take up the reform challenge. In 1993, one school district in southern Ohio, a school district I call "Cedar City,"[1] took up the challenge, applied for grants and waivers, and announced a new program: "Connections."

That spring, as Cedar City's eighth-grade students registered for their next year's courses as freshmen, one of their enrollment choices took the form of a new program encompassing the content areas of English, science, and social studies. This option, "Connections," would also include students identified as having learning disabilities. The four teachers who formed the Connections teaching team represented each of the three content areas and special education. Within a school organized and operated to honor the traditional view of teaching as primarily an individual craft, the Connections teaching team was, indeed, an innovation.

The interdisciplinary and inclusive nature of the program would necessarily affect the way the Connections teachers made daily teaching decisions about, for example, content emphasis, instructional strategies, and student assessment. Formerly the province of individual teacher discretion, such decisions would now often need to be made collectively. The ability of the Connections teachers to collaborate as a collegial community would play an important, indeed essential, role in the program's success.

In the newsletter that welcomed students and parents to the program, the Connections teachers likened the year that lay before them to a journey. The journey metaphor is one with precedents in the domains of change (Fullan, 1993) and interdisciplinary curriculum (Drake, 1993). But as I traveled with the Connections teachers, two other metaphors emerged as more appropriate. As this book recounts the Connections' teachers experiences, those two metaphors frame the story.

As apt as the metaphor of a journey is, the metaphor of an odyssey seems more suitable for telling the Connections story. An odyssey suggests adventures, obstacles, detours, and discoveries—evoking images of Scylla and Charybdis, Cyclops, and storms as well as battles won and a triumphant homecoming—all of which were part of the Connections experience. As an epic narrative, the metaphor of an odyssey also suggests a quest, a destination.

Within the Connections saga, this sense of direction, or vision, emerged as the story unfolded.

The second metaphor framing this telling of the Connections odyssey—ecological systems—also has precedents. Such luminaries as Bowers and Flinders (1990), Eisner (1988), Goodlad (1994), and Yinger and Hendricks-Lee (1993a, 1993b) have offered ecological systems as a conceptual framework for understanding life in schools and classrooms. The ecological metaphor also gets at the process of mutual adaptation, competing and conflicting environments, and contextual dynamics inherent in the process of change. Even more appealing, the ecological metaphor mirrors the interdependence, reciprocity, and interaction implicit in my understanding of collegial community. More importantly, inherent within the ecological metaphor is the notion of equilibrium—an environmental state in which all appropriate systems within an ecosystem connect and contribute to enable an enterprise to be functional, healthy, and productive (Yinger & Hendricks-Lee, 1993a). Because I wanted to understand how Connections (an organism) would evolve as a collegial community in particular environment (the four teachers, Cedar City High School, the 1993–94 school year), the metaphor of ecological systems offered an appropriate conceptual framework for telling the Connections story.[2]

Within the ecology of a program, school, or classroom, meaning and action are produced and composed in the mutual and dialectic interaction of physical, cultural, and personal systems. Just as Connections evolved as a collegial community during the course of its initial implementation, the systems within the Connections ecology would be dynamic, rather than static: individually, in combination, and in webs to Connections' surrounding environment. In essence, there was not *one* Connections ecosystem, but many. At various times during the year, the Connections environment would change—sometimes dramatically, sometimes more subtly. So as this book recounts the Connections' teachers' experiences, the story is framed by a mixed metaphor. At various turning points and ports of call in the Connections odyssey, attention will be given to the various ecological systems operating at that time and in that place—a charting, as it were, of where the Connections teachers traveled in their odyssey toward collegial community.

# CHAPTER 1

# A Prologue to the Connections Journey

*We hope you and your child are as excited about the coming journey as are we!*

—*Connections Newsletter*

In literature, the epic tales of odysseys began with prologues. Before the pilgrimage, journey, or adventure began, such salient facts as were necessary for the audience to know in order to understand the story were announced in the prologue. This chapter is the prologue to the Connections odyssey.

## PORT OF ORIGIN: CEDAR CITY AND ITS SCHOOLS

At the north edge of town, where residential subdivisions give way to the rolling hills of southern Ohio farmland, a municipal water tower proclaims Cedar City as "Home of the Chiefs."[1] Such a proclamation is particularly apt since the tower is neighbor to the sprawling, single story edifice that is Cedar City High School. The proclamation also reflects the prominent place of the schools in the life of the community.

Located within commuting distance of three urban areas, Cedar City and the surrounding township served by the Cedar City schools is a postcard prototype of small towns of the American heartland. With a heritage whose origins coincide with Ohio's statehood, Cedar City is described in the local Chamber of Commerce's visitors' guide in Norman Rockwell-ian terms: "Rich in history [Cedar City] tempts you with its picturesque 19th-century ambiance." Cedar City's location and atmosphere have contributed to the population growth and economic expansion the community has experienced beginning in the 1960s and continuing into the current decade. In coping with the changes growth brings, the community has faced the challenge of maintaining the stability of its historic character. The Cedar City schools have faced the same challenge.

Not surprisingly, the community's growth has had a pronounced effect on the school system. As a district newsletter pointed out, "It is practically impossible to drive in any direction in our district and not see new construction . . . And new houses and new apartments mean new students" (District keeps growing, January 1994, p. 4). Indeed, as the district's 1992–1993 annual report indicated, enrollment had been growing at the rate of about 150 students per year for the last seven years. This pattern of growth led to the current year's addition of eight science classrooms to the high school as well as the beginning of construction of a new building to house grades four and five.

This growth has challenged the district's finances.[2] The current building projects were financed through a bond levy passed in 1992, and a permanent improvement levy was passed in November of 1993. But because the district had not sought an operating levy since 1980 and because state funds to the district had been cut in recent years, a cash balance comparison included in the district's 1992–1993 annual report showed that the general operating budget had experienced a declining balance since 1990. It is not surprising, then, that the district's finances would be a concern during Connections' initial implementation.

The changes in Cedar City Schools had not been confined to physical facilities. Several changes in administrative personnel were made in the three years prior to Connections' implementation. In 1990, Martin Young assumed the superintendency; the next year brought Mike Davis to Cedar City as the assistant superintendent for curriculum and instruction; and 1992 saw several changes in building leadership, including a new high school principal, George Cerny. Under this new leadership, the district adopted a new vision statement and each school created a building mission statement (appendix A), an extensive staff development program was initiated, and curriculum innovations (such as hands-on science for grades K–4) were introduced. All of the changes were envisioned as enhancing an educational program that enjoyed a reputation for excellence (Mike Davis interview, May 11, 1993). The 1992–1993 annual report pointed to the district's North Central Accreditation and the many awards the schools had received, including Blue Ribbon Schools and state recognition for an outstanding drug-free education program. So it was against this backdrop of change within the context of a stable reputation for excellence that Cedar City schools announced the creation of the Connections program on March 10, 1993.

## THE CONNECTIONS JOURNEY SHIPMATES

As Mike Davis and George Cerny prepared for Connections and moved for its adoption, both administrators knew selecting the members of the teaching team would be of great consequence. As Davis put it, "It was critical . . . the teachers needed to be enthusiastic . . . Having teachers that parents would recognize as top-notch was important" (May 11, 1993). With only one year as principal, George Cerny's selection of the Connections teaching team was guided by three factors: the opportunities he had had for observing the teaching and interaction of his staff, the interested teachers' areas of certification and experience with the district's ninth grade curriculum, and the advice of the department chairs. Cerny also knew that he wanted at least one female teacher as part of the team. Given these considerations, the principal chose the Connections teaching team: Sheryl Hart, Tim Schwartz, Bernie Lyons, and Dan Centers. Their introductions will focus on their life and work outside of Connections, but they may also shed light on the stories told in the chapters which follow.

### Sheryl Hart, English Teacher

With twenty-five years in the district, Sheryl was the veteran teacher of the group. During her tenure, she had already taught both English and art and worked in all five buildings in the district.[3] Living and working in Cedar City for so long, it seemed that Sheryl knew everyone, and everyone knew Sheryl. Prior to coming to the high school three years earlier, Sheryl had been part of a close-knit group of teachers at the junior high. It was this "family" that saw her through her divorce and new marriage nine years ago. And family was a theme that surfaced often as I talked with and came to know Sheryl.

The joys of family and home were the focus of Sheryl's life. Homey touches—a pink bud vase with a few artificial pink flowers, a pink and white two-peg coat rack, a personal desk fan, and a thermos for her herbal tea—distinguished Sheryl's desk area. Most prominent on Sheryl's desk was a smiling picture of her three-year-old granddaughter, Katie. The portrait was there not only because Sheryl unabashedly doted on Katie, but because of its inspirational power—"Who could look at that face and not smile?" Sheryl's devotion to family was particularly evident in a May 1994 interview for the local newspaper's weekly "Teachers speak out" feature. Asked for "family information," Sheryl took care to mention each family member: her parents (retired and living in Cedar City); her husband, John; her stepson, Adam (a senior at Cedar City High School); her son, her daughter-in-law, and her two granddaughters.

Balancing her devotion to home and family with her commitment to school, students, and colleagues was not always easy. At times the two blended well—as when John and Sheryl attended Adam's wrestling matches or chaperoned a school dance, or when Sheryl brought Katie along to "'cool" for an hour's work during a weekend. Sometimes they didn't—being a teacher at the school her stepson attended at times cast Sheryl in the role of "wicked stepmother." And often, the finiteness of time brought home and school into conflict. When a teacher friend asked Sheryl to participate in a student-faculty retreat scheduled for a weekend in January, Sheryl, acknowledging that "This is just the kind of thing I enjoy" and that she hated to disappoint her friend and the students who wanted her to come, recognized her need for time at home apart from school was stronger and she declined the invitation.

The conflicted feelings Sheryl expressed in this incident revealed her deep concern and interest in her school family of teachers and students. I often heard and observed these feelings for her school family during the Connections year. Students often visited Sheryl's room, sometimes to work as a student aide or on business related to her role as a class advisor, but at times for no other reason than just to visit. One student in particular, Steven, was a frequent morning visitor. Steven shared Sheryl's interest in science fiction and was in the process of writing a story to be submitted for publication. Half-glasses perched on her nose and her neatly coifed red head bent to the task of editing Steven's efforts, Sheryl spoke with the student about his writing, his thoughts on current events, the books he had read lately, and his plans for the future. This mentoring type of relationship with students was one Sheryl valued. When asked (in the "Teachers speak out" interview) to recall the "proudest moment in your career," Sheryl replied, "Two of my former students that I still correspond with have become English teachers and credit my influence as being the reason for their career choices."

Just as her relationship with students was important to Sheryl, she also valued her ties to her fellow teachers. Often, as fourth period ended, a female teacher would meet Sheryl in the hall or peek into Sheryl's room to ask about plans for lunch. And Sheryl, speaking of her colleagues in the English hall, referred to them as "neighbors." When a teacher survey about staff morale was circulated in November, Sheryl shared her responses with me. Asked to identify her role among the staff, Sheryl had circled "mix with many" rather than "isolated"; she had circled "no" when asked "Do you feel isolated from other teachers?"; and in response to "What can we do to improve interaction between departments?" Sheryl had written "More social get-togethers . . . especially in the A.M. when we're not so tired." As she joined the Connections teaching team, Sheryl's sociable nature would be distinctly evident in the way she built her relationship with Tim, Dan, and Bernie.

Perhaps Sheryl's introduction is best summarized in her own words. The local newspaper profile included Sheryl's comments when asked why she is a teacher: "At the risk of sounding totally corny, I love it. I think it's what I do best. Except for the paper work, I love every aspect of it. I enjoy the reading, sharing, planning, writing, and working with students. I've always wanted to teach."

*Tim Schwartz, Learning Disabilities Teacher*

Tim came to Connections with fifteen years of teaching experience, the last eight within the Cedar City system. Most of his teaching experience, and all of his years at Cedar City, had been as a learning disabilities teacher. But like Sheryl, Tim also had a background in art education. Also like Sheryl, he had taught at the junior high before coming to the high school five years ago. And again like Sheryl, it appeared that Tim knew everyone and everyone knew Tim in this small community. His strong community ties came of being a native son: he was a graduate of the Cedar City Schools.

A look at the area surrounding his teacher's desk revealed much about Tim. What was immediately noticeable was the number of calendars and schedules—among them a desk calendar, a schedule for IEP (Individual Education Plan) conferences, a memo about an upcoming meeting from the local teachers association president, basketball scouting and winter sports schedules. The calendars and schedules reflected Tim's multiple roles at Cedar City High School.

The IEP conference schedule reflected Tim's role as a special education teacher. During the spring of 1993, Tim was honored at the annual county work-study banquet as "Teacher of the Year." As a special education teacher, Tim implemented the IEPs for eighteen learning disabilities students, ten of whom were ninth-grade students enrolled in Connections. But contact with parents and concerns that student goals and educational programs were being addressed were not confined to the week of formal conferences held in April. Regular documentation of student progress in mainstream classes meant constant conversation with other faculty members who taught learning disabilities students. Tim needed to set aside time, at times in blocks of two days or more, for academic assessment using instruments such as Key Math. Tim's "study skills" class, held the last period each day, derived its content from the needs of his students. It was a time for assisting students with their assignments, for providing tutoring or alternative instruction in difficult concepts or tasks, and for working with students individually or in small groups to develop strategies for success with the various elements of the high school curriculum. Filling the role of learning disabilities (LD) teacher had created two professional habits that Tim saw himself as bringing to Connections: "I see myself as one who keeps records; I write a lot of stuff down. And then I see myself as flexible. I can jump off and go wherever I'm needed. I'm used to that as an LD teacher" (September 17, 1993).

The memo from the local teachers association president reflected Tim's role as an elected building representative on the association's executive committee. The role involved both communication and politics. Politics were especially visible at two points during the school year. During the fall, seven candidates vied for two open seats on the board of education. The election took on significance as two candidates appeared to be allied to Freedom 2000, an emerging group concerned with issues of reform and opposing outcome based education in particular. The association sponsored a forum at which all the candidates appeared and later acted to recommend three candidates. Politics and the teachers association were also visible during the spring as the board of education acted to place an operating levy on the May ballot and to make budget cuts that necessitated a reduction in force. As a building representative, Tim would be actively involved in both issues.

The basketball scouting and winter sports schedules reflected Tim's role as an assistant basketball coach. Tim's interest in sports was evidenced not only in the schedules taped to his blackboard behind his desk, but also in the *USA Today* newspaper that was delivered each morning by a student aide. Invariably, Tim would scan the front page but then move to the sports section for more detailed reading. As a baseball card aficionado and collector, Tim's interest was particularly piqued during the early fall and spring by baseball reports. But with November came the scrimmages and scouting duties of his coaching role, a role that had its frustrations. As Tim commented, "Everything that could go wrong with basketball is—injuries, grades, uniforms not in" (November 30, 1993). Nor was the role without its demands, particularly on Tim's time. One morning, early in November, Tim was not at school at his usual early hour. Harried and hurried, Tim entered his room explaining, "I didn't get up until 7:05 . . . I set out my clothes last night because I know how tired I get during basketball season" (November 16, 1993). This year the time demands, even though anticipated, seemed more acutely felt. Another desk artifact helps to explain.

Amid the calendars and schedules sat a picture of Tim's wife, Peg, a fifth-grade teacher for Cedar City. As with Sheryl, the picture revealed Tim's strong family ties. For Tim, family encompassed not only his wife but also his parents and sisters and the house he and Peg had recently purchased. His mother had died two years before, and his father fell ill soon after. Frequent hospital stays led to this autumn's decision to place his father in a nursing home, a decision made easier by one sister's being a nurse there. For weeks, each PA system announcement that "Mr. Schwartz, you have a call" brought an anxious look to Tim's normally relaxed expression. Finally, early in October, Tim's father died.

So throughout the fall, as basketball season arrived, Tim was faced with the duties accompanying his role as executor for his father—duties such as cleaning out his father's belongings and selling his father's car. At the same time, work on a house being built next to Tim and Peg's home created a mess in their yard and the water softener acted up, events that would normally not have ruffled Tim's affable demeanor. But as Tim commented to Bernie one morning, "Normally that small stuff doesn't bother me, but not now" (November 30, 1993).

Just as Tim shared with Sheryl an art background, strong community ties, junior high teaching experience, and devotion to family, he also shared interests and experiences with Bernie Lyons.

*Bernie Lyons, Social Studies Teacher*

Bernie Lyons loved (and loves) his wife, his family, teaching, coaching, and the Cleveland Browns. Balancing his devotions had made Bernie a self-styled "organization freak" (October 5, 1993), paying attention to cycles and patterns of daily life. After fifteen years of teaching, nine of them at Cedar City High School, the rhythms of the school year were familiar to Bernie. For Bernie, the pattern included his usual hours after school coaching soccer in the fall and track in the spring. Bernie's household also had its school year rhythms, rhythms that reflected the work his wife, Karen, does as a county school psychologist serving Cedar City Schools and the needs and interests of their three children: Angie, twelve; Ron, eight; and Mollie, two. This year, the household and school rhythms would each have their moments of change.

Some of the moments were minor, as when Bernie's youngest child's "night terrors" disrupted several nights' sleep. Others could be anticipated in a two career household, for example, when Karen took a course for recertification during the spring while Bernie was coaching track, the household schedule became what Bernie characterized as "el suckola." But other changes were more major.

One such change came in October when the family, including the dog, moved. Each facet of the move—selling the old house, holding a garage sale, moving belongings into the new house, painting, and holding a Christmas open house—merited at least a mention at daily planning sessions with his colleagues. But without question, the change that most affected Bernie was the death of his mother in late October.

Separated by distance (his parents' home was in South Carolina) and voicing the frustration of helplessness in the face of his mother's pancreatic cancer, Bernie—like Tim—spent the early weeks of the school year cringing each time the PA called him to the office to take a telephone call. So in late September, when Tim told the group that his father was near death, Bernie said, "I know what you're saying" (September 21, 1993). The combined stresses of the household move and his mother's death took their toll: "I find myself being short with Karen and the kids. We had to go away over Thanksgiving for Karen's family, but that was hard. We're still not totally unpacked and that bothers me. The swing set's not in—I see it every time I go out the back door. We need to get a dog house. We went Christmas shopping without the kids last night, and the kid trashed the house . . . I can't veg out" (November 30, 1993).

Yet during this time Bernie willingly took on the role of representing the high school on the panel of teachers who posed questions at the teachers association's Meet the Candidates forum.

Change was not limited to home. In addition to joining the Connections teaching team, that same year Bernie teamed with the English department chair, Daisy Nelson, for the last two periods each day to teach the American history portion of an American studies dyad. Being part of this dyad meant meeting regularly with Daisy to coordinate curricula and design learning experiences. For example, together Bernie and Daisy devised a Civil War meal project for the first week of December. Also during that week, Bernie decided to submit his resignation as soccer coach for the following fall. As he explained to Assistant Superintendent Mike Davis in early February, "This is the most work I've ever had teaching."

Yet the year was not without its moments of stability. The normal rhythms of the school year—grading periods, faculty Christmas lunch carry-ins, a winter running club he formed for track team members, NCAA basketball pools, his son's participation in elementary school field day events, his role as coach for his daughter's spring soccer team, the routines of coaching the school's track team, and many snow days—made the winter and early spring a period of relative stability in Bernie's year. But one final dramatic event marked the last weeks of school: Bernie underwent an emergency appendectomy on May 22, 1994.

Certainly Bernie's year was far from ordinary. Glimpses of what is ordinary for Bernie can be seen in an October 1993 district newsletter profile that featured him. The article described Bernie's background, including his master's degree in gifted education, and offered this portrait:

> You know, he's one of those teachers that students say can be very demanding but they really like his class anyway. He's one that lives and breathes his subject—history . . . He is now in his 16th year as a teacher and says he couldn't think of doing anything else . . . His interests include sports, reading, fishing, his family, and, of course, history. When asked about his life's work, he shared these thoughts: "It's a challenge to *motivate* teenagers to enjoy and appreciate history. That's why I tried to include a variety of teaching methods and approaches in my instruction."

Bernie's loves, the changes he experienced during the year, and his busy involvement in the life of Cedar City and its schools—all of these elements would shape Bernie's relationships as part of the Connections teaching team.

## Dan Centers, Physical Science Teacher

Dan worked for ten years in industry before coming to Cedar City High School to teach physical science and physics in 1990. During the Connections year, he was enrolled in a master's degree program in educational technology. Some aspects of Dan's life and work that shaped his Connections year were readily apparent: his extracurricular school roles and his interest and work with technology. But as a quiet, often reticent, and above all a private person, it took time and rare moments of self-revelation to really get to know Dan.

Unlike Bernie, Tim, or Sheryl, no family pictures set on his desk. But as the year went by, such moments gradually revealed the influences family had on Dan. One moment came on a November morning when a student stopped by Dan's room before the tardy bell sounded. The student had brought a piece of creative writing, a "Star Trek" script, he wanted Dan to read. As the student, a classic "nerd," left, Dan commented, "Just my luck, some day I'll have a kid just like that." I asked Dan if his comment reflected that he was like this student when he was that age. "Oh, no!" Dan quickly responded, "I was a lousy student until about eleventh grade, one who would go smoking by the trees."

Through such snippets of conversation a family picture emerged. Born in New York as the last of three children (with a sister ten years older and a brother seven years older), Dan's family moved to a suburb of the city north of Cedar City in time for him to attend the large high school there. Dan's sister now lived in suburban Detroit with her family, and Dan's father made his home with them most of the time. But for about ten days of each month, his father stayed with Dan. Unmarried and living alone in a house in a village north of Cedar City, Dan sometimes found his father's visits disconcerting. As Dan commented one morning, "It drives me crazy. He goes through all my dishes in a day and a half" (June 6, 1994). Dan's father is a widower; Dan's mother died of a brain tumor six years earlier.

So when Bernie's mother was dying, Dan talked privately with Bernie. "I told [him] of my experience, so he could share. I said, 'You know I went through that myself. At least in my case and yours, you have time to say I love you and come to terms'" (September 10, 1993). One legacy Dan's mother left him was a recipe for stuffing Dan made when the family visited his home for Thanksgiving. Cooking and hosting the family gathering, a tradition begun while his mother was still alive, was something Dan enjoyed.

More visibly so than his family, Dan's extracurricular work affected his Connections experience. His role as senior class advisor claimed many a morning before classes began. After a fall fund-raising sale and a Christmas dance, the frequency of these meetings with class officers and representatives increased dramatically as the date of the junior-senior prom loomed ever closer. Myriad details—choosing colors and a song for the theme; preparing wills and prophecies; arranging for pictures, tickets, chaperones, traffic control—needed Dan's attention. As would be his custom in other situations, Dan created a computer file to organize all of these details.

These morning meetings revealed more than Dan's organizing abilities and attention to detail. They were also times when students occasionally witnessed Dan's own brand of humor. As planning at one session became a frenzy of ideas, Dan, referring to his early receding hairline, joked, "I'm getting all charged up! My hair's standing on end! *Both* of them!" Another session produced the wry comment "When I was your age, about five years ago," which immediately drew laughter. But more often, Dan's witticisms were less broad and sometimes escaped students. Such wit would not escape his teaching colleagues.

Just as he was conscientious in his work as senior class advisor, Dan also took his membership on both the district's Instructional Council and Instructional Technology Committee seriously. As one of two elected representatives from the high school to the Instructional Council, the monthly meetings exposed Dan to a wide range of curriculum issues. For example, Dan reported that the January meeting considered issues of grouping, weighted grades, and the continuation of honors English at the ninth-grade level (January 11, 1994). Such issues certainly had political overtones, as did the Instructional Technology Committee's effort to create computer laboratories from units donated to the district. Dan doubted the possibility and efficiency of this effort (November 16, 1993).

This concern for efficiency evident in his extracurricular work was compatible both with Dan's interest and extensive use of computers and with his choice of educational technology as his field of graduate study. As the Connections year ended, he was looking forward to the internship experiences he would have over the summer. A foundations course he had taken during the fall had not generated the same enthusiasm. Part of the educational technology degree program, it was a course Dan appeared to endure rather than enjoy. As the fall term came to a close, Dan commented on the course's lack of organization: "There's no text. The professor rambles" (November 16, 1993).

Dan's dry wit and self-deprecating humor, his skills at organizing, his attention to detail, and his expertise with computers and complex television uses would be evident in the niche Dan carved for himself on the Connections team.

Together, Sheryl, Tim, Bernie, and Dan would be shipmates on the Connections journey. Others also were involved in the Connections journey.

## Sojourners and Fellow Travelers

Sharon Finch, a parent of a Connections student, volunteered her expertise soon after her daughter's enrollment was assured. As a part-time art teacher in a nearby city district, Sharon's schedule left her Fridays open so that she was available during the Connections block. Sharon wanted to devise and instruct students in art projects that would connect with the Connections curriculum. In order to become familiar with the instructional units being planned, she attended meetings with the Connections teachers during the summer. So it was that Sharon Finch came to be a Connections sojourner, visiting approximately one Friday each month to provide art instruction.

Another sojourner arrived as a surprise in mid-September. Terri Gabriel, a third-year English education major at an area university, came to Cedar City High School to observe and participate in field experiences during the university's fall quarter. Terri's arrival came as a surprise because, while she was aware that a student would be coming to Cedar City High School's English department, Sheryl had not understood that the student would be assigned to her. With her broad New York City accent, Terri's "Good morning!" greeting soon became a regular part of the first-period Friday common planning time. But her presence during planning time, like her presence during Connections class periods, was that of an observer. Terri and Sheryl had agreed that during each Friday's visit, Terri would observe and assist with grading papers during the Connections block and gradually assume some teaching duties during Sheryl's afternoon ninth-grade honors English classes. So Connections students would become accustomed to Terri's presence as an observer on Friday mornings, but they would not come to recognize her as part of the teaching team. All too quickly, Terri's university quarter ended and her limited sojourn with Connections was over.

Another university student's sojourn, also a surprise, came just as Cedar City High School began first semester exams. Jim Pelfrey's sixteen-week assignment as Dan's student teacher was a last-minute affair. Jim's roommate had been paired with a biology teacher at Cedar City High School, so when Jim needed a student teaching assignment in physics, Dan was chosen as Jim's cooperating teacher. After an initial period of observing and assisting with lab work and grading, Jim assumed limited teaching responsibilities with Dan's afternoon physics classes. The harsh winter created an unusual number of snow days, so Jim's entre to Connections teaching responsibilities was delayed until February 22. But long before that, Jim's youthful good looks had attracted the attention of female Connections students. A month before the end of the Cedar City school year, Jim's Connections sojourn ended as he graduated.

Unlike sojourners whose ties to Connections were defined by days of the week or portions of the year, fellow travelers were present at Cedar City High School on a daily basis. The freshman class counselor, Barbara Matthews, would deal with student schedules, serve as a school contact for parents of learning disabilities students, and coordinate the ninth-grade proficiency test.[4] Two administrators were also fellow travelers on the Connections journey.

The Connections year was George Cerny's second year as principal of Cedar City High School. With Mike Davis, the assistant superintendent for curriculum and instruction, George had visited a program in a suburban Ohio high school that served as a model for Connections. He had also arranged for the chairs of the English, social studies, and science departments to visit and observe the program. It was also George who wrote the application for a grant of ten thousand dollars used to purchase teaching resources and pay for a summer planning stipend for the Connections teachers. During the Connections year, George would often find occasion to visit Connections classes, and he twice brought visitors from nearby schools with him. At times, his observations were for the explicit purpose of teacher evaluation, a duty he and the assistant principal shared. This year George would evaluate Tim and Sheryl. Bernie, the sole Connections teacher with tenure, was not scheduled for evaluation this year. Dan would be formally observed and evaluated by Frank Barton, the assistant principal.

Frank Barton's travels with Connections would not be limited to the role of evaluating one teacher. As is the tradition in many high schools, one of Frank's major roles as assistant principal was to deal with student discipline issues. Frank had years of experience in this role; the year would be his last before retiring. During the course of the year, several Connections students were summoned to Frank's office to see his aquarium and receive Frank's swift and fair meting out of justice—a few on a fairly regular basis. The infractions would range from tardiness to theft of school property, from continued class disruptions that merited a referral from a teacher to parking violations. But students in trouble were not the only ones who knew Frank. All of Cedar City High School—faculty, students, cooks, custodians, bus drivers—knew Frank as the voice that started each day.

## OF TIDE AND TIME: ROUTINES AND SCHEDULES

The warning bell sounded at 7:30; the tardy bell tolled at 7:35; and, while news aired on Channel One, teachers took attendance.[5] But the day truly began with the morning announcements. Virtually every day, Frank's voice could be heard throughout the building saying, "Good morning, and welcome to [Cedar City] High School." Routinely, after a sports report, after reminders of extracurricular meetings, and after verbal teacher memos had been issued, Frank concluded the announcements with his daily injunction: "Have a great day, and we'll see you in the halls." For the forty-four teachers, three counselors, the athletic director, the two administrators, and more than 750 students, the seven-period day had begun.

The four Connections teachers shared a common planning time during first period each day. The next three class periods formed the Connections block. Each Connections teacher also had a regular planning period during the fifth period, which also included a half hour for lunch. During the last two class periods, Sheryl taught two sections of honors English 9, Bernie taught the American studies dyad, Dan taught two sections of physics, and Tim taught LD classes. (See appendix B for school schedules.)

Within the Connections block, routines and schedules also emerged. At the beginning of the school year, the teachers divided the eighty Connections students into four advisory groups, with each given a color name. The ten learning disabilities students were included in Tim's group of twenty, the Red group. (Tim explained that his choice of name was based on his love for the Cincinnati Reds.) Sheryl's group became the Blue group, and Dan's was the Green group. Not content to give his group a common primary color title, Bernie christened his group Magenta. The three-period block of time allowed the Connections teachers to create various schedule options. There would be times when the entire Connections cohort met for the full block; for example, on the first day, for many of Sharon's art projects, or to see a movie. At other times, the Red group would be parceled out among the other three groups for a three-way rotation based on academic content areas. More complex was a combining of Red-Green/Blue-Magenta in a 1½-1½ period configuration balanced out over a period of three days. The block also allowed for field trips to be planned with minimal disruption to the non-Connections portion of the day.

Yet another major influence on the times and tides that would affect the Connections journey would be the Cedar City High School building itself.

## QUARTERS AND ACCOMMODATIONS: CEDAR CITY HIGH SCHOOL

Cedar City High School was completed in 1969, but many long-time residents still referred to it as "the new high school." Even without the incised concrete sign proclaiming the building's identity, the large parking lot, long driveway, and sports fields all revealed the building's character as a high school. Entering the building removed any doubt. The cinder block walls painted beige, the neutral color of the tile floors, the building directory, the bulletin boards that dotted the main hallway, and, above all, the yellow-enameled lockers all fit the decor common to most high schools. But a look down the main hallway revealed touches that were different as well.

A grouping of four chairs upholstered in a semblance of gold, one of the school colors, was arranged to create a lobby of sorts at the main entrance. Benches had been placed at intervals along the central corridor, and students often clustered there before school or between classes. Interspersed among the bulletin boards, display cases exhibited student artwork. An electronic message board and banners relieved the constant beige of the walls. It was a pleasant and clean atmosphere—no graffiti-covered walls, no signs of inattention to maintenance—that bespoke the character of the town and the student body. It was an environment that was comfortable for the overwhelmingly white, middle-class students of Cedar City.

Exploring the rooms and corridors off the main hall also revealed much about Cedar City High School. The auditorium, with its cushioned seats, large stage, and lighting and sound systems for theatrical productions, was large enough to accommodate the full student body. The gym was also designed to hold large audiences in its bleachers. Two classrooms had been designated for the Air Force ROTC program, and its students proudly dressed in their blue uniforms each Thursday. But the ROTC classroom identity was apparent only by peering into the rooms. All of the classrooms had the solid metal door and rectangular regularity of traditional school design. Signals such as the room numbers above the door, the presence of such fixtures as science laboratories, and individual teacher decoration served to distinguish one classroom from another. But by far the most salient feature, and the one that allowed freshmen to navigate their way through the halls without becoming totally lost during the first days of school, was the configuration of corridors by curricular departments. As I soon would learn, the configuration was not only physical.

This constellation pattern by department had significance for the Connections program. Sheryl's classroom (132) was located at the intersection of the English wing and the library. Bernie's room (138) in the Social Studies wing was separated from the English end of the hall by the library and the main corridor. At the beginning of the year, Dan's room (314) at the end of the science wing was quite distant from Sheryl's or Bernie's, but it was across the hall from the large study hall room (307) that would be allocated to Connections during the Connections block. When the new science rooms were completed at midyear, Dan moved to his new classroom on the extension of the math wing. Tim, whose room was shared with another special education teacher and so was not available to him during the Connections block for the first semester, claimed Dan's old room as his own at the beginning of February. The Connections teachers' scattered classrooms would affect student travel between rooms when the Connections schedule was out of sync with building periods. The scattered geography of Connections classrooms would also affect communication within the teaching team.

## THE PROLOGUE CONCLUDES

Cedar City and the high school, the Connections teachers, administrators, and others who would be part of the Connections odyssey have been introduced. Now it is time for the stories of the Connections journey to begin.

# CHAPTER 2

# *Launching the Connections Odyssey: Spring and Summer, 1993*

[Cedar City] High School administrators and teachers are preparing for what could soon become a norm in educational systems around the country. It's called interdisciplinary learning.
— "High School Prepares for Interdisciplinary Learning"

In early March, a local newspaper article about Cedar City High School caught my eye. The article quoted the high school principal, George Cerny, at length about preliminary plans to implement an interdisciplinary program option for freshmen at Cedar City High School during the next school year. Cerny explained that initial interest in developing such a program came about through a visit he and the assistant superintendent, Mike Davis, had made to observe a similar program at a high school in a suburb of an Ohio city. The article quoted Cerny: "We were so impressed that we sent up three of the school's department heads who, afterwards, turned out to be equally as enthusiastic . . . At this point it's just a matter of presenting the benefits of the class to the board, selecting the teachers to teach the class, and discussing it with parents" ("High School," 1993). As the days of March and early April passed, the events surrounding what would come to be called "Connections" came as George Cerny had predicted.

## THE SPRING OF 1993

### *The Charter for the Connections Odyssey*

Connections' origins could be traced to events that far preceded its March 1993 announcement. Back in 1990, Mike Davis had heard a presentation about the suburban Ohio program and filed it in a corner of his mind. For a time, the idea remained dormant. But by the fall of 1992, when he had been in Cedar City for a year and George Cerny had assumed the principalship at the high school, the environment was conducive to germination. By November, Mike and George had visited the prototype program, and their trip reaffirmed their interest in interdisciplinary classes.[1] That November, at the board of education awareness retreat devoted to envisioning the district's future, Mike Davis presented his agenda for long range goals and new innovations, including an interdisciplinary program for freshmen at the high school. Having perceived a clear message from the board that "We don't want to be the first to do anything" (May 11, 1993), Mike made two key points as he introduced the idea for what became Connections. First, he noted that none of the goals and innovations were "new" ideas: "all ideas are borrowed from successful programs in other districts." Then, noting that he was "cognizant of the conservative nature of the community," he stressed that the planned program would be voluntary. The seed planted, it did not take long to sprout.

The department chairs' trek to visit Connections' prototype took place soon after the board retreat; the processes of sharing their enthusiasm in departmental meetings bore fruit as teachers expressed interest in teaching the class; and a committee (composed of the four Connections teachers, the junior high principal, the junior high guidance counselor, George, and Mike) was formed to draft the proposal for the district Instructional Council's approval at their March meeting. That proposal, in effect, became the charter for the Connections odyssey.

The proposal presented to the Instructional Council (and later to the board of education) outlined Connections' structure, defining the program's three subject areas, identifying the four Connections teachers, suggesting an enrollment of sixty to seventy-five students, and providing for a three-period Connections block and an additional common planning period for teacher collaboration. But preeminent in the proposal was Connections' instructional and curricular charter:

The program—
[1] Will be open to all freshman of all ability levels on a volunteer basis.

[2] Will emphasize different learning styles as compared with the more traditional approach. Critical thinking and cooperative learning will be emphasized.

[3] Will feature essentially the same curricula for the three areas (English, science, and social studies). This will ensure an easy transition for all students to their sophomore classes.

[4] Will have a different focus on the instruction. Much of the lessons will focus on the interrelatedness of different areas. Consider a unit on the "Renaissance." The English teacher would be teaching one of the cornerstones taught to all freshmen, *Romeo and Juliet*. The social studies teacher would be teaching how the needs of the "Renaissance" society led to the exploration and settling of other parts of the world. The science teacher would be teaching the great scientific discoveries of the time and how societal needs fuel scientific discovery. The learning styles expert is meanwhile helping all students to use their own personal learning styles to their best advantage. All four teachers would be crossing over subject areas and supporting each other. (Instructional Council meeting agenda, March 3, 1993)

The "Renaissance" example would often be cited in the weeks ahead—appearing in the district's March newsletter to all Cedar City residents and at the annual eighth grade parent meeting designed to orient parents to high school programs and answer their questions as they completed registration for their children's ninth-grade courses.

By March 10, when Mike Davis held a meeting with the Connections teachers, the Instructional Council had endorsed the proposal, and ratification by the board was expected within a week. So the meeting's agenda centered on the next phase of Connections' launching: voyagers and provisions for the Connections odyssey.

*Voyagers*

The March newspaper article reported that "[Cerny] said no students have been asked whether or not they'd be interested in an interdisciplinary class, however [Cerny] said he believes the students will be eager for this educational opportunity." Consequently, one of the items discussed during the March 10 meeting concerned securing the parental support necessary to a sufficient voluntary student enrollment. While the Connections teachers would meet with eighth-grade students to present the program as part of the registration process, Mike Davis recognized that "Because this program is a significant change, parent[s] will help to spread enthusiasm and excitement for the program" (meeting agenda). The forum for initially generating that parental support was the ninth-grade registration parent meeting held on April 6, 1993.

That evening I observed as George Cerny presided as approximately fifty parents gathered in the high school auditorium. Upon entering, each parent had been presented with a meeting agenda, a list of extracurricular activities open to freshmen, and a Connections information sheet (a 12-point variation on the Connections charter). Following the agenda, George introduced the various faculty members who would acquaint the audience with all that the high school had to offer. After the athletic program, the academic recognition program, and the offerings of each of the departments (in alphabetical order from Air Force Junior ROTC to special education) had been described, George turned the parents' attention to the Connections handout. Stressing that Connections was an option available to students of all ability levels (the first item of the twelve points of descriptive information included in the handout), George summarized Connections' characteristics—the block schedule, the opportunity to work in cooperative groups on projects, the interdisciplinary possibilities—that would "hopefully enhance education" for those students who joined the Connections cohort. Emphasizing that Connections was not "all mapped out" and that the district did not have "further plans" for extending or mandating the Connections format beyond its present charter, George opened the forum to questions. A few parents, perhaps prompted by the handout's sixth point ("sufficient teacher training will take place in the summer of 1993"), asked about the content of teacher training and the texts that would be used. Despite the handout's reassurances that students would be "prepared for the same sophomore classes they would have been eligible for if they had stayed in the traditional program" and that "Connections will be different but not easier or less challenging," more than a few raised questions about the curriculum. Would it remain skill based? Would it prepare students adequately for the state proficiency tests? Would the same course content be covered? Several questioned the program's heterogeneous approach: How would grading be affected by group projects? Would honors students still receive a weighted English grade? Would Connections be able to serve learning disabilities students well while challenging the full range of Connections students?

Assisting George in fielding these questions, Daisy Nelson (chair of the English department) endorsed the program and its teachers, observing that when students study patterns, "they learn more," that the writing requirements would be intensive, and that the Connections teachers "are old pros" capable of meeting a broad range of student needs while balancing important elements of the curriculum. George echoed Daisy's vote of confidence, indicating that the administration had entrusted the program's design to the Connections teachers, believing that they "are professional enough" to "take the information available and develop it." While reiterating that Connections was "not for everyone," George averred that the Connections teachers were committed to offering students "the benefit of the best education we can give them." As the meeting drew to a close, George extended an invitation to parents with questions to contact him so that he might arrange a follow up meeting for them with the Connections teachers.

Three weeks later, on April 27 when the Connections teachers again met with Mike Davis, the first item on the agenda was "Congratulations on a good P.R. job." With some registrations still outstanding, more than ninety students had signed up for Connections. Only one matter remained to be resolved. Apparently, the junior high LD teacher had not received the word that all ninth-grade LD students would need to be enrolled in Connections if Tim was to be able to be part of the teaching team and serve all of his students. So at the spring's annual IEP meetings, the junior high teacher had been telling some parents that Connections would not be appropriate, that the students needed more structure or "can't cut it." But confident that that situation would be settled soon, Mike praised the Connections teachers for the "good things" he had heard about the follow-up meeting with parents and about their recruiting trips to the junior high. Assured of sufficient student "voyagers," the Connections odyssey was a "go."

*Stowaway or Passenger?*

Students would not be the only wayfarers on the Connections odyssey. After reading the about the preparations for Connections in the local newspaper, I telephoned Mike Davis, expressed my interest in Connections as a focus of study, and asked his permission to attend the parent orientation meeting. Davis was more than willing to facilitate my access to Connections, but he asked that I contact George Cerny for his approval as well. Mr. Cerny not only accommodated my request but arranged time to meet with me during the week after the parent meeting. As the days of March and early April passed, I kept in contact with the two administrators. I "stowed away" to attend the April 6 parent meeting, blending into the crowd and remaining anonymous to all except Mr. Davis and Mr. Cerny. As Connections gained sufficient enrollment to assure that implementation would proceed, both Mike and George gave their approval for my studying Connections' initial implementation. But they did so with two caveats. The first was that I would not be permitted to interview students either individually or in groups. Their stated concern was that the student learning experience and routine not be interrupted or disrupted by the time any such interviews would take. The second caveat was that permission to join the odyssey ultimately would need to come from the four Connections teachers—"It's their program" (George Cerny interview, April 20, 1993). So it was that I came to be invited to attend Mike Davis's meeting with the teaching team on April 27.

The last item on that meeting's agenda, "Other," provided time for me to introduce myself and describe my interest in Connections. With but a few minutes remaining before the start of the school day, time did not permit more than a surface introduction of my professional background and a brief mention of the aspects of Connections in which I was particularly interested. Certainly I did not feel comfortable asking the teachers to allow me to accompany them on their Connections odyssey given such a limited introduction and no opportunity for discussion with me or among themselves. So I sent a letter of proposal to the teachers (appendix C) for their consideration, hoping to become a passenger, rather than a stowaway, on the Connections odyssey.

As I later talked with the teachers individually during the first week of May, no concerns were raised; no questions were asked of me. Instead, as they spoke about the journey ahead, each face and voice took on an animated quality. As we talked, it became clear to me that the four teachers felt that they were about to embark on an adventurous journey, an odyssey, and that they would be only too glad to have a passenger who might become a log keeper to chronicle the journey.

*Provisions*

The docket for the April 27 meeting included more than my petition for passenger status and Mike's acclamation for the Connections odyssey's full booking of student passengers. The greatest portion of the agenda concerned provisions for the odyssey: the resources to meet teacher needs, the materials resources Connections would need, and summer planning and training opportunities.

While his meeting agenda noted that he had "no concern about subject matter expertise," Mike Davis did list several "new skills/strategies to learn or strengthen" in preparation for Connections: learning styles, cooperative learning, and performance/portfolio assessment. A district staff development initiative in the area of cooperative learning had been launched the previous summer, and Mike urged those who had not taken that workshop (Dan, Bernie, and Tim) to sign up for the coming summer's session to be held the first week of August. Sheryl was aware of a workshop to be offered in July by an area college, a workshop that promised to stress thematic units in portfolio development. Both she and Tim expressed interest in attending it. Promising to provide whatever support the teachers might identify as necessary to meet their needs, Mike moved on to materials ordering.

Two grants were available to fund materials, one that expired at the end of June and one that would be available throughout the school year. Only one item, a computer, had been specified in either grant. Given his knowledge and expertise with computers, Dan wanted to be involved in the selection of computer hardware, and the other teachers deferred to his expertise in that decision. But with the June 30 deadline looming for a goodly portion of their spending decisions, Bernie asked that the teachers be given a "professional day" before the end of the school year as a time to "crunch ideas." Sheryl concurred: "It would help us to know what to order."

While a significant part of the grant monies would be allocated to books and other teaching materials and supplies, a portion had been set aside for providing a summer stipend for the Connections teachers as they devoted time to "collaborative development" during the summer. By mid-May, the Connections teachers had set their summer schedule: Sheryl and Tim would attend a portfolio assessment workshop during the third week of July; Bernie, Dan, and Tim would devote the first week of August to the district cooperative learning offering; and team meeting dates had been chosen—three in June, two in July, and two in August. The summer, and these seven gatherings for "collaborative development" especially, would be an important milestone in the Connections odyssey.

## THE SUMMER OF 1993

Eschewing the school as a meeting place ("It's not air conditioned"), the Connections teachers decided to convene their summer planning meetings in each other's homes. These meetings were devoted to securing supplies, creating an itinerary, and organizing themselves as a crew for the journey ahead. Sheryl volunteered as the first host.

### Securing Supplies

Sporting the casual garb of summer, the four teachers sat around Sheryl's kitchen table on a Tuesday afternoon in mid-June to share ideas and the strawberries Sheryl had just picked from her garden. Their task, as they pored over catalogs, was to spend that grant money which carried an end-of-June deadline. As Dan concentrated on computer software (and CD-ROM data bases in particular), Sheryl and Tim considered the availability of audiotapes of those books that would be the literature base of Connections' English component. Periodically during their intent catalog searches, a thought would be raised for the group's consideration.

Sheryl mused aloud about "basic materials" like poster board and markers. Tim asked the group's approval for ordering an assignment notebook for each Connections student. Dan wanted to know whether the order would mean that its use would be required of students. Tim's response reflected his experience as an LD teacher—the assignment notebook would be an aid to developing good study habits. Dan also audibly pondered the notion of including the lab book that would be required for science, a requirement he had not submitted to be included in the school fee structure.[2] But he opted to follow the precedent of making this item an individual student purchase. Bernie raised the issue of communications—with administrators, with parents—and observed that "if this is going to fly, we should do it ourselves." Tim wondered if he would have any access to the room he would be sharing with another special education teacher during the morning periods that comprised the Connections block. After all, a computer, typewriter, and individual study carrels were available there. As the afternoon waned, the teachers discovered their task remained unfinished. So Sheryl suggested that they each bring an itemized, prioritized list to the meeting to be held two days later at Tim's home. So it was that on a warm Thursday afternoon, while Bernie's son amused himself by sifting through Tim's baseball card collection, the ordering was completed, and Sheryl and Tim promised to take care of the requisition paperwork. That work completed, the focus shifted to issues of curriculum and instruction, the topics of the next week's session with Betsy Grant, one of the teachers George, Mike, and the department chairs had met while observing Connections' prototype.

*Creating an Itinerary*

Armed with samples of student projects, videotapes of her program's first day and midyear activities, and copies of newsletters, assessment rubrics, and articles about interdisciplinary study, Betsy came at Mike Davis's invitation. Mike and George had perceived Betsy, a science teacher, to be "the strongest" member of the teaching team that had been Connections' prototype. Mike asked her to come to Cedar City and share her experiences.

While Bernie, Tim, Sheryl, Dan, and Mike munched on Bernie's chips and homemade salsa, Betsy displayed student projects and artifacts from her program. Impressive examples of student projects, handouts, and reading lists were passed around and carefully inspected. Adjourning to Bernie's family room, the Connections teachers oohed and aahed at two videotapes. The first recorded Building Bridges, a first-day activity Betsy's team had devised as an introduction and transition to their program's interdisciplinary focus. The second showed the Renaissance Fair, the culmination of the first semester. After outlining the procedures (e.g., reading response journals) and practices (e.g., issuing grades of only A, B, or incomplete) her team had utilized, Betsy was open to questions. Sheryl asked about materials for project displays and how that cost was handled. Mike asked about the scheduling options Betsy's team had devised within their program block. Dan asked about whether she had encountered any difficulties in connecting science to English and history. To each question, Betsy offered her best advice: generally students and parents supplied the materials for individual projects; schedule options included full-block, three-way rotation, and a combination of those two patterns; and "Yes . . . It's okay to not connect" for a two or three-week mini-unit occasionally. Later in the summer, during the second week of August, Betsy would return to Cedar City for consultation of the "nitty gritty" sort—helping to edit the Connections newsletter, looking at the classroom facilities, and cautioning the four teachers to find a way to air the disagreements that were bound to occur.[3] But before leaving the June session, Betsy emphasized what she characterized as the significant lessons of her experience. The work load ahead would be great; the rewards in student work would also be great. In other words, Betsy concluded, her experience had been "the best of times and the worst of times."

Two weeks later, just after the Fourth of July, the Connections teachers were joined by Sharon Finch, the parent who had offered to be a resource person in art, when they met at Dan's home. By this July meeting, the teaching team was ready to adopt two of Betsy's ideas—the bridge-building activity for the first day and the Renaissance Fair at the end of the first semester. Work began on the first week's Bridges unit. Bernie had come prepared with a piece of poster board on which he charted the lesson plans for the week as they were decided. When that task had been completed, the team was ready to consider the unit that would come next: Beginnings. Bernie quickly drew three columns on the remaining space, one for each academic subject area. Starting with history, Bernie then made a list of central concepts, readings, and activities that could be part of a Beginnings unit from a social studies perspective: civilization components, early civilizations (Egypt, Greece, Rome, China), a civilization simulation, a mock trial of Socrates. Brainstorming in incomplete sentences as he wrote, Bernie paused to say, "I like to think out loud, have you noticed that? Are you tired of it yet?" Turning to Dan and Sheryl to follow suit, Bernie poised his marker to record the topics the unit would encompass in English and science. Sheryl, noting that her plans for English would mesh well with Bernie's list, included mythology and *The Odyssey* as the literature base for the unit. She described a project she had developed in conjunction with her teaching of Homer's epic in the past: a "Quest" that required oral, visual, and written components as student groups created an odyssey of their own, complete with five adventurous "stops" on the journey. Sheryl's description met nods and exclamations of approval from her teammates. The contagious theme spreading, Bernie mused about science topics such as technology in early civilizations or the "big bang" theory. But Dan's thoughts about science focused on a question: "What is needed to begin to do science?" As Bernie jotted down the question, Dan itemized appropriate topics to be listed: the scientific method, experimental procedures, and measurement skills. With the lower right corner of the poster board still free of Bernie's notes, Tim raised a topic to fill the space. Drawing Sharon into the conversation, Tim wondered about making connections to the arts. Early art forms, the use of perspective, and symbolic communication surfaced as potential artistic tie-ins. Just as the poster board was running out of space, Sheryl noticed that the planning process had consumed all but a half hour of the scheduled meeting time, so she suggested leaving the development of other units for the next meeting (to be held two days later) and use the remaining time to discuss ideas for student journals and portfolios. Both were seen as valuable: the journals as a tool for reflection and communication; the portfolios as a means to integrate learnings and demonstrate growth. However, by summer's end, as the team's plans jelled, neither found a place on the itinerary. The day's business concluded, Dan invited his teammates to stay for a demonstration of the Hyper-Card program on his computer.

True to the agenda Sheryl had set, the next planning session continued and completed Connections' itinerary of units. The Beginnings unit would be followed by the Middle Ages, then a brief detour to prepare for and take the state proficiency test. The first semester leg of the journey would be completed with a unit entitled Change, with the Renaissance Fair as the capstone. Outlined in less detail, the second semester's instructional ports of call would continue the chronological journey with the Industrial Revolution, the Twentieth Century, and Rights (allowing an appropriate connection between *To Kill a Mockingbird* and the Holocaust). The last stop on the itinerary would be Futures. The year's itinerary established, the meeting proceeded to other dimensions of organizing and preparing for the Connections odyssey.

*Becoming a Crew*

Patterns of organization were the product of this phase of this meeting. Drawing upon their experiences at the junior high, with its organizational pattern of student groups assigned to teacher groups, Sheryl and Tim proposed the idea of dividing the Connections cohort into advisory groups. In this way, the students' bonds to Connections would be cemented by their affiliation with a "color group."

Another organizational schema emerged from a return to the topic of communication, the team's mode of communication both with administrators and with each other. Not wishing to designate one of their number as chairperson, the Connections teachers arrived at the idea of a rotating leadership. Influenced by coaching and extracurricular commitments, the cycle of Connections chairs placed Sheryl in the role for the summer, Dan for the fall, Bernie during the winter, and Tim during the spring. Prompted by Sheryl's suggestions, communication routines within the team's common planning period were also established: Friday sessions would be devoted to "talking about kids," and one day each week would be dedicated to detailed planning of the next week's schedule.

For the next several weeks, attendance at workshops replaced the pattern of meetings in homes, but the work of organization continued. The portfolio assessment workshop Tim and Sheryl attended fell short of their expectations because it focused on elementary curricula, but the conversations that filled the shared drive there and back each day generated a Connections vision statement. During the lunch break on the first day of the cooperative learning workshop, Bernie and Dan approved Tim and Sheryl's thoughts on the statement.

At that workshop, participants formed cooperative learning groups that both illustrated and practiced the principles and strategies that were the heart of the course. Tim and Bernie joined with one other high school teacher in one group, while Dan's group included another science teacher, a social studies teacher, and a health/physical education teacher who also were all from the high school. Being the majority on their team, Tim and Bernie influenced the week's work toward a Connections orientation, devising activities related to the units that had been planned. Amid discussions of the various configurations of cooperative learning, one participant suggested an inexpensive substitute (bathroom wall panel remnants) for the white marker boards shown in an instructional videotape. Bernie, especially, saw the material's appropriateness as a substitute for the poster board he had used thus far at summer planning sessions. So it was that Tim scrounged remnants from a local building supply business and the "official Connections planning white board" came into being.

With the arrival of the third week of August, the workshops had concluded, Betsy Grant had visited once more, materials ordered in June were beginning to arrive, and a meeting of Connections parents loomed less than a week away. In their planning for this meeting, the teachers decided upon the areas that would need to be addressed: content, parental involvement, student work requirements, the variety of teaching and learning components that would be present in Connections, and the program's goals and objectives. Bernie, as the keeper of the planning board, was the logical volunteer for presenting content. Sheryl offered to speak about student work expectations and to recruit a parent volunteer pool. Tim, in his role as the designated learning styles specialist, assumed responsibility for presenting some of the teaching and learning approaches the students would experience. Dan agreed to introduce the Connections vision statement. Just before setting three more meeting times for the week remaining before the first day of school, Tim informed the team of the final tally of the summer's work he had kept for summer stipend accountability. By his reckoning, the Connections teachers had logged 111 hours together in meetings and workshops over the summer, not including individual time doing reading and "homework."

## AUGUST 19, 1993

By Thursday, August 19, only five days of summer vacation remained before the first day of the school year. That evening eighty parents, the four Connections teachers, George Cerny, and Mike Davis gathered in the high school library. Following George's welcome and Mike's introduction of the Connections teaching team, Bernie spoke first, describing for the parents the hours the teachers had devoted to preparing for the year ahead, assuring parents that Connections was not something the teachers had "slapped together over the summer." Then Dan placed a transparency on the overhead projector. The Connections vision statement flashed on a screen.

> Our goal and vision is to produce lifelong learners who have enhanced themselves to meet the demands and responsibilities of the 21st century.
> —Integrate the subject areas of English, history, science, and humanities into thematic units;
> —Build on student interests and curiosity;
> —Use literature as our language focus;
> —Accommodate the various learning styles of the students for continuous and individual progress;
> —Stress critical thinking skills;
> —Draw upon the resources in the family, school, and community.

Sheryl prefaced her remarks by noting that, as a parent herself, she anticipated the parents' wanting to know what Connections would mean at home. She offered a glimpse of homework that would be "different"—involving projects and research at the library. She invited parents to be chaperones, videotapers, and guests at Connections activities.

Bernie highlighted the program's "flexibility and variety" as he outlined the first semester's units and the Renaissance Fair to come. Tim, stating that "Each student is entitled to learn," talked about the learning styles survey students would take during the first week of school. This information would be a "way for teachers to know students and for students to know each other."

When the floor opened for parent questions, there were many: about grades, about how the program would be evaluated, about advisory groups, and about how students with differing ability levels would be accommodated. But the first parent to speak, the one that set the tone for all the questions that followed, offered not a question, but a comment: "It's great to see teachers so enthused!"

## THE ECOSYSTEM SURROUNDING CONNECTIONS' LAUNCHING

Like the first instructional unit the Connections teachers planned, the spring and summer of 1993 were about "bridges"—bridges that would both connect the four teachers and construct the beginnings of a Connections ecosystem. During a telephone conversation in mid-August, as Sheryl reflected on the summer's experiences in preparing for Connections, her concluding remark gave me pause: "We've gotten along so tremendously well so far; it just amazes me!" Sheryl's amazement notwithstanding, Connections' auspicious launching seemed to me more than fortuitous. The congenial dawn of the Connections odyssey betokened an environment in which all of the interacting systems of that environment supported and contributed to "getting along," a state of equilibrium which the Connections teachers not only enjoyed but created during the spring and summer of 1993.

### Physical Systems

As the Connections ecosystem took on shape and form, the dimensions of time and space, elements of its physical system, were central in its architecture. That time—for orientation and preparation—is a necessary condition for successful implementation of an innovation has attained axiomatic status in the study of educational change.[4] The myriad hours devoted to planning, 111 by Tim's reckoning, surely warranted Bernie's reassurance to parents that Connections had not been "slapped together." But in addition to allowing for the thoughtful and careful development of Connections' curriculum, the time the teachers spent together during the spring and summer's planning sessions had another significant benefit. Months later, as Bernie spoke about these sessions with a group of visiting administrators from the area, he observed, "Over the summer we got together maybe forty or fifty hours. Maybe the biggest thing we got out of it was team-building, 'cause we scrapped a lot of it" (May, 17, 1994). Before Connections, ties among the four teachers had been limited. As Sheryl commented, "Tim, I sort of knew; Bernie was a 'hello'; Dan, well, English and science people don't get much chance to know each other" (September 14, 1993). The time spent together in planning the journey ahead changed all that. Yet time was not the only dimension of the physical system that contributed to the bridges across the emerging Connections ecosystem.

During the spring and summer of 1993, Connections' physical world included several locations. But in the months lay ahead, whenever the teachers recalled and told stories of that time, the "place" that figured most prominently in their tales was their homes. While the decision to meet in each others' homes had been based originally on the presence of air-conditioning, the effects of that decision extended beyond the consideration of temperature to other areas of comfort.

Meeting in each others' homes deeply affected how the Connections teachers came to know each other: before becoming acquainted in the context of teaching, Bernie, Sheryl, Dan, and Tim would do so in a more personal setting. Before her teammates knew her abilities in English, they would sample the fruits of her gardening expertise. Getting to know Bernie would include sampling his homemade (and quite spicy) version of salsa. Before knowing Tim as the team's "learning styles specialist," his colleagues would be familiar with his love of baseball (and, in particular, his baseball card collection). Similarly Dan's eagerness to demonstrate his home computer's HyperCard program evidenced his interests. Meeting in each others' homes for summer planning sessions and the early-established ritual of sharing hospitality allowed for reciprocal self-disclosure and gaining knowledge of each other as trusting and trustable. Seeking affinity and bases for personal connection during those first month of team meetings established a sense of commonality—of what Sheryl termed "getting along" and Bernie termed "team building." From my perspective, that of witnessing the formation of personal connections among the Connections teachers, I would suggest another term: team loyalty.[5]

Without the extensive time and personal sense of place peculiar to Connections' beginnings, the teaching team's opportunity for collegial community—to get along, to build a team, to develop loyalty to each other and the program—would have been limited, if not curtailed. In sum, the ecosystem of Connections' launching was marked by a physical system in which the dimensions of time and place supported the creation of the routines and relationships that would be the hallmarks of the Connections culture both during its launching and long into the Connections odyssey.

*Cultural Systems*

Cultural systems are composed of the structures and routines that shape shared patterns of perception and behavior. These patterns of basic assumptions emerge as norms as a group shares a common history and comes to share practices that define the group's identity. During the spring and summer of Connections' launching, an evolving cultural system incorporated routines, structures, and norms which gave expression to Connections' charter.

As Connections was presented to the Instructional Council, the board of education, and parents, an explicit distinction set this program apart: Connections would serve students from "all ability levels." Tim's presence as a member of the teaching team was predicated on this, the first, item of Connections' charter. That this inclusiveness was indeed an innovation for Cedar City High School became quite apparent in the questions raised by parents both at the orientation meeting and the August gathering of Connections parents. Questions about grading practices, especially, reflected parental concerns. Parents of honors students required direct assurances that inclusion would not penalize students—by diluting curricular content, by cooperative learning groups that might either lower grades or lead to Honors students "doing all the work," or by denying "weighted" grades to students who would otherwise have enrolled in honors English 9. Parents of LD students, hearing these questions and having heard a mixed message at IEP meetings, wondered how well their children would be accepted into the Connections student cohort. By the end of the August Connections parent meeting, parental anxieties appeared to have been put to rest. After all, Sheryl would be teaching the non-Connections sections of ninth-grade honors English, Bernie did have his master's degree in gifted education, Dan did have computer expertise, and Tim would provide assistance to LD students.

But more than the teachers' credentials, four elements of the evolving Connections cultural system reinforced the programmatic commitment to heterogeneity. As Tim and Sheryl considered their materials purchases, they gave priority to the audiotapes and parallel editions that would enhance LD students' opportunities for success with Connections' literature base. Including an assignment notebook for each student among Connections' resources requisitions would serve all students, but the notebook was seen as particularly valuable to LD students. Color advisory groups would do more than provide students with a sense of identity within the program: they would be a mechanism for mixing ability levels and would facilitate another significant routine, designating Friday's common planning period as the day to "talk about kids." While the first two elements, literature supplements and assignment notebooks, supported LD students in particular, they were also expressions of another Connections norm: ensuring student success. While the latter two cultural elements, advisory groups and Friday's planning topic, were related to a norm of inclusion or heterogeneity, they also evidenced another norm within Connections cultural system. For the Connections participants, teachers knowing their students (their learning styles and their progress) and students' knowing each other and their teachers would be valued.

Just as the district's commitment to critical thinking and cooperative learning had been manifest in the recently adopted vision statement, this emphasis was also part of the Connections charter. Certainly, Mike Davis's expectation that all of the Connections teachers would have experienced the district's summer cooperative learning workshop codified that particular teaching and learning strategy within Connections' cultural system. As the four teachers planned the learning activities for the year ahead, cooperative learning markedly influenced their efforts. The fall semester would begin with one cooperative group activity (bridge building), culminate with another (the Renaissance Fair), and promise more in between (such as Sheryl's Quest project). More than simply being cooperative group activities, these learning experiences would harken the presence of a project orientation within Connections' cultural system. In Connections' initial planning, such projects—and their placement in the sequence of units—appeared to be the linchpins of interdisciplinary connections among Connections' three academic content areas.

Reflective of the Connections charter, with its focus on "the interrelatedness of different areas," these sorts of learning experiences would reinforce the parallels exemplified in the oft-repeated Renaissance illustration. In addition, Sharon Finch's presence at the July meeting at Dan's home and the artistic activities planned then for the Beginnings unit testified to the importance the teaching team attached to integrating Connections' curriculum. The process by which these projects, whether arts-inspired or more directly content-derived, were planned revealed an interesting dynamic.

The "official Connections white planning board" was both the means and symbol of this process and this dynamic. From its inception on poster board through its more permanent form, the planning board displayed a consistent three-column layout. Although the Connections charter promised difference, it also promised "essentially the same curricula for the three areas." The planning board process balanced these two promises. This balancing process disclosed a dynamic that would persist throughout the Connections odyssey.

For each unit, the planning process began with Bernie, Sheryl, and Dan each itemizing the content and activities for their respective subjects. Then, and only then, did the work of interrelating the three subjects begin. Within the cultural system of Connections' launching, "supporting each other" began with sharing each others' individual instructional plans. For four teachers whose personal and professional ties to each other had been quite limited prior to Connections, this precedence was not surprising—reconciling individual practices to a collective team practice would understandably begin with disclosing the former before negotiating the latter. In this cultural context, Dan's question of Betsy (about potential difficulties in connecting science to English and history) could be anticipated. Becoming familiar with their teammates' "essentially the same curricula" (the third point of the Connections charter) appeared to be a necessary cultural norm and prerequisite to the Connections teachers' "crossing over subject areas and supporting each other" (the charter's fourth point). Given this dynamic, the personal systems surrounding Connections' launching merit discussion.

## Personal Systems

In a healthy ecosystem, individual life histories and experiences create an environment enriched by each person's special strengths and perspectives.[6] During the spring and summer of Connections' launching, the strengths and perspectives Dan, Bernie, Tim, and Sheryl brought to the teaching team began to become visible.

In the eyes of his colleagues, Dan was the resident computer "whiz kid." In matters of instructional technology resources— ordering software and CD-ROM databases, for example—they clearly deferred to Dan's expertise. As Sheryl commented during our mid-August telephone conversation, "I am so impressed with Dan's knowledge!" Dan's personal perspective also surfaced in other matters. In the discussions that created and shaped the routines and structures of Connections' cultural system, Dan often took the role of clarifier. When Tim raised the assignment notebook ideas, Dan sought confirmation that this would be a requirement for students, a matter of student accountability and responsibility. When a briefing with junior high teachers revealed that several soon-to-be Connections students had had attendance problems in the past, Dan solicited his teammates' ideas about a Connections policy in the event of excessive student absences. When the team was planning the August Connections parent meeting and the items that would be included in Tim's presentation on the variety of strategies that would mark Connections' pedagogy, Dan asked for a verification: "Do we all agree that cooperative learning will be 25 percent of the grade at the max?" Dan's concerns and queries illuminated another aspect of the personal perspective he brought to Connections, one he reiterated in one of his end-of-the-year responses (appendix K). The advice Dan would offer to new teachers in a Connections-like program included: "Get together on certain things like tardies, discipline, late policies." A concern for clarity (in policies and in expectation) as well as computer expertise: these were the strengths and perspectives Dan brought to Connections' personal systems.

If Dan was the clarifier in the Connections conversation, Bernie was the initiator. In Bernie's verbal brainstorming, or what he noted as his habit of talking aloud, the flow of ideas usually began with the phrase "what say we." This brainstorming pattern seemed to reflect a very loose style of planning; yet Bernie also furnished the poster board that accompanied the process so that "we can get it set down so we know where we're going" (July 6, 1993). As he tossed out ideas for potential history components for the Beginnings unit, Bernie's listing reflected a shorthand his colleagues would come to know well. Key words and phrases (e.g., contributions, hieroglyphs, commonalities) were connected by arrows and interspersed with self-memos (e.g., the notation about the civilization simulation "one day per group if use whole block"). It was almost as if Bernie had to capture the details of his ideas before they got lost in the flow of his "big picture" thinking style. For Bernie, this propensity for connecting grand ideas across subject areas was not unique to Connections. In the initial talk about possible Connections units of instruction, at the meeting at Tim's home a week before Betsy Grant's visit, Bernie shared the themes that he and Daisy Nelson had developed as a framework for student portfolios in the new American studies dyad: man's role, woman's role, family, values. Bernie's visionary thoughts were not offered without consideration of practical issues, however. As the ideas for projects and activities for the Beginnings unit flowed, Bernie mentioned that he had "already talked to the library people about the noise level" that would probably accompany the Connections students' research. In the midst of planning the areas each teacher would present at the August parent meeting, Bernie suggested that one teacher be stationed at each of the two doors to the library before the meeting to serve as "greeters" and hand out the Connections newsletter. Whether with an eye to detail or to a visionary overview, Bernie's strength as an "idea person" was abundantly present in Connections' personal system.

His experience as a special education teacher and his designation as the team's "learning styles specialist" distinctly influenced the roles Tim assumed within Connections' personal system. Working closely with Sheryl in ordering accompaniments to her literary materials (e.g., a parallel text edition and audiotapes of *Romeo and Juliet*, audiotapes of *Fahrenheit 451*), Tim was the advocate for the LD students among the Connections student cohort. The attention to detailed record keeping that had been essential to his teaching practice transferred to the log he kept of the hours devoted to planning and preparation and the requisition forms (and other central office paperwork) he submitted on the team's behalf. The positive feedback and reinforcement Tim was accustomed to providing students in his classroom also found expression in Connections planning sessions. Consistently and characteristically, Tim met Dan, Sheryl, and Bernie's suggestions with "that's a good idea" statements. Tim was an encourager.

The first to host a summer planning session in her home, and the originator of ideas such as devoting Fridays to "talk about kids," Sheryl was a ritual setter. It was Sheryl who proposed setting aside one day each week for planning the next week's detailed schedule of activities. It was Sheryl who, with Tim's immediate concurrence, advanced the idea of advisory groups. And it was Sheryl who conceived the idea for using the time spent in driving with Tim to the portfolio workshop to create a Connections vision statement. Whether relational (hospitality), organizational (patterns in days of planning), or a synthesis of both (advisory groups, the vision statement), Sheryl's ideas could be seen as focal to the creation of many of Connections' customs. While the Connections teachers were reluctant to designate or claim any one team member to a leadership role, Sheryl's designation as Connections' "chair" for the summer was consistent with the strengths and perspectives she had brought to Connections' personal systems.[7]

The strengths and perspectives each of the Connections teachers brought to the Connections ecosystem were in no small measure the product of personal and professional experiences, including those within the larger ecosystems of Cedar City High School and the Cedar City School District. So it is to the contribution of those larger systems to Connections' ecosystem that I now turn.

## Webs to Other Ecosystems

That the Cedar City environment bore the imprimaturs of tracking and departmentalization was apparent in the initial parent concerns and the original lack of acquaintanceship among the Connections teachers. The plans and preparations of Connections' launching clearly reflected these influences. They also reveal adaptations. The Connections teachers would abide by the norm of having a program chair, but the designation would rotate. Connections honors students would earn weighted grades in English, but they would do so in heterogeneous classes. Demarcations among Connections' subject areas would be observed—in the schedule option known in Connections as a "three-way rotation" and in the separate grades students would receive in each subject—but cross-disciplinary and art projects would blur the traditional boundaries of academic content. Just as Mike Davis had acknowledged and accommodated the nature of the community (including the school community) in his proposals for innovation, the Connections adaptations represented a recognition of the norms of the larger ecosystem in which Connections existed.

Yet this cognizance was more tacit than explicit. In the rarified atmosphere of Connections' launching, the emergent Connections ecosystem flourished with little to no direct competition or conflict from surrounding ecosystems. The Freedom 2000 group which in July had initially expressed concern in the local newspaper's letters to the editor about a variety of reforms—including the "trial interdisciplinary program"—ultimately focused primarily on outcomes-based education. During the summer months, few other Cedar City faculty members were aware of, much less affected by, Connections' launching. Insulated and isolated from environmental distraction or detraction, the Connections teachers enjoyed what could be termed a "honeymoon" period.

Indeed, this idyllic season in the Connections odyssey *did* bear several similarities to a honeymoon. The summer of 1993 *was* a time apart from the ordinary daily patterns of life and work. It *was* a concentrated time spent together that nourished commitment to a relationship. And it *was* a time in which the new union was blessed and supported by a circle of well-wishers. For Connections, such blessings and supports were tangible as well as symbolic, immediately useful as well as ultimately significant.

Tangible support came in an array of forms: observation excursions that secured initial support for the program, grants that funded materials purchases and summer stipends, provisions for training either indirectly through reimbursement or directly through district offerings, and technical assistance and consultation in the person of Betsy Grant. Such support, while inherently and immediately useful, also had symbolic and more far-reaching consequences.

Connections' introduction to Cedar City—to parents, to potential students, to faculty, to district residents—was a shared responsibility, not a one-person, or even a one-team, effort. Notably, the Connections teachers did not present the program at April's parent orientation meeting. Their observation excursions had equipped Mike and George to describe the program's charter characteristics and enabled Daisy Nelson to issue her ringing endorsement of both the program's value and the teachers' abilities. But the parents' requests for details required a follow-up meeting with the Connections teachers. The order of appearance at the August parent meeting reinforced the pattern—George and Mike spoke first and introduced the teaching team, and then the teachers addressed specific issues of implementation. The full weight of authority and public sanction legitimated Connections, but in the crucial matters of curriculum and instruction, the teaching team held sway. As George had told me in mid-April, "It's their program."

The grants George and Mike had secured also had less tangible, but important, impact beyond the requisition orders they funded. To be sure, material resources of texts, software, art supplies, and the like are prerequisites for the successful implementation of any educational innovation.[8] Yet another use of the grant monies conveyed a significant message. The summer stipend offered evidence of the value the school and district attached to the teachers' collaborative work. The Connections teachers received more than programmatic endorsement: they received blessings and support in the form of validating rewards.

For Mike Davis, identifying pedagogical skills and strategies that the teachers needed to learn or strengthen was "not a matter of evaluation" (April 27, 1993). Rather, training would allow the Connections teachers to approach their task from a position of expertise. For the Connections teachers, training also offered other benefits. Especially for Bernie and Tim (as members of the same cooperative learning workshop team) and for Sheryl and Tim (in their drives to the portfolio workshop), training offered opportunities to expand and cement personal relationships. For all of the Connections teachers, participation in training occasions offered yet another piece of evidence of each team member's efforts to learn new practices and of his or her commitment to the program.

That commitment deepened over time—from the early spring's initial expressions of interest in being part of the teaching team to the late summer presentation that led one parent to comment "It's great to see teachers so enthused!" Even though the Connections teachers had been given the freedom and resources to create Connections in their own way, an air of enthusiasm, while anticipated and desired, was not a sure thing. As Sheryl remarked at the May 1994, board of education meeting, "I think we were all apprehensive at first." Faced with the uncertainties inherent in teachers' work in general, and in beginning an innovative program like Connections in particular, initial anxieties were understandable.[9] Fiedler and Garcia (1987) discuss two facets of uncertainty: task uncertainty and relationship uncertainty. When the Connections teachers were initially chosen to implement the program, neither their task nor their relationship was certain. An acknowledgment of those uncertainties, as well as the wisdom of lived experience, was what Betsy Grant brought to the summer planning session on June 24, 1993.

Of all the resources provided to the Connections teachers, Mike Davis's inviting Betsy to be a consultant proved to be the catalyst that secured the transition from uncertainty to enthusiasm. Being able to ask questions of a person who had traveled a

Connections-like journey was, as Sheryl would say later, "productive . . . about nitty-gritty stuff rather than philosophy" (August 15, 1993). In short, meeting with Betsy filled needs. Direct evidence of needs being met can be seen in the adoption of many of the ideas Betsy shared—most notably the bridge-building and Renaissance Fair activities. Less directly, but certainly visible in the many questions the Connections teachers asked following Betsy's presentation, the session addressed personal concerns (about the demands of innovation such as Connections makes and about the teachers' adequacy to meet those demands) and management concerns (about technical issues of process and tasks such as scheduling and grading).[10] Not having been part of the observation excursions to Betsy's program, the June 24 gathering afforded the Connections teachers a glimpse—a visionary flash—of the Connections charter in practice.

In sum, the blessings and supports of the ecosystems surrounding Connections, especially administrative words and deeds, enabled the period of Connections' launching to be both productive and idyllic. The webs to other ecosystems connected and interacted with physical, cultural, and personal systems to create an emergent Connections ecosystem in which collegial community might thrive. From this state of equilibrium, from this friendly port, the Connections odyssey was launched.

# CHAPTER 3

# First Day, First Impressions: August 24, 1993

We hope to expand your child's horizons and help them build memories that will last a lifetime.

—*Connections Newsletter*

August 24, 1993, was the first day of the new school year at Cedar City High School. The day dawned sunny and steamy, promising yet another "dog day" in southern Ohio. Yellow school buses pulled into the long driveway and the student parking lot that had been dormant for the summer filled. Soon the familiar din of first day sounds echoed in the congested halls. Public address announcements could barely be heard over the cacophony of student voices as classmates, separated for the summer, were reunited. The 7:30 warning bell pierced the tumult, and students gradually dispersed to their first period classrooms. By 7:35, only a few lost freshmen remained in the corridors. The first day of Connections had begun.

## THE FIRST FIRST PERIOD

As I entered Dan's classroom, the aroma of coffee greeted me. The two narrow windows had been pushed open, but no breeze wafted in. Dan and Tim paused in their work to say, "Good morning," and then they continued to carry boxes of markers, rulers, white glue, paper fasteners, and scissors from the long counter that spanned the back of the room to the large room across the hall. These materials, part of the resources the teachers had ordered using funds from the grant earmarked for Connections' start-up, would be needed for the day's activity. A glance about Dan's room revealed other evidence of the planning the teaching team had done in preparation for this day.

Dan's writing filled two panels of the blackboard at the front of the room. One panel listed the day's agenda:

> Brief intro
> Break up into advisory teams
> Assign groups (4) and roles
> > materials handler
> > communicator
> > cutter?
> > fastener?

On the second panel, Dan had written:

> Bridge requirements:
> > Up to four pieces of cardboard
> > Aesthetically pleasing
> > Innovative design
> > Hold a brick
> > Free standing

Atop one pair of student tables the white planning board had been marked with calendar-like headings for the days of the week. Bernie was busily filling in the lesson plans for the week-long Bridges unit that would begin Connections. The short unit was based on the first day's activity. Within their advisory groups students would be broken into groups of four, given specified materials, and instructed to build a bridge. A follow-up writing assignment would ask each student to evaluate his or her group's process and product. As an instructional activity, "building bridges" had several purposes. The activity would communicate Connections expectations, provide an opportunity for students to get to know each other, and serve as a source for initial student writing samples. The teachers also saw building bridges as symbolic of the transitions the first day represented for students— from junior high to high school, and from traditional curricular programs to Connections.

Sheryl arrived just a moment behind me and announced that she had brought a home-baked apple coffee cake to share. Her announcement sufficed to create an instant break. Coffee mugs in hand (or in Sheryl's case, tea from her thermos), and pieces of coffee cake on impromptu paper towel napkins, the teachers resumed their last minute preparations. Sheryl had also brought an updated Connections class list fresh from the guidance office. She and Tim conferred about the placement of new students into advisory groups. As they finished that task, Dan took the revised list to his computer, quickly generating new master enrollment lists for each teacher. Bernie looked up from his charting to confirm which teachers would assume primary responsibility for the various orientation lessons planned for the week. The activities, it was hoped, would provide an introduction, or bridge, for students as they embarked on the Connections journey. Tim, designated as the "learning styles specialist" of the team, would, of course, be in charge of administering and interpreting the learning styles inventory students would take the next day. Sheryl estimated she would need one hour to cover the introduction to *Writers, Inc.* (a composition handbook) the group had planned as part of Thursday's work. Bernie offered to incorporate the planned introduction to text highlighting with his introduction to the history text. With those items settled, Bernie stood back from his completed chart to say, "Let's go kick butt!"

Dan was not quite so ready. He turned to his blackboard agenda for the day and asked his teammates to make suggestions. Given his experience in the summer's cooperative learning workshop, Dan thought that two of the role titles he had listed for the student activity were questionable. Bernie offered combining cutting and fastening functions under the apt title of "engineer." Then he wondered aloud, "I'm curious to see how we do on time." In keeping with the bridge-building task, Tim suggested the role of "foreman" for the student given responsibility for being a consensus achiever as student groups would decide how to construct their bridges. Dan made the changes and returned to the job of gathering the resources students would need for bridge building. After grabbing a handful of meter sticks, Dan began transferring paper-wrapped bricks to a cart to be taken across the hall.

Just before three parent volunteers were scheduled to arrive to set up to videotape the morning's activity, Tim wanted to be sure of one last consideration. So he took a pair of scissors and experimented with cutting the corrugated cardboard that would be the primary construction material of the day. As he discovered, cutting was easier with the grain than against, and scoring the cardboard first made cutting easier—discoveries Tim immediately shared with the three other teachers. As the videotaping volunteers (two mothers and an older brother of Connections students) appeared, Bernie and Sheryl directed them to the large room. Others—George Cerny, Frank Barton, and Mike Davis—would also witness Connections' first morning as they dropped in for a few minutes to observe at various points during the Connections block. The bell signaling the end of first period was just a few minutes away.

In the large room, tables in the back corner were now laden with a stack of cardboard and all of the implements students would be permitted to use. The cart of bricks was parked next to the tables. As she looked about the room, Sheryl could be heard telling a parent volunteer, "It's so cool we don't have to do mundane stuff." At 8:37 the bell rang, and Frank Barton's voice came over the speaker to announce, "All Connections students report to room 307."

## BUILDING BRIDGES

Over the next five minutes, eighty students found their way to the large room that would be their Connections home base. A computer-generated banner proclaiming "Welcome to Connections!" had been affixed to the blank hall wall between the twin doors to the double room. Befitting first-day traditions, the students were all wearing new clothes—unscuffed gym shoes, T-shirts that had yet to be laundered, jean shorts still with their fresh-from-the-store stiffness. Over the soft buzz of the two already whirring ceiling fans, Bernie's voice could be heard instructing students to "Sit anywhere you'd like—*in the front!*" The students settled in patterns of friendship and gender, with most of the boys in the front left quadrant of the ranks of desk-chairs and most of the girls occupying places in the left rear quadrant of the room. The teachers allowed a few moments after the 8:42 bell for stragglers to bring the nose-count to expected proportions. Then Bernie, whose voice carried best, took center stage.

"We've got a *wonderful* day—it's 90 degrees!" Eyeing his colleagues, Bernie continued, "We all *like* to sweat! I need your attention for a couple of minutes. This is Connections class." After introducing the teaching team by name and subject area and giving a nod to the three video volunteers, Bernie explained my presence and constant note taking: "This is Mrs. Dorsch. She'll be in observing, hanging out." Before Bernie turned to the next item on the morning's agenda, breaking into advisory groups, he summarized his introductory remarks by telling the students, "I'm excited to start school!"

Admonishing students to "Listen for your name," Bernie called out the names of his Magenta group. Sheryl was next. Before she began calling out the names of Blue group members, Sheryl added to Bernie's introduction. She told students about her family and pointed out the pieces of heart-motif jewelry she was wearing that were part of her collection. As Sheryl finished, Dan announced to the Green group he was about to enumerate, "You guys are the luckiest people!" When it was Tim's turn, he explained that he chose his group's color because, "I'm a Cincinnati Reds fan." With the two classroom clocks now registering 9:00, Bernie told the students, "I'll turn it over to Mr. Centers. He'll give you directions and guidance, and then we'll go after it."

Standing in the middle of the room, Dan began, "I thought we'd just sit here." He paused for effect before adding, "Just kidding." After talking about the roles to be assumed within each of the work groups that would be formed when students broke into their advisory (color-named) groups momentarily, Dan went on to describe the bridge requirements. "First, it has to be freestanding. What does that mean?" A chorus of responses confirmed that the students understood the term. As he continued with the requirement that the bridge be able to support additional weight, Dan held aloft one of the wrapped bricks and dramatically pointed out that thirteen bricks were available. Again with the requirements that the bridges be "innovative" and "decorative," Dan asked the students for their interpretations of the terms, eliciting such responses as "creative,""unusual," "unique." After exhorting students to "put the personality of the group in the bridge," Dan paused to ask if there were any questions and if there were any names that had not been called. Then he walked over to the materials-laden tables to point out the available supplies, stipulating that each group could use up to four pieces of cardboard. The catalog of supplies was quickly rattled off: paper tubing, meter sticks, scissors, fasteners, glue, and markers—including "tropical" colors "for you Jimmy Buffett fans." By the time Dan reached the end of the list, the level of student murmuring attested to students' readiness to begin bridge building. So without further ado, students moved to cluster in their advisory groups in each of the four corners of the room.

As the teachers met with their groups, they followed a common format. Each teacher gave a brief demonstration of scoring the cardboard to ease cutting and reviewed roles and requirements. Bernie, Tim and Sheryl had their students count off by fours to form work groups. Dan explained to the Green group that splitting the cutting and fastening tasks would allow for groups of five and so generated one less group within his advisory. Then it came time to, as Dan phrased it, "rock and roll." For the next seventy-five minutes, the work of Connections was bridge building.

A few weeks later, a local newspaper article described the first Connections morning of bridge building: "Imagine a classroom full of high school freshmen—smiling, laughing, listening to the teacher, learning—not a bored child among the group . . . The students all rose to the challenge and worked together with new friends to build successful bridges that would hold several bricks." The students' first-day enthusiasm could be detected in their immediate and visible engagement in an activity that certainly was not typical of their other first classes of the day. While some of the student chatter revolved around such usual ninth-grade topics as who was going with whom or the potential success of this year's football team, their conversation as they worked also revealed much about their first impressions of Connections:

LUCAS (A MAGENTA STUDENT). What color is magenta anyway?

JESSICA. I want it to be the Jessica bridge—I want my name on it.

R.G. I'm gonna put in those lines, like you know, that divide the lanes on a road. Okay?

KYLE. Let's make the tubes to be pontoons!

JENNIFER. Yeah. And let's make guard rails, too.

AMANDA. Let's put messages, you know, like that get spray painted on bridges . . . We could put I "heart" and then our boyfriends' names.

But by far the most compelling evidence of the students' involvement in their bridge building came at 9:32. The bell signaling the end of second period at Cedar City High sounded, and the attention of not one student was diverted. No one, teacher or student, appeared to take notice. It was only later, as the teachers checked the time to gauge the activity's pace, that they realized that one period had ended and another had begun. This phenomenon, perhaps as much as any other aspect of the morning, proved to be a source of amazement and reward for the teachers. As Tim later told the local newspaper reporter: "When the bell rang for the other students to change classes, they didn't even look up," related [Schwartz]. "They were so absorbed in the lesson."

Throughout the morning, students who did look up from their task would quite likely see the teachers pausing to confer with each other. Those close enough to overhear might have heard comments that revealed the teachers' assessments of the activity's success:

SHERYL (TO TIM). That girl who's doing all the work—she's a general kid who almost didn't make it. I love it![1]

BERNIE (POINTING TO A DOUBLE-DECKER BRIDGE UNDER CONSTRUCTION AS HE TALKS TO SHERYL). You gotta see some of these designs!

TIM (POINTING TO ONE WORK GROUP AS HE TALKS TO DAN). Know what? Three of these are mine [LD students] and I didn't even know it. Look at them!

The frequent interaction among teachers could also be seen to serve as a means for on-the-spot fine-tuning of the morning's lesson plan. Most times the conversations were *sotto voce*; sometimes they were more public.

One instance of the latter occurred after the student groups had staked out their work areas and had some time to negotiate their group roles. After an initial tour of his Magenta groups, Bernie raised his voice to be heard above the loud hum of student voices. His message was framed in the first person plural as an announcement to students: "We're gonna be coming around, asking questions. We'll talk to the communicator. So know each other's names. Be ready to introduce each other and tell about who's taking on which roles." Students quickly grasped the hint and, if they had not done so already, took steps to prepare for the promised teacher visits. Bernie's colleagues also grasped the hint. Previous approaches of initiating contact with a group by querying "You got it all together?" or "How's it going, guys?" were immediately adjusted to "Who's your communicator?" Still, as teachers traveled from group to group, the conversation was not restricted to bridge building issues. Tim and Bernie, in particular, were quick to join in student conversations about sports. The first-day-of-school staple of conversation, summer vacation highlights, also provided teachers with opportunities for personal teacher-student dialogue.

Most often, communication among the four teachers involved sharing their personal on-the-spot adaptations in sequences of one-to-one conversations, each passing on the thoughts of one to another. It was in this way that consensus about the format and requirements for presentations of constructed bridges was developed. To Dan's idea that the bridges be given names, Bernie added the dimension of each group's arriving at an estimate of how many bricks their bridge would support, or in Bernie's words "whether or not you'll push the envelope and risk destruction." Tim suggested that the presentation should include a telling of "how you came up with this." Sheryl, having brought her camera, wanted to take a picture of each group with its completed bridge. So it was that at 10:10 Bernie issued the general announcement that students should try to be finished with construction by 10:25. A few minutes later, Tim elaborated as he called for the students' attention: "As a group, we'll get back together after the break at the bell. Remember you need to name the people involved, talk about the process of organizing, and tell the name for your bridge. Clean up the area—materials person, put the materials back." When the break did come at 10:25, about ten students remained in the room to put finishing touches on their bridges or to just stand back and admire their handiwork. Dan used the time to move a table to the center of the room, creating a stage for the presentations to follow.

Bernie's request for volunteers to be first to present was taken up by the creators of the Suicide Bridge. Confidently the builders predicted that their bridge would support all thirteen bricks. It did! As members of this group were returning to their seats and Tim was taking their bridge across the hall to Dan's room for safekeeping, Bernie told the student audience, "Folks, every time one group finishes, let's have a round of applause!" So, punctuated by rounds of applause and the flash of Sheryl's camera, the parade of nineteen bridges continued. The X Bridge, the King, Beavis the Bridge, the Smooshing Bridge, the Brooklyn Bridge, the Box Bridge, the No Name Bridge, the Pontoon Bridge, and ten more all took up the gauntlet thrown by the Suicide Bridge's risking thirteen bricks. All but three were successful. Bernie and Dan provided color commentary for the proceedings. Dan often mentioned the engineering features he noticed—the use of cylinders as supports, the efficiency of supporting "lots of weight" with a light-weight bridge—or offered encouragement: "a valiant effort, not bad," as the No Name Bridge collapsed after five bricks. Bernie's running commentary often took the form of questions. When the last of the thirteen bricks had been carefully placed on the Pontoon Bridge, Bernie asked, "Why did you guys start over? Why not go with a bad design?" Satisfied with the response he received, Bernie continued the incidental lesson he wanted to teach: "What is the moral of the story? . . . It's an important lesson in life."

At 11:18, Bernie's earlier musing about "how we'll do on time" was answered. Just as the last bridge had been presented, Frank Barton's voice came over the classroom speakers to give students directions concerning the lunch schedule. Students gathered their bookbags. Videotaping volunteers packed their equipment; the teachers' thank-you's were met by responses of "Anytime." With the 11:22 bell, the first Connections block ended.

More than bridges had been built. One of those "memories that last a lifetime" had also been built. The first impressions of Connections for both teachers and students had been formed. Truisms surrounding first impressions abound. First impressions count. First impressions last. First impressions are not easily changed. The story of Connections' first morning is a story of first impressions. What were they? How did they count? Would they last?

## FIRST IMPRESSIONS COUNT

Near the end of the year, I asked George Cerny to reflect on the significant moments in Connections from his perspective as principal. His response was immediate, "We had a good first day . . . It was imperative that they got off to a good start" (interview, April 29, 1994). The teachers also saw the first day as significant. When a group of teachers from an area high school visited in November, stories of the first day were quickly told. Sheryl recounted the phenomenon of the unheard bell. Tim added, "We didn't do rules until the second week. Everybody was involved. It was so much fun." By mid-May when a group of area administrators visited, the story of the unheard bell had become entrenched in Connections lore. Again, Sheryl began the account, "We were shocked how they worked together. They didn't notice the bell ringing." Steve confirmed the tale, "They didn't bolt for the door." Clearly, for the teaching team, this first impression counted.

It is not surprising that the phenomenon of the unheard bell would be the strongest first impression for the Connections teachers. After all, that a teacher's sense of success depends on students is certainly well documented.[2] Accordingly, the students' total engagement in the task of bridge building would provide the teachers with the "good start" George Cerny discerned as "imperative." Yet other first impressions also surfaced when the Connections teachers recalled the first day.

SHERYL. There's so much more family feeling, a growing sense of community. (September 10, 1993)
Most of the presenters weren't honors students. That's cool. (August 24, 1993)

TIM. For the kids I deal with it was a real plus . . . They didn't go off into their own room. (Comment to board of education, March 21, 1994)
The camaraderie of the four of us is good. If something wasn't being done, someone picked it up. (September 17, 1993)

DAN. Everything seemed to fall into place . . . It would be really bad if there was a slacker. Each [of us] seems to pick up on things to do. It's not really discussed. . . The flexibility of the schedule is the best thing. (September 10, 1993)

In considering these first impressions—student engagement, family atmosphere, heterogeneous student cohort, teaching team camaraderie, flexibility—two characteristics are apparent. These first impressions were powerful, and they were complex.

Their power is evident in the place the first day story assumed in the Connections organizational saga.[3] First impressions were consistently reiterated as the teachers invariably included the story of the first day when they were asked to explain Connections to persons outside of the Connections community. The first-day experience seemed to be, quite literally, a defining moment in the Connections journey. Such moments, with their power to shape meanings, are what Denzin (1989) calls "epiphanies." Epiphanies are: "Those interactional moments that leave marks on people's lives . . . They are often interpreted . . . as turning point experiences. Having had this experience, the person is never again quite the same" (Denzin, 1989, p. 15). Epiphanies may be an integral part of the process by which communities are created, providing focus points in the developing history of the community. A collegial community is, in no small measure, a "community of memory" (Bellah et al., 1985, p. 333)—defined by its history and its collective memory of that history. Consequently, the principal's insight that a "good" first day was "imperative" takes on added significance.

While George Cerny was referring to the teachers' need for initial success, the good first day may also be seen as imperative for another reason. With no previous community history, the epiphany of the first day became a source of self-definition for the Connections community. Clearly, the first day was an important port of call on the Connections odyssey—a port whose environment reflected multiple and complex connections between and among parents, students, the Connections teachers, administrators, and the school environment. Examining this web of connections within the first day environment may help account for the marked power of Connections' first impressions.

## AN ECOLOGY OF FIRST IMPRESSIONS

In attempting to explain classroom processes, the construct of ecological intelligence proposes that the classroom environment consists of a myriad of conversations, or connections, involving three central partners: the teachers, the students, and a particular place (Haley-Oliphant & Yinger, 1993). A classroom world, or ecosystem, is created as the teachers and students engage in making connections with the systems that converge within the classroom environment—including physical, cultural, and personal systems. Looking at how the teaching team made connections with students and each other within each of these environmental systems may help to explain the apparent power of Connections' first impressions.

*Physical Systems Connections*

Not surprisingly, many of Connections' first impressions and connections relate to the sense of place emblematic of a physical system. During the first day, Connections claimed a homestead in room 307.

The welcoming banner clearly distinguished the room from all others at Cedar City High School. On the first day, the banner created first impressions: it served as a greeting, or connection, to students from the teachers; and it was an indicator of a separate Connections identity within Cedar City High School. It also provided a landmark as Connections students first learned to navigate the maze of hallways. But it remained affixed between the double doors long after it had served these initial purposes. In fact, the banner, somewhat faded but otherwise untouched by time, still announced Connections' location on the last day of school in June.

The bridge building of the first day illustrated the significance of room 307. For all of the Connections students to meet together, work on the bridge-building project, and present their work, the standard size classroom would not suffice. As a double room, room 307 enabled Connections to have a "home" where all members, teachers and students, could gather together.

This sense of a home place can be seen as enabling both students and teachers to connect and define themselves as a program. Sheryl's first-day impression of a family feeling, a feeling that she valued in her life outside of Connections, would have been more difficult, if not impossible, to achieve had not Connections had a home in room 307. But size was not the only physical dimension of significance.

The physical dimensions of time and location within the building were also evidenced as important on the first day. Not only was room 307 large enough to permit all eighty students and four teachers to connect within a single physical setting, but the room was Connections' for the full three-period block of time. This block of time allowed connections between and among students and teachers to be sustained beyond the standard Carnegie unit class period. Moreover, the block of time allowed for the flexible scheduling that was seen as a distinctive and important Connections first impression. Further, room 307's location at the end of a hallway left the room relatively isolated. Few sights or sounds emanating from the rest of the building, even those associated with the change of classes, could intrude on the world of room 307. In essence, the physical system that was room 307 created a Connections world within Cedar City High School.

Throughout the Connections year, room 307 would be an integral part of Connections' physical system. For the entire first semester, whether the day's plans were for a full morning all together or for a three-class rotation following the bell system, all Connections students met in room 307 for attendance and announcements. On those mornings when room 307 would again be where all students and teachers gathered for the full three-period block, the activity would most often again be project oriented, as was the bridge building.

So it was that Sharon Finch's quasi-monthly art projects—model Parthenons, Egyptian masks, heraldic shields, and the like—were whole group and whole block. Room 307 again saw presentations as well. Sheryl's assignments of student-devised modern-day "quests" with all of the essential components of Odysseus' journey, as well as two projects that involved all three academic content areas (group analyses of events for each decade of the twentieth century and second-semester final projects) were all presented to the Connections audience in room 307. The physical setting of room 307 also provided a staging area for these and other projects (most notably the Renaissance Fair that was the capstone of the first semester) as days were devoted to allowing students time to work together on their projects. Room 307 became a movie theater as well; students gathered as a whole to watch *Romeo and Juliet* and *To Kill a Mockingbird*. Bernie developed his own variation on room 307 as project and presentation center. Bernie, with Tim's assistance, made room 307 a courtroom and a United Nations Security Council. Actually, room 307 was a courtroom on three occasions, for the mock trials of Socrates and Louis XIV and for the Nuremberg Trials. But in recreating such dramatic history, the ratio of available roles to students disallowed a single performance: two full-morning enactments, each presented by half of the students, would be required.

As this discussion of Connections' first-day physical environment and the above litany of projects illustrate, the physical system of time, space, and location that was room 307 was part of a complex web of Connections systems. Connections' project orientation, the program's flexibility, the family atmosphere, and the physical world of room 307 were all bound together. I would suggest that the physical world of Connections' first day—the size, time, and location tied to room 307—set the stage for the first impressions and connections born that day. The physical world of room 307 can be seen as the necessary condition of opportunity for whatever degree of collegial community Connections embodied in its first impressions. But physical system connections alone cannot create a collegial community; other systems within the first day environment must also be considered.

## Cultural Systems Connections

On Connections' first day, cultural systems—those implicit routines that convey a shared pattern of perception and behavior—could be seen both in the bridge-building activity and in the teachers' common planning period.

The choice of bridge building as the first day's activity communicated several first impressions. In April, Mandy and Jason accompanied Sheryl and Tim on a "recruiting trip" for Connections' second year. As the students twice described Connections to eighth-grade audiences, many of Mandy and Jason's comments hearkened back to cultural impressions of the first day:

> MANDY. We do projects all the time. It's project after project . . . It's not as boring; it's different.

JASON. It was kinda fun 'cause you get to work with other kids . . . Whenever you've got a question, you've got four teachers, and they'll get to you.

Sheryl and Tim's presentation to the eighth-grade students also reflected first-day cultural impressions:

SHERYL. If you like to draw, do presentations, a lot of writing, then Connections would be good for you . . . We do a lot of projects. There's more of a family feel with Connections. If you're saying, "Man, this sounds like a lot of work," it is . . . We don't want to scare you. We do a lot of fun things. You don't have to be a "good" student [to be in Connections].

TIM. Our number one goal in Connections is to make sure you're successful in the classroom . . . [Success] is not dependent on whether you're academic, honors, or general . . . I know these [Connections] students better than any other students I've had in sixteen years of teaching . . . In this program, you have a lot of responsibility.

By recalling the words, actions, and events of Connections' first morning, it is possible to see whence many of these impressions came.

Words, actions, and events communicated cultural messages. Themes may be discerned in these cultural messages. First, consider: the choice of bridge building as an activity that required student involvement in groups; the designation of student advisory groups; teachers visiting groups, asking questions, and sharing stories. All of these cultural messages seemed designed to promote interaction, or connections, between and among students and teachers. Moreover, Connections' structures would encourage, or render acceptable and normal, active learning and group work. These cultural messages recognize the pressing need of adolescents to connect to an adult who gets to know them and care about them (Astuto & Clark, 1991).

Other words, actions, and events conveyed other cultural messages. Recall that work groups were created by chance, without regard to student ability-level designations, and that everyone was given the same task and materials. Note the message in Bernie's encouragement for a group that scrapped its original unsuccessful design to begin again. Consider the messages conveyed as students presented their bridges: so many different bridge styles, but all able to support the weight of many bricks; a "general" student chosen as group communicator; the applause that followed each presentation. These cultural messages communicated Connections' heterogeneous orientation of ensuring success for all: It would be acceptable, or normal, for students from three ability levels to connect with each other, to engage in the same academic work, and to be subject to the same standards of performance.

On the first day, students also witnessed teachers openly conferring with each other. They saw parents videotaping and administrators stopping in to visit. These cultural messages created the impression of the Connections classroom as a very public forum, one in which Pauly's (1991) characterization of classrooms as places of "unrelenting mutual scrutiny" (p. 40) is not a threat, but acceptable.

Schools and classrooms are "message centers" where "the messages show teachers and students what their future holds" (Pauly, 1991, p. 94). The cultural messages, or first impressions, communicated during the three periods of bridge building on Connections' first day were multiple and complex. But they were not the only cultural messages of the first day. Connections' first-day cultural system could also be seen in the teachers' first common planning period.

On the first morning of school, the aroma of perking coffee and Sheryl's coffee cake came as no surprise. Neither did Bernie's work on the white board nor Dan's turn at the computer seem anything but routine. The summer's meetings of planning and preparation had given rise to routines and relationships that later found their way into the cultural system of the common planning period. Considering the well-documented uncertainty of teachers' work,[4] and given the uncertainty inherent in initial implementation of any educational innovation, such predictability takes on major significance. It is no wonder then, that both Dan's and Tim's reflections on their first impressions focused on being able to depend on their colleagues. As Dan put it, "Everything seems to be falling into place. [There's] no situation where nobody would take up tasks. Everybody is so reliable" (September 10, 1993). There is a sense of serendipity in Dan's words, a sense that the cultural system embedded in the first day's planning period was as much a result of the fortuitous blend of these four teachers in this time and place as of deliberate effort. The question then arises: can serendipity create first impressions that last? The answer may lie in the personal systems within Connections' first-day ecology.

*Personal Systems Connections*

Implicit in personal systems is Bruner's (1986) concept of "stance." Within the language and actions of classrooms, stance marking occurs as teachers and students convey their perspectives on the scene. Within the context of Connections' first day, one stance looms larger than all others.

Bernie's statement that "I'm excited to start school;" Sheryl's comment that "It's so cool we don't have to do mundane stuff;" and Tim's recollection that "It was so much fun"—all of these expressions point to a common stance about Connections: excitement. Teaching and learning in Connections would be an adventure. As the Connections newsletter told parents, "We hope you and your child are as excited about the coming journey as are we!" For Mike Davis, this air of excitement was "critical. The teachers need to be enthusiastic" (May 11, 1993). To some extent, this air of excitement could be anticipated. After all, it was the first day of school and Connections was a brand new program at Cedar City High School. And the bridge-building project was most certainly an exciting departure from "normal" first-day-of-school activities.

While the sense of excitement, shared in common by teachers and students, was the hallmark of personal first impressions, other dimensions of Connections' personal system could be seen as well on that first day. Teacher perspectives about the nature of teaching and learning and about subject matter can also be discerned in Connections' first-day experience.

Throughout the morning of bridge building, teachers tacitly imparted shared views of teaching and learning. They had structured the task, but learning would, quite literally, be student constructed. To be sure, teachers would facilitate the process (as with Bernie's incidental lesson on the value of starting over), but the presentations would be made by students, not teachers. In addition, while traveling from group to group and engaging students in conversation, each teacher clearly regarded making personal connections with students as part of the teaching process.

The task involved risk, an acknowledgment that in Connections teaching and learning would involve risk, but Connections would be a place where "pushing the envelope" (to use Bernie's phrase) would be safe. Applause was given to all efforts. All students, regardless of ability level, would experience success in the learning task of the first day.

The perspective of teaching as craft could also be seen. In keeping with Huberman's (1993) tinkerer model, teachers openly conferred to create on-the-spot adaptations of their basic lesson plan. Teachers sought and accepted the suggestions of their colleagues.

The activity of bridge building could not be considered as within the province of any of Connections' three subject areas. The first day's content was distinctly metacognitive. Concerned with group strategies and processes, the teachers applied the lessons of their cooperative learning training with gusto. Group work and critical thinking strategies were the subject matter of the first day, and all four teachers communicated the perspective that such subject matter would have validity in Connections. Later in the week, Sheryl's English perspective would surface as she would ask students to write about their group experience. Dan's science perspective surfaced briefly in his comments about the bridges' structures and efficiency. But overall, any individual teacher's perspectives about his or her individual subject areas were subdued as the single activity of bridge building transcended subject area boundaries.

United in place, time, and activity, the four teachers presented a seamless interweaving of personal systems on Connections' first day. Active, student-constructed learning, the value of cooperative learning, ensuring success while acknowledging risk, teaching as craft, and an interdisciplinary focus—all of these perspectives seemed to be claimed by all four teachers in equal measure. Undeniably, the elements of interdependence and communication so necessary to collegial community were present in the personal systems of the first-day ecology.

In considering Connections' first-day ecosystem, it becomes clear that the personal, cultural, and physical systems are inextricably bound together. Linked in mutual reinforcement were the shared physical system of room 307; the cultural messages of family, camaraderie, heterogeneous students, active learning and group work, and flexibility; and the personal perspectives placing value on excitement, adventurous teaching and learning, student construction of knowledge, cooperative learning, teaching as craft, and an interdisciplinary focus. Yet one other dimension of the first day ecosystem remains to be examined briefly for the ecology of first impressions to be complete.

## Webs to Other Ecosystems

In creating a teaching team whose members were from four separate academic departments, in mixing students from various ability group designations, and in structuring the flexible scheduling of the Connections block, the Connections program deviated from the ecosystem in place at Cedar City High School.

While the teachers' first morning was spent in the Connections world of room 307, their afternoon work would return them to the traditional environment of Cedar City High School. For the first morning, at least, the two worlds were successfully compartmentalized. The larger school system—even its bell signaling the end of second period—did not intrude on the Connections ecosystem. Yet the larger school and district environment had exerted some influence in creating Connections.

As their visits to room 307 attested, Cedar City administrators were very interested in Connections. Connections' entitlement to room 307, the teachers' extra planning period together, the application for waivers allowing Tim to teach non-LD students, the securing of grants—all had resulted from administrative actions in the larger system. As Tim told a group of visiting administrators in May, "If [Connections] didn't have the backing of the administration, this would never have flown."

On the first day, the perceptible influence of the school and district environments was limited to the visible expression of administrative interest and support. This is not surprising. In the life of schools, first days are unique. Cedar City High School proved no exception. After the summer break, the return to school carried an almost palpable air of excitement. Rhythms and routines had not yet settled in. The school's vision statement, adopted the year before Connections' implementation, had given a tacit endorsement to Connections. But on the first day no one yet knew what Connections would mean at Cedar City High School. On August 24, the customary politics of departments had been displaced by the more immediate and pressing political concern about the potential threat of Freedom 2000 to the upcoming board of education election. On the first day, district financial pressures had yet to be felt. So on the first day of school, the ecological web connecting Cedar City High School and Connections was far from intricate.

## THE LASTING POWER OF FIRST IMPRESSIONS

The euphoria of success permeated the environment of Connections' first day and assured that day a prominent place in Connections lore. But research in the area of implementation sounds a cautionary note in the midst of such euphoria. Gross, Giacquinta, and Bernstein (1971) warn that "Initiation is not enough to ensure implementation" (p. 208). Odden (1991) cautions that teacher commitment is of two different kinds: the commitment to try the new program and commitment to the new program— the latter usually emerging at the end, rather than at the beginning, of the implementation process. In his analysis of the development of community, Peck (1987) distinguishes between community by accident and community by design, between pseudo community and genuine community. Peck admonishes groups to "Beware of instant community. Community-making requires time as well as effort and sacrifice. It cannot be cheaply bought" (p. 88). Would Connections' first impressions be the basis for the development of community? Or would they be an elusive chimera of community that would appear infrequently, if ever, again?

The power of Connections' first impressions cannot be denied. In the teachers' consistent recollection of the first day, a vision of the object of the Connections quest began to form. But after the first day—the first port—the question remained: would the environment in the ports to come on the Connections odyssey be as hospitable to this emerging vision as the first day ecosystem?

# CHAPTER 4

# Second Impressions:
# September 14, 1993

> Although the program [Connections] has only been in place for
> about two weeks, it appears to be running smoothly.
> —"Connections make [Cedar City]
> freshmen smile, laugh, listen, learn"

Unlike the first day of school, the halls of Cedar City High School
were quiet as I made my way to Dan's room. The day before, the
fourth week of school had begun with the news of a student death
over the weekend. Other events of the first weeks—football
games, yearbook picture-taking, days of early dismissal due to
extreme heat—that had been prominent in before-school conversation faded as students (especially junior classmates) seemed to
be bracing themselves for the next day's funeral.

The somber mood was dispelled as I entered Dan's room.
Again, like the first day and all of the other days in between, the
aroma of brewing coffee indicated that Dan or Tim had performed the customary early morning coffee-making chore. But
only Tim and Sheryl were seated in their habitual places at one
pair of tables as the 7:35 bell rang.

## THE COMMON PLANNING PERIOD

This mid-September morning found the Connections program
well into the Beginnings unit. In planning for the unit, the teachers had envisioned that each content area would relate to the central theme of "beginnings." Sheryl would focus on literary beginnings in Greek mythology and *The Odyssey*; Bernie's instruction
would center on early Greek, Egyptian, and Roman civilizations;
and Dan's teaching would explore the beginning elements of the
scientific method, particularly measurement and the format for

experiments. This morning, Tim had brought in a workbook-type text on ancient Greece that he had found at the local public library. He had chosen the book in preparation for conducting a lesson on Greek art and architecture the next day. He showed the book to Sheryl, and she took several minutes to thumb through it. In the process, she found several ideas that were relevant to the unit's English focus. Bernie peeked in for a moment just as Sheryl was telling Tim, "This is such a good book!" In a voice that grew more hoarse with each word, Bernie told Tim and Sheryl he would return soon but that he had to get to the photocopier to "run off the Soh-crates [a Bernie-ism for Socrates] packets." While they waited for Bernie and Dan, Tim showed Sheryl the activities he had chosen from the book for the next day's lesson.

Shortly after 8:00, Bernie returned with a stack of uncollated papers in his arms. "Quick, folks, I need a brainstorm idea!" As he had been photocopying, it had suddenly occurred to Bernie that there was a problem with the day's planned schedule. In last Thursday's charting of the week ahead, this day had been designated as one on which Tim's Red group would be parceled out among the three other color groups to follow a "three-class rotation by the bells." But today's history time would be devoted to preparation for Friday's dramatization, the Trial of Socrates. It was to be performed twice—once by Red/Magenta and once by Blue/Green. So Bernie needed to meet with students today in those groupings. Just as Bernie had explained his dilemma, Dan came into the room.

"Good, we need a mathematician!" It took all three teachers—Bernie, Sheryl, and Tim—to explain the complexities of the desired schedule, one that would allow Bernie to meet with two color groups at a time for 1½ periods each while the remaining two color groups would switch between Dan and Sheryl for 3/4 period each. The task was sufficiently complex that Dan needed to "play with it" on the blackboard before he could encode the schedule with color-keyed markers on smaller white boards for students (and his colleagues).

While Dan was busy working out the schedule's details, Sheryl pulled out her list of chaperones for the upcoming field trip to a local Renaissance Festival, and Tim and Bernie tackled the chore of collating and stapling Socrates packets. As they worked,

Bernie briefed Tim on his plans for the day's classes. "We'll do the pre-trial survey, and then get them in groups for a little pseudo cooperative learning stuff . . . Then the reading; then more info on the Greeks."

A PA system interruption—"Mr. Lyons, you have a telephone call"—prompted Sheryl to make the comment she would make many times in the days to come, "We need a phone, guys!" While Bernie went to the office to take the call, Tim continued collating. Dan finished working on the schedule and started laying out materials for the day's science activity on student tables. Sheryl looked at her grade book. To no one in particular, she noted, "Marsha Bates had her fourth absence yesterday. We need to refer her to George." Then, as Bernie returned and resumed packet assembling with Tim, Sheryl asked, "Have any of you had trouble with Jason?" She explained that her concern sprang from Jason's inattention (he had slept) during the school librarian's standard freshman orientation to the media center the day before. But Sheryl's question remained unanswered as the bell signaling the end of the common planning period rang.

## A THREE-WAY ROTATION

*Room 307*

When the Connections students reported to room 307 for what had by now become the daily ritual of attendance and announcements, several noticed the white marker board schedules Dan had created. One asked, "Is this going to be a confusing day?" Dan promised an explanation later. By this fourth week of school, each advisory group had claimed a quadrant of room 307 as its own— Sheryl's Blue group in the left front, Tim's Red group in the right front, Dan's Green group in the left rear, and Bernie's Magentans in the right rear.

During the next few minutes, Dan called out Green group names while Bernie and Tim took attendance silently. Sheryl announced that she would be collecting late work from last Friday's art project. (In her first visit to Connections, Sharon Finch had talked about the visual language of cave dwellers and students had each designed a visual expression, or logo, for Connections.) By 8:45, students and teachers were ready for Dan's promised explanation of the day's structure.

"Okay, guys, listen up, please." Displaying one of the color-coded white boards, Dan went through the schedule, explaining the sequence for each color group. As he finished speaking, Bernie noted, "That explained a lot easier than how we planned it!" Since Dan was still displaying a white board, Sheryl issued a not-so-subtle hint to students, "Guys, you might want to jot some of this down." A general rustle indicated that at least some students had taken Sheryl's hint, retrieved their assignment notebooks, and copied the schedule. (Each Connections student had been given an assignment notebook during the first week of school, and the teachers had been working on making their use habitual.)

Before dismissing the students from room 307, Dan reminded them that Mr. Barton had spoken with the four teachers about the need for Connections students to move through the halls *quietly* when they were not following the school's bell schedule. "So how do we go through the halls?" The response came in chorus, "Quietly."

## Room 138

Bernie set his grade book and the stack of Socrates packets on his desk in the left rear corner of his windowless room. As he moved front and center, he told the combined group of Red and Magenta students, "I'm going to need your help today. I'm not as energetic as usual. We've got some neat things to do this week." As students listened to Bernie's reprise of earlier talks about the Greeks, students could again notice the two signs Bernie had placed below the classroom clock. One conveyed the single word "Gridlock." The other displayed a Nixon quotation, "I'll take the responsibility but not the blame."

As Tim arrived with the white boards and markers students would soon use, Bernie launched into the conversation that would set the stage for this day's activities and the Socrates trial to come: "How many would agree that 'the masses are asses'? This is where we left off yesterday. Folks, you're young adults; you need to have opinions. Will Mr. Schwartz laugh? Will I? We may disagree, but we won't laugh. Neither will the class. We have good people here." A brief digression later (wherein Bernie noted he has found print media more informative than television and Tim reinforced the thought), Bernie distributed a survey and asked students to "go through and circle your opinion." (See appendix D for a copy of the eight-question survey.) During the few minutes students were circling their responses, Bernie and Tim met at Bernie's desk to confirm the time line of the extended period's activities.

When most students had put down their pens, Bernie made the purpose of the survey clear: "These questions are what got Socrates in trouble. We're going to put him on trial in Athens in 399 B.C. as recorded by Plato. You remember Plato; you played with Play-Doh when you were little." Snickers indicated that most students understood Bernie's pun.

This transition made explicit, Bernie was not done with the survey yet. He asked students to form teams of three or four by proximity, to take ten minutes to identify within each group the three most important opinions the group could agree upon, and to record their consensus on the white boards that Tim would distribute. While the students were so engaged, Tim left the room to get paper towels to serve as erasers, and when he returned Bernie went to refill the coffee he had been sipping to soothe his sore throat. Both Bernie and Tim toured the groups, Tim silently checking progress, and Bernie pausing to ask students to defend their positions.

Drawing the class back together, Bernie began the discussion by telling Tim to "feel free to jump in." After a few groups had reported their group's decisions, Bernie eyed the clock and noted that only a few minutes remained until the school's bell would interrupt and leave only twenty minutes for the rest of the extended period's agenda. So before that could happen, Bernie interjected, "I'd like to hit a couple of the hard ones with you." Pointing specifically to items five and seven (individual versus societal rights and the limits, if any, on freedom of speech), Bernie raised two contemporary issues to illustrate the implications of the survey's general statements: gay rights and antiwar protests.

The first provoked animated debate among the students, with some insisting that "special" rights were not just. One student's argument, "God is the judge, not men," drew Bernie's praise—

"That's an enlightened idea." The second prompted Bernie to recall, "I gotta tell ya, Mr. Schwartz, me, and Mrs. Dorsch back there, we were around during Vietnam. [Dissent] caused a lot of problems then." Tim nodded vigorously, but any comment he might have added was interrupted by the sound of the school's bell.

A few students remained in room 138 during the five minute break. Despite the PA's summons for specified students to "come to the office," they were able to hear the stories of Tim and Bernie's recollections of Vietnam era protests. Bernie took advantage of their presence, asking them to place a copy of the Socrates packet on each desk. When all the students returned with the bell, Bernie drew them back to the lesson, "Back to the Greeks. They had the same dilemma. Socrates was critical of the war effort." Referring to the first page of the packet, Bernie offered a synopsis of the historical context of the Athens-Sparta war. "Turn-o el page-o."

With time quickly running out, Bernie (to the accompaniment of a few groans and a voiced "Oh, man!") told students which pages needed to be read as homework—"This is important, okay?" Assured that the homework assignment had been given, Bernie directed the students' attention to the page listing the roles to be dramatized in Friday's mock trial. With only two days to prepare, Bernie deliberately pointed out the roles that would require more research and significant speaking time, particularly the central role of Socrates. Yet four students raised their hands to volunteer for the demanding role. Bernie turned to Tim, "How shall we do this?" Tim suggested a "pick a number" strategy, and the allocation of major speaking roles continued until all had been assigned. To the remaining students, Bernie said, "The rest of you are jurors. An Athenian jury had five hundred men, but we'll make do with twenty-five or so."

In the few minutes before the "split" time indicated by the white board schedule, Bernie asked students with speaking roles to "come to my office" to get a background sheet describing their part in the trial while Tim handed out a paper, "duties of jurors" to each of the jury members. As students began to gather book bags, Bernie reminded them to "read the background info for tomorrow," to wipe off their boards and stack them on a table along the left side of the room, and place their seats back in rows. Promptly at 9:55, Tim also issued last-minute reminders: that Magenta would go to Mr. Centers's room, that "my group" would go to Mrs. Hart's room, and that "in the halls, do not make noise, and do not stop at the rest room."

## Room 314

The Magenta students who traveled next to Dan's room for science took their places at lab tables arranged in facing pairs. After closing the door (ensuring that stragglers would be noted as tardy), and during the time that students were settling in their seats, Dan focused on preliminary tasks. He asked for any permission slips and money for the field trip, and one student stepped forward. He asked for lab notebooks, and another student held one out for Dan's inspection. "This one is unacceptable. It's not bound." So this lab book would not be added to the forty-four accumulated on Dan's front counter thus far (eleven of which were in a separate stack for those a day late). He asked for any late submissions of vocabulary sheets, and one boy brought his forward. Glancing at the sheet, Dan noticed that a few entries were missing. So he asked the class to recall the procedure if a given word was not in the text's glossary. Immediately, responses of "Look in the other book" [students had been permitted to choose between two texts] and "Use a dictionary" indicated that these Magenta students were already well versed in Mr. Centers' expectations. "I don't mean to sound like a meanie, but I am a meanie. [A pause, a smile.] No, you've had plenty of time."

Preliminaries completed, Dan pointed to the materials list he had written on the blackboard and began the introduction to the day's prelab activity. Before the "real" lab scheduled for Thursday, this activity was designed to provide practice in formatting a lab report and in accurately measuring with both a ruler and a balance. For this prelab, students would need a pencil or erasable pen, a ruler, a balance (Dan had already placed one on each student table), and a wood block. As he itemized the list, Dan cautioned the students that the balances were not designed to accommodate more than six hundred grams, and he further explained that placing more than a pound on the balance would make the balance edge dull and therefore inaccurate. As he finished reading off the list, Dan told the students that he was missing some rulers and that they might have inadvertently taken one the day before—"I know it was not on purpose." But he asked the students to "look anyway." While some were looking through their book bags, three girls came up to Dan's desk to buy pens and pencils. As he conducted the transaction, Dan reminded the girls, "Please remember, if you have to buy something, buy it before class."

"Today, we're going to measure three dimensions of a wood block." Holding one block aloft, Dan asked, "Where is the length?" First one girl, and then one boy pointed to the same edge of the block. "Well then, where would you measure the width?" The first girl chose another edge of the block. "Where would you measure height?" Dan flipped the block in his hand so that the girl would indicate a previously chosen edge, ensuring that Dan could make the point that the students would need to be consistent in their orientation to the block as they measured. Other points also needed to be made. "Do you line up the edge of the ruler to the edge of the block?" "How many decimal places?" "To calculate volume, what do you do? Add?" Still ensuring that students would follow correct procedures, Dan then continued to explain that in measuring mass to the nearest hundredth of a gram, the students would need to estimate the last digit. Dan's quick drawing of a balance scale on the blackboard illustrated the estimation process.

Explanations and demonstrations completed, Dan told the students they could "get working. I'll come around and pick up what you did from yesterday. If you didn't understand, you will today and be able to finish." While Dan distributed wood blocks (one to each pair of lab partners) and rulers, a few students still had questions:

E. J. Do we each do our own sheet of paper?

DAN. Yes, and then compare with your partner.

CHRIS. I don't have a partner.

DAN. It's okay to not have a partner.

CHARLIE. Is this a lab?

DAN. No, this is practice. Keep it. There'll be a lab on Thursday.

In the course of his rounds among the students, Dan overheard one student exclaim to his partner, "Hey, this is exactly five!" Addressing the class as a whole, Dan repeated the student's observation and asked, "What do you do if it's exactly something like four?" Lucas raised his hand and blurted out, "Make it four-point-oh." "Right."

Dan's rounds continued through the 10:27 bell, ignored because this morning's rotation provided a "split" at 10:40. As he glanced at the student's recorded measurements, Dan sometimes paused to ask, "Do you want to reconsider that?" or to assist students in reading the balance scale. In a room that held few items that could offer any visual distraction (other than a large periodic table of elements that dominated the right wall), most of the students exhibited an undistracted concentration on their task.

One exception proved obvious. Shortly after his 10:30 warning of "Guys, we need to change at 10:40. You have ten minutes left," Dan noticed Jesse copying his partner's paper. Quietly, Dan took Jesse's paper, crumpled it, and told Jesse to do the measurements again. When his stroll took Dan by Jesse's table again two minutes later, Jesse's paper was again magically complete. Again, but more audibly, Dan took the paper, crumpled it, and told Jesse, "If I see this again, I'll ask you to go into the hall." No such opportunity arose this day—10:40 was approaching rapidly.

"There are only two minutes left. Hang onto your papers. These will be your guides for the lab on Thursday. So save them." On his last tour of the tables, as students were gathering their belongings, Dan collected rulers, offering a "thank you" to each student who handed him one. As the Magentans were leaving Dan's room and heading to Sheryl's, one girl told another, "Mr. Centers whines and bickers too much."

## Room 132

When the Magenta students entered Sheryl's classroom, many noticed the change in the side bulletin board. What had been an empty space, covered only with royal blue paper, now was a carefully arranged display of their Connections logo projects from last Friday. Some also noticed "A composition includes:" in Sheryl's neat script on the front blackboard. As students were becoming aware of Sheryl's teaching patterns, a few might have seen the fragment, realized that prewritten blackboard cues usually foreshadowed the day's class topic, and concluded that today's instruction would depart from the Greek myths that had been the English focus for the past two weeks. In fact, at least one student did make the connection as she complained to Sheryl, "I thought we were talking about the story we read last night."

But Sheryl explained that today's talk about composition was necessary to prepare students for a major "fun" group project they would be undertaking as part of their upcoming study of *The Odyssey*. She did not reveal more about the promised project, but observant students might have noticed that the back bulletin board now displayed poster board maps illustrating previous student "Quest" projects. Instead, Sheryl told the students, "You will need a piece of paper for notes about composition and the final copy." Even though Sheryl said, "I'm not going to check notes," students had discovered the week before that Sheryl permitted students to use their notes while taking a test, so they readily complied with her directive.

Alluding to an earlier combined history-English assignment in which students had written about the components of civilization, Sheryl explained, "We didn't give you very much information about your compositions. We wanted to see how you approached writing. Now it's time for structure." Structure would come in a series of guiding questions / student responses / teacher elaborations.

Pointing to the blackboard where the fragment "A composition includes:" awaited completion, Sheryl began by writing the numeral "1" on the board and asking, "What's the first part of any composition? It's in your *Writer's Inc.*" Several students offered, "the introduction." "Exactly." As she wrote the response on the board, Sheryl added, "the main idea, the topic." Asking students to think about their own writing for the Components of Civilization essay ("Many of you did a great job of this"), Sheryl queried, "What are some ways to vary it to get the audience involved?" Within a few moments, Sheryl had expanded the blackboard notes to include the students' suggestions: dialogue, questions, grabbers. As she wrote her own addition to the list, Sheryl asked for its meaning, "What's an anecdote?" Lucas blurted out, "It's a medicine." Smiling, but successfully suppressing laughter, Sheryl corrected Lucas, "You're thinking of antidote; an anecdote is a little story."

"Okay, now the second part of a composition is the important stuff. Just like in a letter, it's"—Sheryl's rising inflection and pause allowed the students to fill in the blank with "the body." Again, when Sheryl wrote the students' response on the board, she amplified, adding "important details, dialogue, examples," and asked students to think about the examples they had used in their Components of Civilization essays. Then Sheryl asked Greg to stand. "Greg is like a composition. His head is like the introduction. His body, up to his feet, is the body. But if we just stopped there, Greg would be walking on his ankles." Greg, given the class's attention, buckled his ankles, producing laughter he (and Sheryl) obviously enjoyed. "So we need to give Greg some feet; we need a what?" Greg supplied the answer: "A conclusion." "Exactly."

Once again, as Sheryl wrote "3.) Conclusion" on the board, she amplified the concept by explaining that this part of a composition should "tie up loose ends" and restate the topic. "But never put 'the end' on your paper. When the words stop, I'll know it's over."

With the left panel of the blackboard now filled, Sheryl began writing on the right panel, "Tips for final copy." As she wrote, she announced: "Now we're going to switch gears. Final copy form means something to me. It needs to mean the same thing to you. Otherwise, you'll be rewriting." No longer asking questions, Sheryl enumerated her "final copy" criteria. First on her list was neatness—"It needs to be legible." Second was "ink (typed)." She explained the parentheses: "In tenth grade you'll have keyboarding, so final copy from then on will mean this." Third was "margins." Lastly, Sheryl explained that for Connections work, students should use a heading that included their name, the date, and their color group.

"It's neat, in ink, now what?" As she wrote "M U G S" on the blackboard, Sheryl said, "I know those of you who had Mr. Martin or Mrs. Nelson at the junior high probably recognize this. Anybody remember what these letters stand for?" With a little prompting, students recalled the eighth-grade acronym: Mechanics, Usage, Grammar, Spelling. To those who had not had the teachers mentioned and whose faces bore expressions of puzzlement as mechanics and usage were listed, Sheryl explained: "Mechanics is the paper's set-up. Usage means avoiding saying things like 'He ain't got no good English.' So far, I've only looked at spelling and mechanics on your papers . . . Final copy means a perfect paper, not just the way it looks."

One last item on the day's agenda remained for the last several minutes before the 11:22 bell would sound. "Let's move to the assignment book." On each of the remaining days of this week, Sheryl explained, students would need to bring their literature books, "the orange or white books."[1] Sheryl reminded the students that by Thursday, these books should have covers. "Tomorrow, also bring your atlas from history. In our introduction to *The Odyssey*, we'll talk about locations." Sheryl also reminded the students that Friday would be the day for "the big test over the heroes" and that, as before, they would be permitted to use their notes as they took the test. "Any questions?" Apparently there were none, so students had free time for the few minutes left before the bell. Just as students used the time to visit, Sheryl also paused to converse with several students as she strolled toward the classroom door. "Nice game Friday, Casey . . . I love the logo you did, E.J."

*Second Impressions Also Count*

Unlike the first-day story, the story of September 14, 1993, was never included among the Connections stories recounted by the teachers. In his discussion of organizational sagas, Clark (1972) distinguishes between a saga's initiation and its fulfillment. Moments of epiphany give rise to, or initiate, a community's saga. But without fulfillment, a saga "can be removed quickly from the collective understanding of the present and future . . . and the events that set the direction of belief can be readily reversed" (Clark, 1972, p. 179). In other words, if the ecosystem of Connections' first impressions were to remain viable and support the life of a collegial community, then second impressions, like those of September 14, would also count. The ecosystem of days like September 14, 1993, would also need to support collegial community. September 14 would need to serve a fulfilling role. Therefore, an analysis of the September 14 ecosystem, with its component subsystems, is needed in order to address the issues raised in the conclusion of the preceding chapter.

## AN ECOLOGY OF SECOND IMPRESSIONS

In contrast to the first day, September 14 was more fragmented: it was no longer unified by place, time, and activity. As the Magenta students traveled from room to room, they not only entered varying physical systems but also entered distinctly differing cultural and personal habitats. The extent to which these differing habitats were in harmony or discord is the focus of this analysis.

### Physical Systems of September 14

On the first day, Connections' physical world was limited. Its horizons extended from room 307 across the hall to room 314, but no farther. By September 14, the bounds of Connections' physical system had come to encompass room 132, room 138, and the connecting halls of Cedar City High School. Connections' physical world had grown.

**Room 307** The room had not changed since August 24, but its use had. Now as students entered the room, they automatically assumed seats in areas of the room claimed by the four color groups. As Sheryl had observed on September 3, 1993, "We've got our territories staked out now." By September 14, a routine had developed that would be observed throughout the first semester. Regardless of the schedule for the day, the first five to ten minutes of each day would be spent in room 307. During those several minutes, attendance would be taken, the schedule for the day would be announced, general announcements (about field trips, for example) would be made, and individual teachers would often also issue reminders about assignments that were now or soon, as Sheryl put it, "due, d-u-e, not d-o." With those housekeeping chores done, the students would then be dismissed to follow the day's schedule, one that more and more often would be a three class rotation.

If the metaphor of family were applied to Connections (and in the teachers' talk it often was), then the gathering each morning in room 307 could be seen as being very like a family gathering for breakfast. Each person's plans for the day would be shared, parental reminders would be issued, and then family members would, on most days, go their separate ways for the day. Like most of the families of the students' and teachers' personal experience, being together as a family for the full day was the exception, not the rule. So "breakfast" might be the only time in any day when there would be the opportunity to see and converse with each other, to touch base with each other's lives. So, too, those occasions when the family did spend the day together around home and hearth for a special activity would be cherished days. It is no wonder, then, that when students were polled at the end of the first semester, they overwhelmingly chose the full-cohort/full-day schedule option as their favorite. For Connections, home and hearth was room 307.

**Room 138**    For Bernie, the ever-open door to room 138 led to his home and hearth at Cedar City High School. It was there that a picture of his wife and children sat on his desk. It was there that his cache of chewing gum was secreted in a desk drawer. It was there that his repository for teaching materials and student work (two long tables along the left side of the room) could be found. So despite the crowding, when Bernie wanted to meet with a double Connections grouping (like the Red/Magenta of September 14), he often chose to meet in "his" room. As he explained during one common planning period (October 1, 1993): "I feel homeless. That's the problem floating here and there. [I'm] not in my room with the table all the time. I have stuff in the big room [room 307], in Daisy's room, in the athletic office." Although the room itself and many of its furnishings were standard issue, room 138 was distinctly Bernie's.

Unlike most Cedar City High School classrooms, the teacher desk in room 138 was at the back left corner of the room, behind the rows of student desks. Bernie's desk, and the two file cabinets within arm's reach, formed what he called "my office." But in many ways, Bernie's "office" extended beyond that left rear corner of the room. The handmade signs of "Gridlock" and the

Nixon quotation were unframed—and unexplained to students. Like the book that lay on his desk during the fall, *Dave Barry Slept Here* (a malapropist retelling of American history), the signs appeared to be more a reflection of Bernie's sense of whimsy about his subject area than instructional devices.

More directly related to Bernie's teaching were the posters and pictures that covered the bulletin boards. But these thematic announcements (on September 14, a map of Greece; later, Civil War–related materials) were seldom changed throughout the course of the year—Bernie's priorities did not apparently include room decoration. Nor did his teaching methods include a great deal of writing on the largely unused blackboards. Indeed, for much of the second semester the blackboard on the right side of the room was covered with flags from Great Britain, France, the Soviet Union, and the Third Reich. True to form, Bernie did not use the blackboard on September 14. But when he did use the blackboard as part of his "giving notes" to students, Bernie usually limited his scrawled print to lists of key phrases that would get circled and arrowed to each other as he spoke. In many ways, what students could read on the blackboard was a chalk version of Bernie's manner of speaking, staccato blips that were a shorthand for a stream-of-consciousness thought process.

The student desks in room 138, although ordered in rows at the beginning of the day, often were regrouped during the course of a class, as they were on September 14. Among Bernie's record-keeping archives, no seating chart could be found. In fact, although he used the grade/attendance and lesson plan books common to all Cedar City High School teachers, Bernie's primary mode of organization was piles, whether stacks on *the* table, or on the floor along the back wall (as would be the case with November's family tree project).

In short, for Bernie, what the physical system of his room looked like was far less important than the learning that went on there. Yet in its own, somewhat disheveled, way the physical elements of Bernie's room conveyed messages—messages of love for his subject matter, of informality, and of the importance of big ideas over small details. They were messages that could be expected to resonate in the cultural and personal systems of the room 138 habitat as well.

**Room 314**    Room 314, Dan Centers' room, also conveyed messages, ones that were quite different from those of Bernie's room. No personal touches adorned Dan's desk, but then Dan worked more often with his chair turned toward the computer than toward his desk. (The computer stored files of student grades, handouts for each lab, and tests.) Unlike Bernie, Dan made it his habit to close the door to his room as he began each class period. Unlike Bernie, whose use of his room's blackboard was sparing, Dan's use of the blackboard was integral to each lesson. As on September 14, students would often enter Dan's room and see a list of materials for the day's lab already written on the blackboard. The blackboard was also Dan's chief visual aid. Explanatory drawings (e.g., a sketch of an enlarged balance scale on September 14), math calculations, and sample charts or graphs of an experiment's findings regularly found space on Dan's blackboard. But more than these differences of desk decor and blackboard use, two features in the physical system of Dan's room stand out as significantly different.

As was true of all science classrooms at Cedar City High School, heavy tables with oak legs and durable black surfaces served as student desks. Each table was designed to accommodate two students, and Dan had arranged the unwieldy tables in his room in eight facing pairs, perpendicular to the large demonstration counter, which, following traditional science classroom arrangement, spanned much of the front of the room. Like Bernie, Dan kept no seating chart. But, although he did not issue the injunction on September 14, Dan often enjoined students, as they took their seats, to "Remember, pick a person with whom you won't be tempted to talk" (November 9, 1993).

Laboratory counters, with sinks, gas outlets, and storage cabinets, ringed the sides and back of the room. The below-counter cabinets housed most of the lab equipment (balances, spring scales, graduated cylinders, and more), but still much of the counter space was taken up with various supplies, including Connections' art supplies. (As the year progressed, the counter space would also be the repository for Connections art projects— Parthenon replicas, pyramids, heraldic shields, and the like.) The students' access to the counter area, and so to lab equipment, was limited. As was true on September 14, Dan customarily got out the materials needed for the day's lab before class began and placed one of each needed item on each student table.

By design or by deference to the stationary demonstration counter, the front of the room was distinctly a teacher zone. From left to right across the full breadth of the room, beginning with shelves of teaching materials next to the windows, the teacher zone continued to the cart laden with Dan's Macintosh computer, monitor, and printer. Next to the cart was the teacher desk that formed a continuous line with the demonstration counter and the file cabinet set at the right end of the counter. The zone's right terminus consisted of the door to the storeroom shared with the next science classroom and the room's sole bulletin board (and only visual display other than the periodic table), a collage of schedules and memos. On September 14, the preliminary tasks all occurred within this zone. But it is noteworthy that Dan conducted his instruction about and explanations of the lab from the center of the room.[2]

A curiously mixed message emerged from these two components of room 314's physical system. The implied friendly informality of facing pairs of student desks clashed with the distancing effect of a clearly demarked teacher zone. However mixed or ambivalent the message conveyed by the room's arrangement of furnishings, as was the case with room 138, the messages of room 314's physical system could be expected to find echoes in the cultural and personal systems present in the room's ecology.

**Room 132**  The physical system that was Sheryl Hart's room also conveyed messages. Sheryl's room, like Bernie's, came equipped with the same standard issue individual student desks. Like Bernie, Sheryl kept no seating chart—at least not until November 16 when she announced, "I did a seating chart with Magenta. I've had it with their mouth." But given basically the same architectural shell as Bernie's room, Sheryl had created a physical system uniquely her own.

In room 132, bulletin boards were the preserve of student work, whether they displayed the logos that had been artistically and carefully arranged for students to see on September 14, the Connections "Quest" project maps that would soon replace those from the year before, or the "Dear Abbess" letters that would be part of the study of *Romeo and Juliet*. Students could clearly see that Sheryl saved their work, displayed it with care, and would use samples of student work from earlier years as models for future classes.

In the left front corner of the room, Sheryl had created a work area where organization and homey decorative touches blended. On her desk, Sheryl had placed a pink bud vase next to the rack of folders that organized her work. Each Connections color group, and each afternoon honors English section, had its own pocket folder that held current student work to be graded or returned. (No folder ever became very thick; Sheryl prided herself on grading and returning student work promptly.) At times, when students were settled in (taking a test or taking advantage of time Sheryl allocated in class for reading), students would see Sheryl seated at her desk grading papers or reading from the same text as they, periodically peering over her half-glasses to see if students had questions and were on task. But during most of Sheryl's time with students, as on September 14, Sheryl, like Bernie, stood front and center to lead the classroom conversation.

Just as her desk area reflected both artistry and organization, so, too, did Sheryl's use of her front blackboard. On September 14, as was her custom, Sheryl initiated the classroom conversation with the beginnings of an outline already written on the blackboard in her characteristically neat script. As the conversation continued, the blackboard outline was expanded to include the conversational turn-taking of both teacher and students. By the end of the class meeting, the blackboard had explicitly become both agenda and minutes.

Like Bernie, and unlike Dan, Sheryl customarily left the door to room 132 open during class time. Yet on September 14, as on most days, no distracting sounds from neighboring classrooms intruded. The open door meant that, as was also the case with Bernie's classes, students had the ability to slip into class a few seconds late without great risk of detection. But that appeared not to concern Sheryl.

What did concern Sheryl was quite visible in the physical system she created in room 132. Student work was important. Her room was a home, welcoming and carefully decorated, but also organized and functional. And as with Bernie and Dan, the physical system of Sheryl's room would have corollaries in personal and cultural systems.

**Tim's Non-room**    On September 14, and until Dan moved into his new room in the newly constructed science addition early in the second semester, Tim shared a classroom with another special education teacher. But this room, room 133, was not Tim's to use during the Connections block. With no physical space of his own, Tim became a nomad. On September 14, and on many other days, Tim was an inhabitant of room 138, Bernie's room. Later, and especially during the time when *Romeo and Juliet* was Connections' English focus, Tim would inhabit room 132, Sheryl's room. When either Sheryl or Bernie was absent, Tim would assume "house-sitting" authority for their rooms and their classes. If Tim needed to work with a small group of students intensively (listening to an audiotape of *Romeo and Juliet*, for example), he would meet with students in the large room, room 307.

I heard Tim voice frustration about his room-less status on only one occasion. During the common planning period on September 10, as the discussion centered on a few students already in need of some assistance in "catching up," Tim said, "That's the bad part of not having a room. [I have] no access to my encyclopedias, my computer, to work with kids."

Not having a physical territory he (and students) could call his own meant that Tim's modes of communicating the personal and cultural dimensions of his teaching were relatively restricted. Tim's non-room would also affect the content of those personal and cultural systems, directly influencing his role within the Connections ecosystem.

**The Corridors of Cedar City High School**    Unlike the first day, when the physical system of Cedar City High School was all but irrelevant to the Connections ecology, its intrusion was beginning to be noticeable by September 14.

Other teachers and the assistant principal had spoken with Connections teachers about the noise level in the halls when Connections students rotated among rooms off the regular bell schedule. Consequently, Dan's reminder as students prepared to leave room 307 for the three class rotation would often be repeated in the days following September 14.

Similarly, Bernie's recognition of the bell and the PA summons during the break he observed were concessions Connections made to the physical systems operating at Cedar City High School. Other concessions were forthcoming; for example, a shutdown of instruction during "activity period" times, an interruption of one of Sharon Finch's art sessions for an all-school assembly, substantial alterations in the Connections schedule for the required student participation in the anti-drug D.A.R.E. program, and the surrender of room 307 to Ohio Proficiency Test testing and interpretation sessions. As Connections' physical world expanded, its boundaries with the physical world of Cedar City High School both overlapped and blurred.

The few weeks between the first day and September 14 had seen Connections' physical system dispersed among four classrooms. As I consider the story of September 14, it seems that with this dispersal came dilution. Although I question whether the intensity of the first day, made possible through a full morning together in room 307, could (or even should) be maintained over time, there is no question that the first day's intensity had diminished. There is also no question that Connections' expanded (and no longer unified) physical system of September 14 played a significant role in this diminution. The familiar architectural principle, "Form follows function," seems relevant here. If this axiom holds, the physical system of September 14, dispersed in separate classrooms as it was, would presage changes in other systems of Connections' ecology and thus to Connections' community identity as well.

*Cultural Systems of September 14*

As I considered the cultural systems evident in the September 14 Connections block, the phrases "culturally diverse" and "pluralistic" came to mind. On that particular day, the routines of instruction, patterns of interaction, rituals and symbols that compose a cultural system seemed to vary by time, room, and/or teacher. Some of these cultural dimensions appeared to be consistent with the cultural system of the first day; others did not.

**Common Planning Time Culture** By September 14, the ritual of brewing coffee had become almost sacrosanct; so sacrosanct that the week before Tim had brought in special Kona coffee that he reserved for Fridays, "when we really need it" (September 7, 1993). But on September 14, only Tim and Sheryl had arrived in room 314 as the coffeemaker sputtered the last drops of the brewing cycle. Dan and Bernie were elsewhere.

Within the first few weeks of school, finding all four Connections teachers together in room 314 at the beginning of the common planning period had become increasingly uncommon. Being elsewhere until about 8:00 had become the norm. Whether he was photocopying Socrates packets, typing an American studies dyad budget, or arriving at the last minute, delayed by a before-school coaches' meeting, Bernie often did not make his appearance in room 314 until well after the first-period bell had sounded. Even the usually prompt Sheryl and Tim were occasionally waylaid by drawn out class meetings or difficulties in "chasing down" the LD students' mainstream teachers for progress reports. Except for rare occasions when he needed to get to a telephone in an attempt to reach "a parent I've been trying to connect with for a few days," Dan's presence in his own room was predictable. His attention was not. Whether setting out lab equipment, as on September 14, or at his computer, Dan now rarely sat at the table where his colleagues had claimed habitual seats.

A creeping "strategic individualism" (Hargreaves, 1993, p. 63) had entered the common planning time culture. Hargreaves notes that many teachers thrive on collegiality and collaborative planning as a source of creativity. Certainly, when Tim showed Sheryl the book he had found, Sheryl's interest was piqued. It seemed that Tim and Sheryl, at least, were among those teachers who thrive on the idea exchange that a common planning period was designed to facilitate. Perhaps that explains why, as the year went on, Tim and Sheryl appeared to be so devoted to prompt and active participation in common planning period discussions. Yet Hargreaves also posits that planning time, even an extra planning period held in common, may not be the best time for collaborative planning. Hargreaves (1993) suggests: "Prep time is a scarce resource that . . . needed to be spent on the many little things that made up the endless list of teachers' jobs . . . Prep time was a way to cope with the immediate demands of instruction, focused on the short-term practical requirements of the teacher's class" (p. 63, 72). Bernie's words confirm Hargreaves' thoughts: "I've become an organization freak, and that's not always possible . . . Out of necessity as a coach, I use planning time as planning time" (September 7, 1993). Clearly, for Bernie, his tardiness to the common planning period on September 14 reflects strategic individualism on his part.

While recognizing the phenomenon of strategic individualism, Hargreaves (1993) also distinguishes it from what he calls "elective individualism," where a teacher chooses to work alone "even when there are opportunities and encouragement to work collaboratively" (p. 63). However, the distinction between strategic and elective individualism may not always be clear. Perhaps that is why Sheryl, especially, was at times irritated if Dan and Bernie seemed not to be as devoted to common planning time as she was. "I hate to do much of this [planning] without Bernie" (September 23, 1993).

Physical presence or attention is not the only form individualism may take. To be sure, the flexibility, camaraderie, and collaboration of the first day's common planning time remained visible on September 14. Dan and Sheryl proved flexible in their willingness to meet Bernie's scheduling needs, and Dan was quick to lend his expertise to working out the details of the revised schedule. Yet this flexibility and collaboration seemed to be reduced to accommodation of a colleague's instructional needs.

The teacher talk and work of that morning's common planning period bespeaks a subtle shift as well. Sheryl's voiced concerns about Marsha's attendance and Jason's sleeping in class provoked no response. Evidently, within each teacher's classroom, matters of discipline—such as attendance, tardiness, student behavior—were the province of the affected teacher. Similarly, the work of the planning period conformed to an individualistic pattern. Sheryl's work on the field trip's chaperone list was a solitary task. Bernie shared his instructional plan for the day with Tim, but not with the group as a whole. Seeing Dan setting out lab equipment sparked no curiosity about the day's science lab lesson. The still-present white board corroborated this minimal level of sharing of teaching plans.[3] Although general alignment around the theme Beginnings had been negotiated collaboratively, it appeared that there was a tacit assumption, never made explicit, that each teacher retained instructional autonomy within his or her subject area.

In the same way, a creeping individualism intruded on the first day's cultural emphasis on learning through projects. Sheryl's upcoming Quest project was just that: Sheryl's. The dramatization of the Trial of Socrates was Bernie's—and, by extension, Tim's—project. Two weeks earlier, all of the Connections students had been out on the football field counting the blades of grass in a square inch as part of an Orders of Magnitude lesson. Sheryl, Bernie, and Tim had helped supervise the students, but the lesson was quite clearly Dan's; no co-teaching occurred that day. In sum, unless immediate or near-future plans required collaborative planning for a cross-disciplinary project, the common planning period did not reflect the unitary agenda so prominent on the first day. This is not surprising.[4] Given a three-class rotation in which each subject area was addressed separately, and given the tacit cultural norm that each teacher retained relative autonomy in his/her academic discipline, the more individualistic tone of the September 14 common planning period was to be expected.

At different times during the Connections odyssey, common planning time proceedings fit anywhere along a continuum from autonomy to collaboration. Wherever a Connections common planning period might be situated on any given day (and it appeared to move closer to autonomy between August 24 and September 14), that cultural placement was a function of the Connections teachers as a group. Within individual classrooms the autonomy of each teacher was unquestioned—each Connections teacher was "in control" of his or her room. So whatever cultural system prevailed during common planning time, it was subject to "pluralism" or "cultural diversity" among rooms 138, 314, and 132 for the remainder of the day. So it is to the cultural systems of these individual classrooms that I now turn.

**The Room 138 Culture**    Clear cultural messages were embedded within the activity of preparing for Friday's Trial of Socrates. From his beginning announcement, "We've got some neat things to do this week," to his end-of-class invitation, "Come to my office," the unique classroom culture Bernie cultivated was evident. In *The Culture of the School and the Problem of Change* (1971), Seymour Sarason cites Bloom's conclusion that four themes define "outstanding" teachers: immediacy, individuality, informality, and autonomy. While Bloom applied these themes solely to teachers, Bernie's classroom culture demonstrably elevated them to the status of cultural norms and values that extended to students as well.

When the students demurred at Bernie's reading homework assignment, his immediate response was, "This is important, okay?" The reading was important because it was necessary. It was necessary if students were to be able to bring meaning to their participation in the living history they were about to reenact on Friday. And participation was not only expected in the culture of Bernie's room, it was a "neat thing." Moreover, as students discovered on Friday (if they had not already done so through the previous weeks' Civilization simulation and "dig" through contemporary cultural artifacts), participation was fun. Yet the experience of donning bed sheet togas, of hearing the impassioned pleas for mercy from "Mrs. Socrates," and of witnessing "Socrates'" unhistorical acquittal was more than fun. In the "debriefing" that followed the trial, Bernie again (as he did on September 14) carefully related the issues arising in ancient Greece to the immediacy of current democratic struggles. The first day's cultural emphasis on learning through projects, active learning, and group work took on a uniquely Bernie cast in the immediacy he attached to projects like the Trial of Socrates.

In the cultural system of Bernie's room, students were not only expected to participate, they were to express their individuality in the process. In the discussion Bernie initiated about gay rights and antiwar protests, Bernie encouraged all students to voice their personal thoughts whether they had raised their hands for recognition or not. Bernie directly encouraged individuality during the course of the discussion: "Folks, you need to be able to say what you think. Under the Constitution, it's a protected right. The majority isn't always right. We need to respect the courage of dissent." True to his promise made at the beginning of the class, no laughter greeted any offered opinions. This placing of cultural value on diverse, individually held, opinions was but one way in which Bernie's classroom culture honored the first day's cultural value of heterogeneity.

Similarly, the first day's cultural value on student teacher interaction was honored in the informality of Bernie's classroom. His invitation to Tim to "feel free to jump in" applied to students as well. His Plato/Play-Doh pun bespoke Bernie's frequent use of humor in his classroom. His seemingly impromptu grouping of student consensus-seeking groups, while not in strict accord with cooperative learning models, also reflected Bernie's deliberately informal mode of teaching. But more than any of these examples, Bernie's informality and his way of interacting with students could be seen in the language of his teaching. Interspersed with the jargon of history were phrases like "the masses are asses." The vernacular of Bernie's classroom was a language of informal conversation, not one of lecture. On September 14, class began with Bernie's conversational note about his not feeling especially energetic that day. On other days, class might begin with a conversation about the weekend's football game, an anecdote about his youngest daughter, or a request for a piece of gum when his cache was depleted. Such informal conversation is indicative of what Cohen (1988) calls "adventurous teaching," where there is "an extensive exposure of self, where students and teachers engage each other more fully within the context of a classroom . . . Teachers must both intensify engagement while reducing and easing the risks for students. This is no mean trick" (pp. 72, 74). With Bernie's self-revealing informality came risk, but if students were to take the comparable risks of expressing individuality and engaging in a relationship with their teacher, it was a risk Bernie seemed more than willing to take.

Closely tied to the themes of individuality and informality was the theme of autonomy that emerged in Bernie's classroom on September 14. Assigning roles for the Trial of Socrates was a matter of student choice. Within the parameters of the project, students were free to choose roles with which they felt comfortable or challenged. Other than a general outline of trial procedures, the Socrates packets contained no script. With autonomy came the implicit cultural imperative of responsibility. Publicly, Bernie allowed no room for doubt that students could rise to the occasion. For those whose behavior was less than expected, Bernie's "debriefing" early the next week hit home: "The theme of bearing responsibility is at the heart of Socrates' teachings. Meletus's son is responsible for his own downfall . . . Ultimately, you have to take responsibility for what you do and what you don't do" (September 21, 1993). That said, Bernie in effect encapsulated the culture of his classroom by adding, "We've got good people here—there's lots of potential." The cultural norms of immediacy, individuality, informality, and autonomy seemed to be central to Bernie's efforts to tap into that potential.

**The Room 314 Culture**    Just as the physical system of Dan's room conveyed ambiguous messages, so too the cultural messages conveyed in Dan's class of September 14 were difficult to sort out.

As part of his variation on the first day's celebration of the heterogeneous nature of Connections' student cohort, Dan permitted students to choose one of two texts as the book they would use to complete reading and vocabulary assignments. (Hence the reference to looking in "the other book" for vocabulary words not found in the student's personal text.) But, as Dan pointed out, "Both are on the same level. One is neither higher or more cerebral than the other" (September 7, 1993). Instead, Dan suggested that students be guided in their choice by such factors as pictures, diagrams, and vocabulary in bold type. Another part of Dan's variation on the theme of heterogeneity was the unitary curriculum he followed. Like Bernie, Dan did not differentiate assignments or tests by student ability groups. But unlike Bernie (who often made his tests of a take-home variety, allowed students to choose roles, and graded essays with individual student abilities in mind), Dan held all students to the same grading standard. At a meeting of the four teachers with George Cerny and Mike Davis (February 1, 1994), Dan explained how he implemented the cultural values of heterogeneity and success for all: "General and academic physical science [has been] a little bit of a problem. The biggest difference [has been that] I let the general [science] kids do the work in class. So I don't get as far."

Similarly, the first day's cultural norm of group work took on a different shade of meaning in Dan's classroom. While the students were paired as lab partners, the copying incident revealed that this was to be a limited partnership. In sharp contrast to the informal groups of Bernie's class the period before, the work of lab partners was *not* to achieve consensus. Rather, the function of lab partners seemed to be restricted to sharing equipment and checking each other's measurements. Lab work partnerships appeared to be more of a physical arrangement than a learning process.

In Dan's science class, the first day's cultural norm of active learning translated into "doing labs." The parameters of "doing labs," however, were more proscribed than those of bridge building. In the bridge building activity, materials were specified, but results were judged by a minimal criterion. With lab work, not only were the materials specified in a highly detailed manner, but results were expected to be presented in a highly prescriptive form. Students were expected to observe a set format for lab reports (introduction, hypothesis, procedure, data, analysis) and to record those reports in a lab book that met Dan's specifications. In the culture of Dan's room, the active learning of "doing labs" was characterized by precision and organization.

Yet precision was not absolute, in either lab data or vocabulary assignments. The last digit of the students' measurements of mass would need to be estimated. Similarly, in an earlier class, Dan had made it clear that vocabulary assignments were not exercises in copying. So while he chastised one boy for incompleteness, soon several students would find their vocabulary papers returned with Dan's admonition to "put it in your own words" written in the margin.

Judging by the parting comment I overheard on September 14, finding balances between "getting it right" and "putting it in your own words," and between working with a partner and individual work evidently frustrated at least one student. Subsequent events, to be related in the sixth chapter, would indicate this student was not alone in her frustration.

Perhaps as perplexing to students was the cultural norm governing teacher-student interaction in room 314. As he moved to the center of the room to explain the lab, as he assured students that he did not consider the missing rulers a deliberate occurrence, and as he freely offered assistance to those who asked, Dan created an aura of friendly approachability. He also used his own brand of humor to soften what amounted to his rejection of the incomplete vocabulary paper, smiling as he said, "I don't mean to sound like a meanie, but I am a meanie." Bowers and Flinders' (1990) discussion of kinesics seems relevant to this pattern of teacher-student interaction.

> [G]ood teachers . . . move toward students to engage them more directly . . . smile frequently, and use humor to lighten the atmosphere . . . Smiling communicates warmth, support, and the other values associated with a nonthreatening environment. But it does not, by itself, insure a positive learning environment, particularly if the other aspects of the communication send a contradictory message to the student. (p. 83)

The cultural climate in Dan's room varied widely. At times Dan exuded amicability, as when he distributed Jolly Rancher candy (leftover from Halloween) to students with correct responses to review questions (November 2, 1993). At other times, particularly in response to student behavior he deemed inappropriate, Dan issued less friendly messages. One exchange on September 7 illustrates:

DAN. Are you supposed to be talking?

STUDENT. Um-m-m . . .[pause] no.

DAN. It shouldn't take you that long to think. See me after class.

Thus, depending on student behavior, teacher student interaction in room 314 ranged from harmonious to antagonistic. Considering the parting student comment I overheard on September 14, at least some students found such a cultural climate disconcerting.

**The Room 132 Culture**    Like the other teachers whose rooms the Magenta students entered on September 14, Sheryl created her own cultural version of the first day's norms and values. In Sheryl's classroom the first day's cultural themes of a project orientation, teacher-student interaction, a heterogeneous orientation, and predictability would again emerge.

While the day's focus on the structure of formal composition and final copy seemed a digression from the Greek myths of the past two weeks, Sheryl saw the departure as essential to student success on the upcoming Quest project. This project, like others

Sheryl would assign throughout the year, related to the subject matter currently under study but intentionally provided students an opportunity for self-expression as well. Each student group would be free to determine the object of its quest, be it the perfect candy bar or the mythical five swords needed to combat evil, so long as Sheryl's basic criteria for the written narrative and oral/visual presentation were met. Just as Bernie characterized the Socrates trial as "neat," Sheryl saw the projects that punctuated her instructional units as "fun."

The "homey" atmosphere of Sheryl's classroom found its teacher-student interaction counterpart in the conversational nature of Sheryl's instruction. Sheryl had confessed that in moving to the high school three years earlier, she did not want to sacrifice the give and take of her conversational style to a perceived high school norm of lecturing (November 2, 1993). Aware that within the classroom teachers and students would be involved in a lengthy and sustained way, Sheryl wanted to know her students personally and individually. Her comments to Casey and E. J. were not offhanded remarks made to pass the time of day. Rather, they reflected the same motivation revealed in her reaction to the students' response to an assignment she gave in November. Asking that students consider various Shakespearean adjectives used to describe characters in *Romeo and Juliet* and choose those that applied to themselves as the basis for a short essay, Sheryl was pleased by the self-revelation within their writing. "I enjoyed finding out things about the kids" (November 12, 1993). By the animated way in which the students eagerly supplied answers to Sheryl's queries on September 14, it appeared that they entered the classroom conversation/lesson aware of Sheryl's interest both in their personhood and in their personal success. This sense of genuine interest was central to Sheryl's placing high cultural value on a very personalized teacher-student interaction.

Sheryl's investment in student success was also apparent in her way of attaching cultural value to the heterogeneity of the Connections students. Like Dan, Sheryl used two textbooks for her teaching of Greek myths and *The Odyssey*. But, unlike Dan's texts, the literature books were correlated with the students' ability grouping. Later in the year, Sheryl would use a specially purchased parallel edition of *Romeo and Juliet* as well as supplementary audiotapes to assure that her subject matter was accessible to all students. Her test construction practices were planned just as carefully. When students took the promised "big test over the heroes" on Friday, they would do so with three separate test forms. Because Dan would assist in proctoring the test for the combined Blue/Green and the Red/Magenta students, Sheryl told him that "This is a parting of the ways day" (September 17, 1993). The honors version of the test would include several essay questions; the academic version required a few paragraph responses; the general version contained the "objective" sections common to all three versions, but only one question that asked for any writing beyond a few sentences. Furthermore, Sheryl explained to Dan, all students would be permitted to use their class notes during the test.

This custom of encouraging students to use their notes during tests reflected the cultural norm of predictability that was so characteristic of Sheryl's classroom. While the learning activities in Sheryl's classroom could not be seen as routine, some rituals, like the beginning fragments on the blackboard, were predictable. A general rule of thumb came to be part of each student's understanding: if anything was important enough for Mrs. Hart to write on the blackboard, it merited note taking. Sheryl's expectations of students were also highly predictable. As she told the students, "Final copy form means something to me. It needs to mean the same thing to you." Moreover, in (quite literally) spelling out the MUGS acronym, Sheryl clearly communicated the standards by which she would grade final copy. But before there was final copy, there would be first drafts (and the possibility of second drafts); rewriting would allow for a greater chance that all students could be successful in Sheryl's classroom.

Certain cultural themes pervaded Sheryl's room on September 14: "fun" projects; a pattern of teacher-student interaction that betokened Sheryl's genuine, friendly interest in her students; a mode of instruction that recognized student heterogeneity while preserving a common curriculum; and rituals whose predictability was designed to ensure student success.

**E Pluribus Unum?**    As the Magenta students left room 307 and entered three culturally diverse classrooms, two entities served as cultural ties that bound their Connections world together, however loosely. The first was Tim Schwartz. The day before, Tim had been Dan's teaching assistant. On September 14, and for many other days, Tim served as what Bernie drolly called his "lackey." Within a few weeks, Tim would act as Sheryl's substitute when she was ill, a role he duplicated for Bernie when Bernie's mother died. Later in the year, during Sheryl's instructional units on *Romeo and Juliet*, the structures of grammar, and *Fahrenheit 451*, Tim would work intensively with students who could benefit from extra assistance in English. In other words, when Tim asked his colleagues "Where do you need me today?" (September 3, 1993), it was a sincere offer to work wherever he could be useful. Bernie and Sheryl were consistently happy to take Tim up on his offer, and they were disappointed on days when IEP conferences or testing duties meant Tim was not available in his helping role. Dan rarely requested that Tim join him in room 314. So on most days, Tim, roomless as he was, could be found in room 132 or 138. In Sheryl's room and Bernie's room, Tim adapted to and was adopted by the cultural system that was his habitat for the day. It is because of this adaptability and adoptability that I came to view Tim as a "cultural tie that binds" within Connections. As on September 14, Tim was free to leave Bernie's room to get supplies or run errands. This freedom made Tim more than a gofer. He acted as a communications tie among the three other Connections teachers. Tim's formal role as LD teacher authorized him to know in detail about the assignments and expectations of all three classrooms. So what the white board and common planning conversation did not reveal about each teacher's subject area instruction, Tim knew. In his quiet way, without overt and visible leadership, Tim served as a vital connection in Connections' cultural system.

The second cultural tie binding Connections together was the still-present daily gathering in room 307. Here in Connections' first home, students still saw the four Connections teachers working together, reinforcing use of the assignment notebook and coordinating the daily schedule. Here, projects such as one Friday's logo design and another Friday's Trial of Socrates still took place with reassuring semiregularity. Here the flexibility of the Connections block was attested to daily as students received the day's schedule. The cultural system of the first day was still alive, and in many ways well, in room 307. Room 307 was still home.

That these two cultural ties were needed is clear from the fore-going discussion of the diverse interpretations of the Connections cultural system. Why the interpretations were so diverse will become clear in an analysis of the personal systems of September 14.

## Personal Systems of September 14

Within the complex ecology of September 14, the physical and cultural systems in evidence were not isolated from, but rather connected to, the personal systems that shaped each habitat the Magenta students entered that day. The ways in which the Connections teachers organized and decorated their physical milieus and the cultural norms and values expressed in each teacher's practice were, to a great extent, shaped by their personal, practical knowledge of their craft. Certainly falling within the realm of personal systems is Milbrey McLaughlin's (1993) observation that "Teachers' classroom choices are a product of their concep-tions of subject matter . . . and their conceptions of their students as learners" (p. 98). Within the latter, McLaughlin further observes that

> Teachers' classroom responses to students fell into three general patterns:
> (1) Maintain traditional standards . . .
> (2) Lower expectations for coverage and achievement . . .
> (3) Adapt practices and pedagogy. (p. 85)

This last pattern had clearly prevailed on the first day. Whether it continued to prevail when the teachers' individual conceptions of subject matter and of students as learners were no longer subject to the unifying influence of a shared time, place, and activity may be seen as this section once again revisits rooms 138, 132, and 314.

**Room 138**  The themes of immediacy, individuality, informality, and autonomy that were manifest during Bernie's introduction to the Trial of Socrates illustrate the pedagogical assumptions inher-ent in relational teaching.[5] Building on the foundation of the stu-dents' lived experiences both within and without the classroom, relational teaching engages students in the interpretation of a text. In Bernie's classroom on September 14, the text was the Trial of Socrates, and students were encouraged to interpret this text using the lenses of their personal opinions about current events.

Importantly, the students' personal opinions were sought *before* they encountered the text. Bernie's introduction to World War I offered another prime example of this approach to instruction. After researching governmental, religious, and economic structures (Judaism/Christianity/Islam, democracy/dictatorship, capitalism/communism, nationalism/colonialism), but before considering the causes and effects of World War I, Bernie engaged the students in a discussion. Providentially, this dialogue occurred on the day of the week designated for ROTC students to wear their uniforms. Following a group presentation about the views of one religion, Mickey had asked about the stance a religion might take about the morality of killing during a war. So on this day, February 3, 1994, Bernie recalled Mickey's question— "Let's go back to what Mickey says: It's okay to kill in a war"— and took an instant poll of the students' opinions. Asking volunteers to "expand on your point of view" generated an intense discussion. Mickey, in his ROTC uniform, offered that "We need to serve our country." Patrick, also in uniform, raised the issue of the morality of following orders unquestioningly. Bernie likened Patrick's question to the central issue in a current movie, *A Few Good Men*, and asked, "Where do you draw the line?" Patrick was adamant that "In the military, you follow orders no matter what"; this prompted Bernie to ask, "Why?" To which Patrick responded, "You will be living with these guys . . . An American life is worth more than anybody else's." Bernie limited his response to a softly spoken, "Wow!" before alluding to films that raised moral questions about the conduct of the war in Viet Nam (*Platoon, Apocalypse Now*) and asking students what they would do if confronted by a village containing both enemies and innocents. Before more than two students could respond, the bell ending the class period sounded. But the conversation had planted seeds of thought that would be watered again as the class discussed the evolution of the central character in *All Quiet on the Western Front*. This pattern of involving students in a shared classroom discussion or experience so as to facilitate the emergence of "big picture" ideas and their implications for the students' lives was a recurring pattern in Bernie's practice. Whether he engaged students in the Trial of Socrates or any of the other dramatizations and simulations that were part of his repertoire of history activities, Bernie's conception of history shone through. For Bernie, history was an ongoing and evolving pattern of circles and chains embedded in stories of the enterprise of human civilization. This conception lay at the heart of Bernie's expressed reservations about organizing the study of history by thematic rather than chronological units: "Thematics misses the flow of cause and effect" (November 30, 1993). Quite explicitly, Bernie drew attention to this sense of "flow" in the classroom discussions, inviting students to, for example, connect the original French notion of a left-to-right political spectrum to the development of fascism and Nazism (February 22, 1994).

The pedagogical "hook" Bernie used to initially engage students in the classroom dialogue was storytelling, both personal and historical. His account of the Athens-Sparta war, which on September 14 he rendered in all its gory detail, foreshadowed other dramatically told historical stories. Later in the year, students would be treated to a graphic description of Spartacus's mass crucifixions, of Louis XIV's sumptuous lifestyle at Versailles (complete with slide show), and of the specific effects of Zyklon-B. Students also would hear Bernie's personal stories of fishing trips, college adventures, and family life that on a surface level appeared to be digressions. But as Huberman (1993) points out: "Teacher selection of [tinkerer responses are] based on a criteria of productivity that may not be immediately apparent. The curiosity and engagement generated in going off on a tangent will pay off later. But this is a nonlinear thought" (p. 43). This nonlinear way of thinking, so evident in Bernie's storytelling, had its physical and cultural system counterparts in the blackboard scrawlings and the informal language described earlier.

But more than a device for generating student curiosity and engagement, classroom dialogue and storytelling also dynamized Bernie. His sore throat and general malaise notwithstanding, Bernie obviously became energized during the conversational exchange of September 14. Such delightfully unanticipated "enlightened" ideas as "God is the judge, not men," proffered by students were clearly rewarding to Bernie. In seeing such moments as both unanticipated and rewarding, Bernie's conceptions of teaching and of his students as learners are appeared to rest on the premise that the teaching and learning process involves transforming and assimilating thought on the part of both the teacher and the learner.[6] This stance recognizes that teaching is not the mere transmission of knowledge that resides in the teacher but a dialogic process that both recognizes and depends upon the confluence of valid student knowledge and the classroom's ecology. It is a process that is inherently both uncertain and risky. But Bernie appeared comfortable with such a level of uncertainty and risk. Bernie's perception that Connections was about ensuring success for all students was his overarching consideration.

In McLaughlin's (1993) terms, Bernie's response to students fell in the category of "adapt practices and pedagogy." As McLaughlin explains, this response pattern requires teachers to broaden (but not lower) their definitions of achievement, to create new classroom arrangements, and to provide active roles for students. In so doing, McLaughlin observes: "Students generally prosper, but teachers often are left exhausted, *or* they experience exhilaration, depending on the character of the collegial environment. Which occurred depends on the teacher conception of the task as framed and supported by the [community]" (p. 85).

During Connections' initial implementation year, Bernie would experience exhaustion ("This is the most work I've ever had teaching," February 1, 1994). He would also experience exhilaration ("If I had to do this again, I'd do it in a minute!" May 17, 1994). If, as McLaughlin suggests, experiencing exhaustion or experiencing exhilaration is a function of the collegial environment, then understanding how Bernie came to express *both* feelings will be possible only through looking at both the environment within the Connections teaching team and the environment within Cedar City High School.

**Room 314**   For Dan, the work of learning science was the work of doing labs. As the course syllabus Dan distributed to students during the second week of school announced, "Much of our time will be spent in the laboratory working through experiments." Moreover, as the syllabus continued to explain, the work of doing labs would be structured in precise ways (appendix E). The language and format of Dan's syllabus reflected his perspectives on the nature of science as a discipline, on students as learners, and on appropriate and effective pedagogy. Those perspectives differed from Bernie's in two important ways.

Like Bernie, Dan sought to integrate student knowledge and experience with the instructional content at hand; however his approach evidenced a subtle, but important, difference. Dan often used examples from the students' experiences in daily life to illustrate, but not to introduce inquiry into, a concept. For example, as the review of vocabulary on November 23 reached "inertia" and "momentum," Dan went to a cupboard to get "old Bob" (a bowling ball). Rolling it along the classroom floor, the point was clarified: force would be required both to get the ball rolling or to stop it once rolling. Similarly, a February presentation on the history of theories of elements and atomic structures included Dan's explanation of Rutherford's experiment: "Let me make an analogy here . . . [If I shot a BB gun at a chainlink fence] what would happen to most of the BBs?" Such verbal illustrations and concrete examples, as well as drawings (e.g., those he drew on the blackboard on September 14), were consistent features of Dan's teaching strategies. Combined with the emphasis on lab work, Dan's view of teaching seemed, indeed, to be "hands-on." Yet his allusions to student and daily life experiences served as explanations via illustrations—a step removed from inquiry-based learning or from Bernie's use of student experience as a "hooking" strategy.

If Bernie viewed history as circles and chains, Dan's view of science seemed more linear. Each unit of study followed a pattern: a vocabulary assignment, a series of labs and lab reports, and a unit test. A sequence was also detectable in Dan's syllabus: measurement preceded other lab work; the study of atoms and elements preceded the study of chemical reactions; physical properties were studied before chemical properties. This sequential, linear view of his subject matter places Dan in a conceptual context that has been noted by many studies of the subject subcultures present in secondary schools.[7]

Attempting to mesh the beliefs and practices that were implicit in his disciplinary socialization to teaching with an interdisciplinary view of his subject would prove difficult for Dan, as the language of his syllabus suggests. The inclusive language of "we" used at various points in the syllabus coexisted with "you," "mandatory," and "no excuses." Just as with the cultural mixed message about the function of lab partners, the syllabus's double messages of "discovery" and "required," of "we" and "you," seemed mixed.

In Dan's September 14 class, however, one theme emerged unambiguously. After his explanation and demonstration, Dan told students its was time to "get working." The operative word was "working." When teachers adopt a work orientation to their practice of teaching, classroom systems promote order and learning as intertwined tasks. Thus, "students can be seen as workers and teachers as supervisors whose main function is to ensure quality work" (Marshall, 1988, p. 10). On September 14, despite assistance that hinted at Dan's desire to be seen as approachable in student-teacher interactions, the main purpose of Dan's tour among the lab tables seemed to be about quality control and maintaining order. Consistent with this concern for order and organization were the preliminary tasks of September 14 and the comments Dan offered in an interview on September 10, 1993. When asked to characterize his role within the teaching team, Dan summed up his role as that of "efficiency expert."

In keeping with the work orientation, both the syllabus and the activity of September 14 inextricably linked lab work to lab reports. This linkage implicitly conveys the message that learning is about doing work, that is, generating "products" to be evaluated. In other words, if students do their work, learning will occur. As Dan explained to the students when the first quarter's report cards were issued, "If you got all your work done, you got no lower than a D" (November 12, 1993). The implied corollary, of course, was that students who failed had failed to do the work.

This "technicist" paradigm (Bowers and Flinders, 1990) equates learning with observable behavior, conceiving teaching as a rational process whose patterns, once detected, reduce the uncertainties of practice. Dan's syllabus, his step-by-step instructions, and the progression from the September 14 "practice" lab to the "real" lab two days later all reflect a way of organizing lessons that has been associated with the discipline of science. Certainly, this pattern also reflected Dan's past experiences in learning. Contemplating the difficulty of connecting the science units of his syllabus to the overarching Connections units, Dan remarked: "I wasn't taught that way. With science, I saw the connections as I learned more and could put it in perspective. I'm not sure that freshmen are ready to do that" (May 10, 1994). The generalization that teachers tend to teach the way in which they were taught certainly seemed to be true for Dan.

The personal systems evident in the classroom ecology of room 314 on September 14 included a work orientation; a conception of science as ordered, organized, and efficient; a rhythm of teaching that followed a carefully delineated syllabus; and a level of adaptation or improvisation that seemed comfortable with being flexible about schedule options, but not about content. In such a habitat, the risks and uncertainties of teaching can be reduced. In other words, the teacher is able to exercise a greater degree of control. Accordingly, it is not surprising that, in McLaughlin's (1993) schema of teacher responses to students, Dan's teaching on September 14 could be seen as "maintaining traditional standards."

**Room 132**    As the events of September 14 suggest, Sheryl's conception of her subject matter held that the elements of literature, writing, and speaking intertwined in the progression of the language arts curriculum. Her Quest project embodied this conception. Based on the students' reading of *The Odyssey*, the project would include a written formal paper and an oral presentation. Moreover, the project would build on previous learning (the MUGS acronym from junior high and the myths read and discussed in the weeks before) and extend to future learning (keyboarding and advanced composition classes). In this way, the classroom conversation of September 14 was but a part of an ongoing conversation of learning.

This notion of teaching as an ongoing conversation is a central feature of "responsive teaching."[8] The tension and constant movement between preplanned routines and situationally adjusted responses appropriately describes the conversation about the structure of formal compositions that Sheryl had planned for September 14. Beginning with a minimal prompt, Sheryl continually adapted to and shaped whatever students offered to the basic ideas she wished to convey during the course of the thirty-five-minute period.

Of course, Sheryl could have foregone the conversation and its demands for constant adaptation and improvisation and unilaterally presented her personal list of compositional elements instead. But that was neither her style nor her conception of teaching. The students' participation and engagement in their learning was important to Sheryl. The opportunities for self-expression afforded in her assignments, test essay questions, projects, and class discussions were the results of quite deliberate pedagogical decisions on Sheryl's part. As we talked after class on September 14, Sheryl offered her perspectives on teaching and the teacher-student relationship:

> I like the ten minutes of gathering time [in room 307]—it gives us a few minutes of personal time with the kids. I walk by classes and see lectures. It's so bad. Connections is fun. There's so much more family feeling. It is so nice that Bernie does history, and now we have the art tie-in that I love. I love it, and I think this is what teaching is supposed to be.

Sheryl clearly valued the conversational nature of her practice and the dimension of involvement with students that entailed; so much so that if teaching in this way was demanding of her time and energy, she was willing to meet those demands. Sheryl's response to the heterogeneous mix of Connections students involved still more self-imposed demands. At the midterm point of the first quarter, Sheryl noticed a trend in the Connections students' grades across subject areas. Telling Tim about her observation, she explained that honors students were "on the whole doing well," and that the academic students formed "the middle," but she was concerned about the general students: "I wonder if untracked competition won't discourage general kids who never get the really good grades." She hoped that using different books and tests would level the field of competition, even though (as she explained to a group of visiting administrators in May), "It takes real close and careful planning." By the year's end Sheryl felt that her practice had been rewarded: "Seeing the LD students rise to the occasion so often has been significant. I think the general students overall have come a long way in this program. I don't think they flourish very often in a "tracked" classroom" (May 19, 1994). For Sheryl, watching students flourish was teaching's chief reward. She, for example, took great delight in a heretofore low-achieving general student's "winning" the designation of "best logo" as chosen by her afternoon classes. She regarded this kind of achievement with a craftsman's pride.

Above all, as her artistic background may have presaged, Sheryl regarded teaching as an art and a craft. A significant part of that art lay in the involvement she sought with and asked of her students. Even as she had expectations of her students (e.g., final copy requirements, tests), she took care to ensure that those expectations were within the students' grasp (e.g., first drafts, the notes to be used during tests). Among the three response patterns set forth by McLaughlin (1993), that of adapting practices and pedagogy aptly describes Sheryl's personal system—as it does Bernie's.

**Tim's Non-room**    In the choice he made to be part of the Connections teaching team in the designated role of "learning styles specialist," and by the role he created for himself during the year, Tim took a defining stance of "ensuring success." This stance encompassed Tim's relationship with both the Connections students and his teaching team colleagues.

The nature of Tim's relationship with students was best depicted in two autumn moments. The first occurred on October 8, the day Tim returned to school following his father's death. During the gathering time in room 307, just as attendance and announcements were concluding, Bernie told the students, "Mr. Schwartz has something to say." In the absolute quiet that followed, Tim spoke softly, "I appreciate the card you all sent last week and some of you coming up and saying nice things, and I just wanted to thank the group as a whole." Then, just as softly, one boy's voice could be heard saying, "You're welcome."

The second moment came on November 2, when Bernie's mother had died and Tim taught in Bernie's place. Tim had talked to Bernie by telephone at length, and he was well prepared to conduct the Renaissance review scheduled as the history portion of the day's three-class rotation. But as class began, Tim announced, "Okay, a couple of things before we start. I want to talk about the end of the nine weeks." In the ten minutes that followed, Tim set the stage for a brief assignment of his own. Among the thoughts, sentiments, and ideas he shared were the following:

> The majority of you have done work that met our high expectations at one time or another. I want to talk for a few minutes about goal setting. What were your expectations [for Connections]? . . . [Students suggested grades, activities, field trips] . . . I had very little opportunity to do these kinds of things . . . What you learn and how you approach it is up to you as an individual—it can't be taken away from you. For example, if you don't make your car payment, the car will be gone. If a disaster strikes, your home may be gone. But nothing can take away what you've learned and what you've learned about yourself . . . What I want you to do—take out a half a sheet of paper . . . You don't have to share with me, your friends, or your parents. I want you to be truly honest with yourself. Looking at this class, take a look at this next nine weeks. Be brief and be specific. [Write] something you would like to obtain in this class this next nine weeks. When you're finished, tuck it away somewhere where you can find it, and look at it again at the end of the nine weeks. I know I have goals for myself in the classroom, for basketball, and personally.

As Tim was speaking, no other sound could be heard in room 138, a reaction common whenever Tim spoke to the students as a group. Even on those rare occasions when he seemed angry and was chastising the group for their misbehavior, students paid attention to and thus indicated respect for Tim. What transcribed words cannot fully convey—and what Tim's tone of voice, facial expression, and gestures could—is the complete and sincere feeling of caring he consistently communicated to students. As he freely meted out deserved compliments or encouraged them to finish the science vocabulary due the next day, the students *knew* Tim wanted them to be successful. At the year's end, Tim's first response to being asked about significant Connections moments was this: "The growth of the majority of the students. Not only their educational growth, but also as individuals" (May 19, 1994).

For Tim, his stance about ensuring success was not limited to students. He also worked to ensure his colleagues' success. At times, as on September 14, that meant being a "lackey." But tending to details (like stapling, bringing white boards, or getting paper towel erasers) was not in any way demeaning either to Tim or his colleagues. At the start of the second semester, it was Tim (in his communicating cultural tie that binds role) who suggested, assembled, photocopied, and distributed weekly Connections schedules. Allied with Sheryl for much of the third quarter's study of grammar and providing intensive assistance to students struggling with reading Shakespeare or Harper Lee, Tim saw this work as more than helping students. In both situations, doing the detail work or tutoring, Tim expressed the benefits of his role as "I can free [the other Connections teachers] up" (November 9, 1993).

His often asked "Who needs me today?" clearly places Tim as a teacher who responds to students by adapting practices and pedagogy. His past experience as an LD teacher enabled Tim to be comfortable with improvisation, flexibility, and the notion that "expectations and quality of work is going to be different from student to student" (May 19, 1994). But the Connections year, in Tim's estimation, with its opportunities to "step in and teach other subject matter as well as other students" provided real experiences in professional growth.

**Personal Punctuation**    Over the course of the first few weeks of school, the sense of excitement that had pervaded the first day's personal system ebbed. If the first day's personal system could be thought of as an exclamation point, then the personal systems in evidence on September 14 might be seen as variously representing a comma, a semicolon, and a period. In Bernie's room, September 14 was a comma, a brief pause for breath before the excitement resumed with the Trial of Socrates. The first day personal system elements of personal connection with students, the dignity of risking self-revelation, the view of teaching as craft, and the sense of adventurous teaching and learning were still present. So the day's comma was one that marked items in a related series. In Sheryl's room, September 14 was a semicolon, with the excitement of the Quest project removed by a greater pause. But the sense of craft, of adaptation, of the possibility of success, and of personal connection still were very much a part of Sheryl's personal sphere. So the day's semicolon punctuated related clauses. In Dan's room, September 14 was a period, the end of one thought, but with some hope that the paragraph would continue. The hands-on lab work resembled the student-constructed knowledge of bridge-building, but the sense of personal connectedness was unevenly felt. Success in fulfilling the teacher's learning expectations was no longer a sure thing.

Like the physical and cultural systems, personal systems of September 14 seemed a dilution of Connections' first impressions. The degree to which the larger school ecosystem influenced this dilution will be explored in the next section.

## Webs to Other Ecosystems

Unlike the first day, the bell system of Cedar City High School (and its concomitant public address announcements) were heard in Connections on September 14. Physical intrusions also asserted themselves in another significant way. As students traveled from room to room, the injunction to "be quiet in the halls" offered a constant reminder that Connections was no longer a world unto itself. The physical separation of the Connections teachers' class-rooms was seen as a distinct hindrance to the program's flexibility. In May, when a group of visiting administrators asked the Connections teachers to identify drawbacks, Sheryl responded, "There is a disadvantage we should cite. We're spread out. We're coming from all over the building." Then Bernie, who had often expressed his wish that Connections and the interdepartmental dyads could be given the abandoned old science wing as a corridor of their own, repeated Sheryl's thought, "Yeah, we're spread out." During the year, George Cerny had considered Bernie's wish, but he had his reservations about the idea: "I don't know if teachers want to be removed from their departments, or if that would be a good thing. It's a fine line between promoting teams and giving them physical proximity and isolating them. I don't want to split the staff" (April 29, 1994).

George's thought points to the strong influence of the depart-mental structure at Cedar City High School. That structure also influenced Connections on September 14. With their individual sequences of course curricula, each department's members had clear expectations of what each course would "cover." As Sarason (1971) points out, those expectations of coverage are powerful: "From the standpoint of the teacher, the curriculum is not a suggestion, but a requirement" (p. 77). Hence, Dan's syllabus represented, for him, an accepted or tried-and true way of meeting a perceived mandate. Similarly, Sheryl was keenly aware of the future course demands her students would face, and she was determined that her students would be able to meet the demands she knew would come in their advanced composition class. Since Bernie's course was an elective within the social studies department course sequence, he did not have that stricture placed on his curricular decisions.

More than delimiting course sequences, Cedar City High School departments also recognized the time-honored effect of the school's tracking system. Both Mike Davis and George Cerny spoke at various times during the year about an "elitist" mentality that existed within the community, and the parents' initial concerns about Connections (especially among parents of honors students) offered evidence that Connections would feel community and district pressures. Sheryl, especially, was mindful of the tracking influence since Connections honors students would receive weighted English grades. So beyond the consideration of providing challenging educational experiences, Sheryl felt obligated to include more rigorous requirements for honors students in their tests and projects.

The departmental course sequence and the school's tracking system conjoined to shape the teaching experience each teacher brought to Connections. Normally, students who enrolled in world history were sophomores, so Bernie was unaccustomed to teaching freshmen. Normally, the freshmen who enrolled in physical science were honors and/or academic students, so Dan's experience had been primarily with such students, whether the freshmen of physical science or the seniors of physics. Normally, Sheryl saw her English 9 classes separated by tracking groups, each with its distinct curriculum. General English 9 students did not read *Romeo and Juliet*. Normally, Tim's learning disabilities students were largely general students, and he had no contact with other students, nor did he normally teach directly from the "regular" curriculum. So each Connections teacher faced, in varying degrees, a change in his or her teaching assignment during the Connections year.

Cedar City High School norms also affected Connections in the area of teacher evaluation. The district's master teacher contract delineated the evaluation procedures that would be applied to the Connections teachers. Because Bernie had tenure within the Cedar City system, he was not formally evaluated each year, and the 1993–94 year was an "off" year for Bernie. But Dan, Sheryl, and Tim would be part of the yearly cycle of evaluation.[9] By September 14, notice had been given to all teachers "up" for evaluation as to which administrator would conduct his or her evaluation, and each teacher had been asked to develop yearly goals. As Dan devoted much of one day's (December 7, 1993) planning period to cleaning his room in preparation for being formally observed/evaluated, and as he had told me earlier that he was the confidant for his neighboring teacher's evaluation-related woes, I wondered (in an aside in my field notes) about whether the evaluation of teachers could be an inhibiting factor for pedagogical risk-taking. Sheryl, on the other hand, with her twenty-five years of experience, regarded the procedure more as a nuisance: "He [George] insists on coming during Connections" (December 7, 1993). But she was otherwise unperturbed about evaluation. Without rancor, but as a statement of neutral fact, Sheryl had told me: "I have told George that I will be here long after he's gone. With twenty-five years here, it wouldn't be politically feasible for George to really give me any trouble" (November 9, 1993). In an interview at the year's end, George had come to question the role of evaluation in innovative programs like Connections. "I would not evaluate teachers from this point on working on a pilot program." When I asked for clarification, about whether that meant he would observe their afternoon classes instead, George replied, "I would waive the process entirely." But that would be subject to negotiation with the teachers' association and would require some fancy political footwork on George's part. For as George also noted during our April interview, Cedar City High School had a strong union presence. It was to this presence that George at least partially attributed his sense that "This school is highly fragmented."

On September 14, that fragmentation had had but a limited influence on Connections. The only rumblings disturbing the calm relationship between the Connections teachers and the rest of the faculty had been the request that Connections students be quiet in the halls when traveling off the bell schedule. But in mid-September, the early stages of planning for a state grant that would be directed in large part toward improving staff morale had begun.[10] So these early rumblings could not be ignored. Whether they would grow, and how they would affect Connections, is part of a later chapter.

Despite having undergone the process of developing a school mission statement the year before, the Cedar City High School staff was not, in the perception both of its principal and at least two of the Connections teachers (Bernie and Sheryl), a unified community. The norms of self-reliance, mutual noninterference, and professional isolation that traditionally have pervaded schools were present at Cedar City High School, contributing to a pedagogical pluralism among the faculty that was mirrored in the Connections teaching team. The school's norms of mutual noninterference were clearly observed in the surface talk of the morning's common planning time. The daily pressures of teaching had allowed a creeping strategic individualism to enter the emerging Connections community. In a subtle shift from the first day, each teacher's individual practice had assumed a greater centrality in the Connections picture, and the images of Connections' first impressions were blurring with the shift in focus.

Yet amid the pedagogical pluralism there were some areas of commonality, particularly between Bernie and Sheryl. As Sheryl observed that day, after the bell ending fourth period had rung, "I tend to feel that Bernie and I are the focuses. I don't know if Dan feels like an outsider looking in." Her remark points to the clear differences between the cultural and personal system similarities she and Bernie shared and the cultural and personal system so manifest in Dan's room.[11] The differences, while perceived and felt, were not confronted on September 14. On September 14, the Connections teachers had not yet openly begun either the work of openly acknowledging their differences or the work of reconciling those differences with the first impression vision they held so dear.

But the seeds of difference and the need to deal with those differences was clearly foreshadowed in the ecology of September 14. This inevitable work of acknowledgment and the reconciliation necessary to forging the interdependence of collegial community would occur at another port of call.

# CHAPTER 5

## The Best of Times

In the real world of teaching, knowing the best of times only happens when you know the worst of times.

—Mike Davis

When Betsy Grant met with the Connections teachers as they prepared for the year to come, she described her experience in a Connections-like program with Charles Dickens's opening lines from *A Tale of Two Cities*, "It was the best of times; it was the worst of times." Implying that the Connections teachers would also encounter both exhilaration and frustration in the year ahead, Betsy's words echoed Huberman's (1993) observation: "Collective experiences of rejoicing, grief, and fellowship . . . are, without a doubt, important preconditions for collaborative work . . . Collaborative cultures grow like plants—they cannot be grown by swift expedience" (pp. 32–33). Betsy's reflective thought, Huberman's assertion, and Mike Davis's remark all point to a common understanding: the journey toward collegial community, like an epic odyssey, is fraught with both obstacles and triumphs. If this is so, and I believe it is, then understanding what triumphs and obstacles occurred in the Connections odyssey would be important to discovering the ecological dynamics of creating and sustaining a collegial community.

*How* those obstacles and triumphs were met by the Connections teachers collectively would be even more important. The extent to which the processes of reciprocity, interdependence, and democratic communication would be present in the face of both the best of times and the worst of times would have everything to do with whether the Connections teachers would either create and sustain a collegial community or fragment.

The stories of the first day and of September 14, recounted in the preceding chapters, were portents of other stories—stories of both the best of times and the worst of times to come in the Connections odyssey. Just as Connections began with a triumphant first day, I begin this chronicle with "the best of times."

Like the story of the first day, other stories of the best of times found their way into a growing Connections saga. Interspersed throughout the year were what I term "milestone meetings"— occasions when the Connections teachers were called upon to recount their successes. Whether to visitors (in November and May), to potential enrollees (in April), to the board of education (in March), to administrators (in January and February), or to each other (most notably in January and June), four "tales" were consistently included in the recounting.

## FOUR TALES OF TRIUMPH

Each tale of triumph focused on a particular event, or series of events, in the Connections odyssey. I have entitled these tales the *Romeo and Juliet* Tale, the Renaissance in the Snow Tale (also known as a Coming Through Tale), the Emma Lazarus Tale, and the Nuts and Bolts Tale.

### *The* Romeo and Juliet *Tale*

First told in November by the parent of a learning disabilities student, the Romeo and Juliet Tale was most significant to, and most likely to be repeated by, Tim and Sheryl. But at the board of education meeting in March, Mrs. Archer wanted to personally tell the story she had originated.

> My son has a learning disability. I was skeptical at first. At the parent meeting I heard parents of honors kids concerned about their children being in with LD students. I thought, "What's going to happen to my son?" But I went ahead and took Mr. [Schwartz's] and Mr. [Cerny's] advice [and enrolled Nathan in Connections]. One day I came in from work. Nathan had *Romeo and Juliet* in his hand, and he said, "This is so cool; have you read it?" I asked Nathan, "What do you like about Connections?" He said, "The special projects." I asked if he liked working with honors kids. He said, "It's really neat." (March 21, 1994)

Mrs. Archer was not alone in her Connections testimonial. During the annual conference days in November when, as Bernie observed, the second day is "normally a time to catch up on paper work," all available time slots were quickly taken up by Connections parents eager to meet with the Connections teachers. (In fact, Sharon Finch had told Sheryl she was upset that she was unable to obtain a conference appointment.) Many had stories like Mrs. Archer's to tell: one mother spoke about her honors son who "gets up at 4:30 to study"; another parent, referring to Bernie's use of colloquial language, explained that her son liked Connections because "Mr. Lyons cusses"; and yet another parent described his child's change in late-night-reading-by-flashlight reading materials. To be sure, some parents had concerns (one of which was part of a worst of times story to be related in the next chapter). But the conference days as well as the impromptu telephone and in-person conferences that occurred throughout the year attest to a connection with parents that the teachers and administrators valued.

The *Romeo and Juliet* Tale, however, was about more than parental connections. Mrs. Archer's story was also about a change she noticed in her son. As she concluded in her remarks to the board of education, "His attitude is great—academically he's doing great, better than in years." Nathan's delightfully unanticipated interest in reading (of all things) *Romeo and Juliet*, reflected themes within the second tale of triumph.

*The Renaissance in the Snow Tale (or Coming Through)*

The culminating activity of Connections' first semester had actually begun far earlier than the second week of January. Long before students were introduced to the worlds of Elizabethan England, Michelangelo, and Louis XIV in Sheryl's and Bernie's classes (and to a lesser extent, the Age of Adventure and Scientific Curiosity in Dan's classes), the first Connections field trip foreshadowed the midyear extravaganza to come. On September 23, the eighty students, four teachers, and several volunteer parent chaperones boarded buses for a "student day" at the Ohio Renaissance Festival. There they saw a living history reenactment of a joust presided over by Good Queen Bess, a bawdy version of

Beowulf, and assorted minstrels and vendors in full Elizabethan regalia. More than providing a visualization of Renaissance England, the field trip's purpose was to stimulate ideas for the Renaissance Fair that would serve as both a Connections showcase and a major component of the students' English and world history first-semester exam grades.

As gloomy and rainy a day as September 23 was, and as diverted from the academic purpose of the trip as some students were by the "cute" men and women they "scoped out" while there, the field trip provided a powerful impetus to the assignment that came in mid-November. (See appendix F.) Armed with ideas garnered from the first field trip, a subsequent field trip to an art museum, and Sharon Finch's November art project, as well as the topical assignments spanning November and December (e.g., viewing *The Agony and the Ecstasy*, building a data base of inventions of the period, and the daily progress through *Romeo and Juliet*, to name but a few), students were to return from the Christmas break prepared to mount a Renaissance Fair.

But in a pattern of nature typical of southern Ohio, the better part of January's first week of school was cancelled for what truly were "calamity days." As welcome as the television and radio announcements of "snow days" normally are to both students and teachers, the Renaissance in the Snow Tale was an amazing contradiction. The first snow day came on the day the Connections Renaissance Fair was to take place. Several anxious parents and students called George Cerny's office, wondering if the fair would be merely postponed or suffer cancellation. On the reset date, yet another snow day forced another postponement. As desolate and untravelled as Cedar City's roads were, the Cedar City telephone lines were abuzz with activity. Snowbound in their homes, the Connections teachers conferred with each other and administrators in a series of calls and decided on a plan. Each teacher would call the students in his or her color advisory group with the news that the fair *would* indeed be held on the exam day that encompassed the Connections block.

On January 12, the Connections students and their teachers journeyed the half mile to the junior high auditorium/gymnasium to set up for the Renaissance Fair. In various states of medieval garb, students set up their display areas, including a replica of a castle that dominated one end of the room. Bernie rented a Sir-Thomas-More-like costume, Sheryl put together an outfit befitting a wench from Verona, and Tim appeared in full peasant regalia. Dan, who attended the fair in standard teaching habiliment, had created and printed a program for the event on his computer. Sheryl, whistle at the ready, called for attention just before the first contingent of junior high teachers and students arrived. Bernie exhorted students to "get into the part; stay in character." Shortly after noon, all was ready. Those junior high students and teachers (along with a smattering of Connections parents and administrators) who entered the transformed auditorium/gymnasium met a host of Renaissance characters and reproductions: kings, queens, knights, popes, and peasants; cathedrals, castles, armadas, and gory representations of the Black Death. As Sheryl, Bernie, and Tim toured the room, they required each student (or group of students) to present and explain their exhibit, to evidence their status as "mini-experts" in their chosen topic. As could be expected, a few students had obviously engaged in rather slapdash efforts. But the vast majority had just as clearly expended great time and effort to rise to the occasion. Most had "come through."

Just as the Renaissance Fair had been the capstone of the first semester, the final project was the year's culminating event. Like the Renaissance Fair, this project replaced traditional final exams—this time not only for English and world history, but for science as well. A natural extension of the Futures thematic unit, the final project required that students engage in higher order thinking skills as they considered one of three themes: the meanings within modern technology, the identification and analysis of a local problem, or the need for a future invention. (See appendix G.) For the entire day of June 1 and the morning of June 2, students presented their work. Seated together at a table like a panel of judges, the four Connections teachers witnessed a wide array of student-chosen projects. As on the first day, rounds of applause punctuated the parade of presentations. Explanations of CD-ROM technology, nuclear energy, and virtual reality; expositions of Cedar City issues in the areas of housing, crime, and school finance; and demonstrations of slicer-dicer, fighter plane, and warship prototypes alternated in a presentation order determined by drawing numbers. The Connections year ended much as it had begun: in room 307, with excited students talking, and a project that transcended subject areas.

In between, other "coming through" tales became prominent in Connections lore. Stories of students "rising to the occasion" (Sheryl) were recounted with pride. Most often these tales were associated with projects. Bernie told such a tale at the October 12 common planning session. He had "run into" a Connections parent in town, and the parent had excitedly approached Bernie with a story to tell. As Bernie told his colleagues, "He said [his son] had sat him down and *read* him his Quest. He said, 'This is the first time this boy has really been interested in school.'"

The parent had been impressed by his son's work, by his "coming through" on a project; but he had been more impressed by his son's interest. Closer to the end of the year, another project elicited a similar reaction, this time from Sheryl. The teachers had devised an impromptu mini-unit to span "this huge block of time we were leaping over" between the Reactions unit (*To Kill a Mockingbird*, World War II, chemical reactions) and the Future unit (*Fahrenheit 451*, a mock United Nations meeting on current and future global issues). Students organized themselves into groups of their own choosing; then, in a random drawing, each group picked a decade of the first half of the twentieth century. The students' assignment was to create a list of significant events, persons, and technologies that emerged during their given decade, create a visual representation of their findings on posterboard, and present their research to the rest of the Connections students. Sheryl concluded her recounting of the story to May's contingent of visitors by saying: "The kids got so totally involved that we extended it for the whole week. Hey, they're good. They amaze us sometimes." Sheryl's comments about the time line project and the parent's words about the Quest project parallel an important dimension of the Renaissance in the Snow Tale.

As successful as the Renaissance Fair was when it was finally held, the Renaissance in the Snow Tale, as told and retold at milestone meetings, was more about what happened during the snow-day telephone calls to students. As Sheryl told the board of education in March, "Kids were *upset* at being out on snow days." Each of the teachers talked with parents pleased about their child's level of excitement and engagement with Connections in general and the Renaissance Fair project in particular. Each of the teachers talked with students eagerly anxious to display their projects and disappointed at the postponement. In his year-end reflections, Tim wrote, "The Renaissance Fair I thought was a turning point for many students academically." Tim's thought points to the predominant theme of a third tale of triumph.

### The Emma Lazarus Tale

This tale's title derives from the name of Emma Lazarus, who wrote "The New Colossus," the poem that provides the inscription for the Statue of Liberty. Inviting the "homeless, tempest-tossed" to the "golden door" of the American Dream, the poem expresses an egalitarian view of access and opportunity. Like the poem, this tale in the Connections saga was concerned with access and opportunity.

Not tied to one specific event, the Emma Lazarus Tale took many forms. At the February 1 meeting with George Cerny and Mike Davis, Bernie encapsulated his version as he remarked, "Some [of the students] we were told by the eighth grade [teachers] were absolute zeroes have done well . . . The good has been, we've pulled some kids up." Tim's version, related at the March board of education meeting, focused on a dimension of the tale that was especially important to him: "For the most part, LD kids have been able to grasp and take off. We have been pleased with their progress." Sheryl's version was implicit in her April comments to potential next-year Connections students, "We like lots of well-rounded people; you don't have to be a 'good' student." Dan's version, though rarely recounted, centered on one underlying factor that all of his colleagues agreed contributed to the tale's significance: flexibility. As he told May's contingent of visitors, "The best thing has been flexibility of time."

As Sheryl and Tim, most especially, recounted the Emma Lazarus Tale, their comments about student success transcending ability-level designations were always preceded or followed by examples of flexibility and adaptability. Whether pointing to the use of parallel texts (e.g., *Romeo and Juliet*), audiotapes (e.g., *Fahrenheit 451*), differentiated tests, field trips aligned with classroom topics (e.g., to the local courthouse in preparation for the trial scenes in *To Kill a Mockingbird*), videotapes that appealed to visual learners (e.g., "Castles"), or to simulations that required exploration and application of key concepts (e.g., the "Dear Abbess" letters, the mock trials), the Emma Lazarus Tale explicitly linked student academic success to egalitarian teaching strategies. As Bernie (in a comment reminiscent of his "Staff Profile" remarks) concluded, "We need to 'hook' them" (January 25, 1994). "Hooking" students, encouraging them to cross the threshold of the "golden door" through methods and projects that were designed to both engage student interest and enable student success, was the Emma Lazarus Tale's theme.

## The Nuts and Bolts Tale

In this fourth tale of triumph, the teachers offered tangible evidence of Connections' success in terms of standard measures of programmatic success. Like the Emma Lazarus Tale, the Nuts and Bolts Tale was tied not to a single event but rather to perceived trends that bespoke success. Comprised of testimonials about attendance, state proficiency test results, and grades, this fourth tale was couched in a language that all outside the Connections community would understand.

May's visitors provided an audience of, to use Mike Davis's terms, "curriculum director types" (or in Sheryl's terms, "the suits") who were clearly seen as a group that would appreciate the significance of a Nuts and Bolts Tale. Before any of the other tales of triumph had been told, but after an initial question about the program's acceptance by "high ability parents," George Cerny prompted the Connections teachers, "Tell them about the proficiency results."

As they had at the February 1 milestone meeting with Mike Davis, Bernie and Tim outlined the Connections students' performance on the tests they wrote at the end of October. At this May conclave, Bernie prefaced his narrative with the explanation that the four teachers (like many of their non-Connections colleagues who taught ninth-grade students) had devoted the two weeks prior to the testing days to preparation, review, and practice for the high-stakes, state-mandated tests. With a twinkle and wink of his eye, he told the visitors, "I don't want to say we taught to the test; nobody does that, right?" Smiles of recognition acknowledged Bernie's frank account of the realities of meeting state accountability mandates. The students also had recognized the practical value of their Connections teachers' tactics. The month before, as Mandy, a Connections student, had described the program to eighth-grade students, she had pointedly told them, "If you're worried about the proficiency tests . . . they [the Connections teachers] have the time to help you." The "help," consistent with the central theme of the Emma Lazarus Tale, had worked. Connections honors students, with one exception in math, had passed all four parts of the test. Academic students had all passed the reading and writing portions. General students were, in Bernie's words, "a mixed bag," but they were not a source of disappointment. Tim described the results for the nine LD students who had taken the test: "Two passed all four parts. Most passed two. Only one didn't pass any. To be honest, he wouldn't have passed no matter where he was." Overall, as the local newspaper reported on March 16 (in an article detailing the district's Instructional Council's approval of Connections' continuation past the first year): "Of students who took Connections, 99 percent passed writing, 95 percent passed reading, 91 percent passed citizenship and 75 percent passed math on the first try . . . These figures include both gifted and learning disabled students." As impressive as the proficiency test results were, they were but one part of the Nuts and Bolts Tale.

The May meeting with "the suits" continued with Bernie's observation: "Attendance on the vast majority of these kids has been really good. They know they're really gonna miss something [if they're absent]. My attendance book is almost empty." Attendance had also been discussed in George Cerny's summary of Connections' success at the March Board of Education meeting. Proudly, he told all assembled: "Of the 150 students with perfect attendance, twelve are in Connections. I asked Dan to figure the Connections attendance rate. It's 98 percent." Given that the first of the high school's annual goals, as listed on the cover of the student handbook, was to achieve an overall student attendance rate of 94 percent, George's pride seemed justified. Such an attendance rate had not come about passively. At the customary Friday common planning periods devoted to "talking about kids" (and on other days as well), teachers would voice their concern (usually Sheryl or Tim) about student absences. If telephone calls home to parents had not resolved attendance questions, Sheryl was usually the first to say, "We need to talk to George about [Misty] big time" (October 29, 1993).

The grades portion of the story came almost in the same breath as the attendance part of the Nuts and Bolts Tale in May's telling of the tale. Sheryl noted the relatively few midterm reports she had sent out for the fourth quarter, and Bernie characterized the overall Connections grades as "pretty positive."[1] Made only at George's prompting and without the elaboration that accompanied other tales, these comments revealed that the teachers, while cognizant of the significance of grades to both students and their May audience, did not attach as much value to grades as they did to the other tales of triumph they shared. Grades appeared to be significant primarily as they reflected themes of those other tales, the Emma Lazarus Tale in particular. George Cerny's quoted comments in the March 16 newspaper article illustrated this connection: "Some students have said that they used to get all D's and F's and now have plans for college."

*Four Tales, One Saga*

By definition, all of the stories that become part of a group's organizational saga are success stories (Clark, 1972). Yet the four tales of triumph just recounted share more than their saga role as exemplars of Connections success. Their themes weave together.

Nathan's rapt reading of *Romeo and Juliet* reflects the student engagement so apparent in the Renaissance in the Snow Tale. In turn, this student interest and involvement generated (and/or maintained) the high level of parental support evidenced in both the *Romeo and Juliet* Tale and the Renaissance in the Snow Tale. Moreover, student interest and involvement in their learning was clearly the linchpin of the "hooking" theme in the Emma Lazarus Tale. Further, the standard measures of programmatic success evoked in the Nuts and Bolts Tale were affirmations of the efforts the Emma Lazarus Tale prized. Like an interdependent web, the themes of Connections' best-of-times tales betoken a common ecology.

THE BEST-OF-TIMES ECOSYSTEM

If the first day story (chap. 3) marked the initiation of the Connections saga that first created a Connections community identity, and if that community was to be sustained, then the stories of Connections' best of times would need to evidence the saga's fulfillment. A saga is fulfilled when a community's members adhere to the values expressed in the saga and the community's practices embody those values (Clark, 1972). In other words, because the four tales of triumph assumed places in the Connections saga alongside the first day story, they could be expected to reflect a similar ecology of physical, cultural, and personal systems. Thus the analysis that follows explores the extent to which the ecology of the best of times correlated with the ecology of the first day.

*Best-of-Times Physical System*

The significant first day's physical system hallmarks (room 307 and the Connections block) had set the stage for Connections' project orientation, flexibility, and family atmosphere. Proximity of time and space had created the opportunity for collegial community on the first day. Within the best-of-times tales of triumph, the effects, if not always the causes, of the first day's physical system hallmarks retained their significance.

The Renaissance Fair, like many of the projects in which the students' "coming through" was significant, was tied to a public forum. Expositions of learning, like the first day's bridge display, were a Connections trademark. With the notable exception of the Renaissance Fair held in the junior high school auditorium/gymnasium, room 307 was the site for these exhibitions.

Yet other projects (for example, Bernie's family tree assignment, Sheryl's research paper, Dan's invention database) were not the objects of a public display. However, the "coming through" dimension was *still* evident in the students' work on these projects. Like an intermittent schedule of reinforcement, public exhibition of several projects concentrated in the beginning weeks and the longer-term promise of public exhibitions to come appeared to sustain both Connections' project orientation and the value placed on "coming through" with a best-work effort.

What appeared to be integral to the sustaining power of the intermittent displays of learning was the schedule flexibility component that had been such an important part of the first day's physical system. The Connections teachers' ability to configure a variety of schedule options—full-day-full-cohort, full-day-half-cohort over two days, 1½-1½ balanced over three days—was the catalyst for many of the "hooking" strategies so prominent in the Emma Lazarus Tale. The continuity that came from being able to conduct a learning activity in a single day (as opposed to the fragmentation that came with following the standard schedule) was important to the teachers as they planned their "hooking" teaching tactics. At May's meeting with visitors, Dan asserted that being able to conduct as many as three related labs in one session had allowed him to "cover as much material . . . more effectively and efficiently." At February's meeting with Mike and George, Bernie spoke of being "able to do things I've never been able to do [before]." From Bernie's perspective, conducting simulations (e.g., games such as Civilization and one exploring the pre–World War I competition for colonies) and mock trials in one extended session increased both student involvement in the activity and student understanding of the concepts embedded in the activity.

Similarly, at February's meeting Bernie (with Sheryl's strong concurrence) spoke about the "good" videos Connections teachers had been able to integrate into their instruction. Being able to show such films as *The Agony and the Ecstasy* and *All Quiet on the Western Front* to all Connections students in a single seating was seen as a distinct pedagogical advantage. The "hooking" power of visual approaches to content was seen as much greater in a single viewing than in the fragmented showings (usually over a three day period) teachers had known in their individual practices before Connections. Consequently, both Sheryl and Bernie reported that they were much more inclined to use movies, *and* able to use them to greater effect, than ever before. Such showings were enhanced when, at Sheryl's instigation (as faculty advisor to the Class of '93), approval was secured in February for using funds from the class gift of the Class of '93 to purchase two large-screen televisions. Moreover, Tim suggested that these televisions be stored in the supply anteroom between room 314 and room 312, so they would be readily available for Connections' use in room 307, just across the hall.

The physical system elements of time and space were also important to another, perhaps more subtle, aspect of Connections' best-of-times tales. The *Romeo and Juliet* Tale, the Renaissance in the Snow subtale of the boy reading his Quest paper to his father, and the planning required for implementing many of the "hooking" strategies of the Emma Lazarus Tale were all allied to the common planning period. The stories of Nathan's reading of *Romeo and Juliet* and the son's sharing of his learning with his father were stories made more powerful as they were passed on during the common planning period. In the best of times, stories of success, whether they originated in a parental comment to one teacher or in the events in one teacher's classroom, were stories to be *shared*. In the best of times, being "able to detect and celebrate patterns of accomplishment within and across classrooms" (Little, 1990, p. 171) became a tacit part of common planning period time. In the best of times, the triumphs of one became the triumphs of all.

This sense of shared work found a more practical, and far more explicit, expression in the time devoted to planning during the first period of each day. On a surface level, this shared planning involved imparting information about individual teaching needs and accommodations,as in the planning period of September 14. Other occasions (such as planning for field trips, the Renaissance Fair, the second semester's final project, and other elaborate and extensive ventures) required close coordination and interdependence as each teacher assumed responsibility for specific tasks. In the Renaissance in the Snow Tale, when snow days precluded the opportunity to meet in room 307, the Connections teachers substituted a series of telephone calls for their daily common planning time. Close coordination could also be seen in Tim's daily conversations with whomever he was working at the time. Indeed, on any given day Tim's work was defined by his agreed-upon role/duties discussed during common planning period sessions. So important was this shared time for the practicalities of planning and coordination that George Cerny's query (February 1, 1994) about next year's Connections needs—"Can you do without the extra prep?"—was met with an immediate response. Quickly, Dan responded, "No," and Sheryl added, "Two years down the road, *maybe*."

The opportunities inherent in Connections' best-of-times physical system enhanced the themes in the tales of triumph— "hooking" students, ensuring success for all through engaging learning activities, providing projects for which "coming through" became an explicit norm, and experiencing the shared triumphs and coordinated planning of the common planning time. Like accounts of the first day, Connections best-of-times tales betokened a physical system distinctive in its provisions of both a home space and, more importantly, flexibility of time. But, in and of itself, the opportunity afforded by physical systems could not and did not assure collegial community during Connections' best of times. Other systems within the ecology of the best of times were also needed to establish the equilibrium that, by definition, marked Connections' best of times.

## Best-of-Times Cultural System

The cultural messages embedded in these tales reveal the essence of the imagination-arresting power, the inquisitiveness-igniting influence, and meaningful interactions associated with healthy classrooms (Haley-Oliphant, 1994).

The imagination-arresting power within the best of-times cultural system was evident in both the students' disappointment at snow days (the Renaissance in the Snow Tale) and the student attendance figures of the Nuts and Bolts Tale. Clearly, the students liked being part of Connections. One reason for this student attitude was articulated by Nathan Archer in the *Romeo and Juliet* Tale. When his mother asked Nathan what he liked about Connections, his immediate response was "the special projects." The first day's emphasis on active learning, especially in groups and in conjunction with a project, remained a hallmark within the Connections best-of-times cultural system. Yet more than the mere existence of projects, the *nature* of those projects was important to understanding their imagination-arresting power.

Built into each of the major projects (e.g., the Renaissance Fair, the twentieth-century time line, the Quest, the second-semester final project) were two common elements: choice and a public forum. The choice of whether to work individually or to join with others to form their own self-selected groups lay with the students. The choice of topic, within given guidelines, also lay with students. The choices were of consequence. Attached to their efforts would be not only a grade but a public exhibition as well. Always before their peers, sometimes before administrators (who "popped in" for portions of project presentations), and notably before the more extended audience (the junior high teachers and students, the parents able to attend) of the Renaissance Fair, Connections projects were legitimated not only by their status of "counting" significantly in a grading rubric but also by their public exhibition. Attaching the cultural mandates of choice and a public forum to the cultural value placed on projects vastly increased the projects' imagination-arresting power for both students and teachers. Just as the first day's bridge building had captured imaginations in a powerful *first* impression, the best-of-times' continuing project orientation created a *lasting* cultural impression.

As imagination-arresting as the projects were, the four tales of triumph were not limited to instances in which choice and a public forum played a significant role. The students exercised no choice in reading *Romeo and Juliet* or in taking the state-mandated proficiency tests. They had no public forum for their individually prepared family trees or research papers. A source of igniting power, one that went beyond the cultural message of a project orientation, also lay embedded in the best-of-times tales.

The first day's cultural messages of Connections' heterogeneous orientation and flexibility found expression in both the Emma Lazarus Tale and the *Romeo and Juliet* Tale. Significant sources of the best-of-times' igniting power lay in these cultural messages. The shared values and culture characteristic of effective schools include high expectations for student performance, a genuine caring and respect for individuals, and mutual trust (Cohen, 1987). In effect, these elements create a moral order in which the norm of collegiality is evidenced through a sustained focus on solving the problems of students.

A sidebar to the proficiency test portion of the Nuts and Bolts tale points to this important dimension within the best-of-times tales. As Sheryl planned the timed practice sessions for the writing portion of the test, she used prompts gleaned from her own imagination and previous tests. By serendipitous coincidence, one of the prompts students found on the "real" late-October test was one Sheryl had selected for practice. At the October 29 common planning period Sheryl reported the students' predictable reaction: "The kids were *very* impressed!" The students were impressed by more than Sheryl's apparent psychic powers. The fortuitous incident had dramatically reinforced a best-of-times cultural message. In the best of times, the students understood that the teachers cared deeply about their success in the program and could be trusted to provide the instruction and direction necessary to that success.

In such a cultural context of trust, caring, and concern for student needs and problems, Nathan's absorbed reading in the *Romeo and Juliet* Tale, as delightfully unanticipated as it was, should not have been seen as surprising. Rather, Nathan's reading and all the other evidence of student involvement within the four tales of triumph occupied a common place in a cultural cycle.

In this cycle the "hooking" strategies for success that were the focus of the Emma Lazarus Tale were inextricably linked to the projects and the "coming through" focus of the Renaissance in the Snow Tale. Both the cultural message of a project orientation and the cultural message of ensuring success created a cultural environment in which students "came through." In turn, the students' "coming through" increased the teachers' commitment to a flexible pedagogy for success. Consequently, the "good start" George Cerny saw as an important first day legacy was but the beginning of a cycle that created its own sustained igniting power. The early successes of (for example) Sheryl's Quest project and Bernie's Trial of Socrates foreshadowed both the extensive and demanding efforts involved in preparing for the Renaissance Fair and its ultimate success. In a like manner, the use of a parallel text and audio tapes (distinctly Emma Lazarus Tale strategies) contributed directly to Nathan's rapt reading of *Romeo and Juliet*; this in turn validated the use of similar strategies in future literature-based studies. Teacher inquisitiveness—to design ever more intriguing projects or to develop a wider repertoire of teaching strategies for success—begat student inquisitiveness in an ongoing cycle.

Serving as the catalyst within this cycle, and implicit in the trust and caring that were significant in the Emma Lazarus Tale, was the cultural indicator of "meaningful interactions." In the best of times, the teachers' words and actions (for example, preparing for the proficiency tests, telephoning students individually about the postponed Renaissance Fair) bespoke a relationship in which the teachers cared about the students and could be trusted to ensure their success. The reciprocal of that best-of-times relationship was also evident. Most notably with the advent of the second semester, and again at the year's end, the Connections teachers actively sought the students' suggestions for improving Connections. Numerous parental anecdotes about the students' interest and engagement had reinforced the teachers' tacit acknowledgement that the students cared about Connections. Moreover, multiple occasions had proved that the students could be trusted to "come through." The teachers' words evidence their understanding of this distinctive best-of-times relationship:

> BERNIE. The kids want engaging stuff . . .They want assignments and direction, but then "let us go." (January 25, 1994)

> TIM. Taking suggestions from the students on how to improve the program has been a real plus. There has been a lot of one-on-one contact. (March 16, 1994)

> SHERYL. In the long run, they [the students] "came through" beyond my expectations on major assignments. Another change, that I have mixed emotions about, is that they felt free to question our requirements and/or conditions, and I didn't necessarily relish that. (May 26, 1994)

Sheryl's "mixed emotions" notwithstanding, the Connections best-of-times teacher-student relationship, strongly impressed by the first day's cultural system, was one of meaningful interaction characterized by mutual caring and trust.

The meaningful interactions within the tales of triumph were not limited to teachers and students. The best-of-times culture also included parents. The *Romeo and Juliet* Tale and the Renaissance in the Snow Tale both incorporated themes of parental involvement. Thus it was not surprising when George Cerny proudly told both the May contingent of visitors and Mike Davis (earlier, at a February meeting) about the evidence of parental support for Connections he had witnessed: many parental inquiries (from parents wanting a Connections-like program for tenth grade) and an unprecedented level of parent volunteerism (to videotape, to chaperone field trips). In their year-end reflections, the four teachers evinced a shared regard for the importance of the parental connection:

> TIM. The parents for the most part were very supportive . . . I know many of the parents thought Connections was a great learning experience for their child.

> SHERYL. I thought there were more connections made among . . . parents than in a "normal" structure. I thought there was more caring, more concern, than is usually present at the high school level.

> DAN. Support from the parents [was important].

> BERNIE. Several parents regard [Connections] as a second chance for kids who have had a poor time at [the junior high].

The connections with parents that had begun with the initial parent meetings and the first day's parent volunteers continued and strengthened during Connections' best of times.

Similarly, the ties among the Connections teachers as a teaching team that had been evident in the first day's cultural message of camaraderie were also evident in the four tales of triumph. As with the first day's cultural system, camaraderie was closely tied to dependability and predictability. Nowhere was this more evident than at a morning planning session held during the Christmas break. Gathered together at a local restaurant for breakfast (the ritual of sharing food remained throughout the year), the teachers devoted the better part of a vacation morning to planning for the Renaissance Fair. Dan volunteered to compile and prepare the program. Sheryl assumed responsibility for preparing the necessary parental notes. Bernie took charge of logistics, which included contacting the junior high about equipment and space needs and arranging for buses. Tim, while taking notes, offered to make contacts to videotape the extravaganza. Sheryl, ever mindful of details, mentioned calling the local newspaper and then asked, "Who's going to remind George about subs for the Fair day? Who's on good terms?" Evidently Bernie was, for the task fell to him. Arrangements completed, the conversation turned to another common topic of Connections teacher talk.

Again, as at each Friday's (and many other days') common planning time, the talk turned to the few Connections students who "refuse to participate" and whose success, despite the Emma Lazarus teaching strategies, remained elusive. The teachers had not given up on these few. The case of Billy had proved that tenacity had its rewards. By early October, it was clear that Billy was in trouble. Sheryl reported Billy had earned a 48 percent average in English, Bernie figured Billy's current world history grade at 49 percent, and Dan's records revealed a 9 percent for physical science. At the October 8 common planning session, the teachers prepared for a conference with Billy's mother, to be held at 11:30 that day. In response to Bernie's "Are we all set on Billy baby?" the consensus was that Billy would be given until the end of the quarter to improve significantly. If he did not, then "he's out." During the November 19 common planning time, Sheryl issued a progress report: "I'm happy to report that Billy has gotten eyeglasses. He's kind of disassociated himself from the jerks and he's been doing better academically."

In Billy's case, parental contact supplemented the two conditions all of the Emma Lazarus Tale variations consistently linked to ensuring student success. The first was the flexibility of time and methods distinctive to Connections as a program. The second condition lay in two Connections resources, one created by the teachers, and one inherent in the teaching team's composition. The teachers had created both the color advisory system and the tradition of dedicating Fridays to "talk about kids." The other resource was most explicitly identified in Sheryl's comments to May's contingent of visitors. In talking about the accommodation of Connections' heterogeneous students in a unified curriculum, Sheryl concluded with, "Plus we have Tim. He took those kids—anybody who was struggling with it [*Romeo and Juliet*], and slowed it down." In the best of times, the meaningful interaction among Connections teachers included both shared planning and responsibility for major (and minor) events and shared concerns about students.

In the best of times the three cultural messages of a healthy ecosystem were all present: meaningful interaction among teachers, students, and parents; active learning through projects that captured imaginations; and the igniting power of a heterogeneous orientation and flexible teaching strategies. These cultural messages had been present in the first day's cultural system. But throughout the Connections year, they became more pronounced and interwove ever more tightly. As bound together in a continuous cycle as these cultural indicators were within the best-of-times cultural system, they were also intricately related to the best-of-times personal system.

*Best-of-Times Personal System*

It is a truism of the profession that the greatest rewards of teaching come from students—from their "eureka" moments, their achievements in assignments and on tests. This truism suggests an extension of the cycle evident in Connections' best-of-times cultural system. When students "come through," teachers feel rewarded, and their commitment to the teaching methods and strategies that engendered such "coming through" is reinforced. In effect, when students "come through," the risks of adopting a pedagogy of flexibility and adaptability are reduced. Consequently, the teacher so rewarded is likely to continue an adventurous pedagogy. This complex cycle of students "coming through" → teacher feelings of being rewarded → increased commitment to students → increased willingness to take pedagogical risks is precisely the cycle manifest in the best of times personal system.

When the Connections teachers met with George Cerny and Mike Davis on February 1, the Renaissance in the Snow experience was still a fresh memory. Near the end of the meeting, Mike Davis asked the teachers if they were planning a similar culminating event for the second semester. Bernie responded: "Sure, we'll cook something up. The snow days made the Renaissance Fair difficult, and we would do some things differently. But you gotta start somewhere."

"You gotta start somewhere" was an illuminating phrase. "Somewhere" denoted a measure of uncertainty, while "gotta" denoted a resolve to proceed in the face of that risk. Bernie's adventurous stance explicitly expressed a significant part of the best-of-times personal system cycle. Within the four tales of triumph, explicitly or implicitly, all four elements of the personal system cycle were manifest.

The element of "coming through" began on the first day when all but a few student-constructed bridges both risked and sustained the weight of thirteen bricks. The vast majority of Connections students "came through" repeatedly, most noticeably with projects (e.g., the Quest project, the twentieth-century time line, and the final project successes described above). As the narrative of the Renaissance in the Snow Tale indicated, "coming through" became a regular cultural feature within the Connections ecosystem. Just as regular were the expressions of teachers feeling rewarded when students "came through."

As the teachers recounted the tales of triumph at milestone meetings, they not only described the various projects and learning activities they had undertaken but also, quite pointedly and proudly, described the students' success in these learning ventures. During May's conversation with "the suits," Bernie made the general observation, "Even the so-called general kids are writing better than my junior class students." Later, when Sheryl was telling the visitors about the twentieth century time line week, Tim retrieved a 1960s poster created by two learning diasabilities students to show the guests. His choice was significant. The two boys who had created this particular poster were not academic shining stars, and neither had compiled a particularly impressive academic record in Connections. But this work had impressed Tim, and he eagerly displayed it.

The teachers' telling tales of feeling rewarded by student success were not limited to milestone meetings. Quite the contrary. As Bernie's initial sharing of the Quest-reading story and Sheryl's first sharing of the *Romeo and Juliet* Tale illustrate, the common planning period was often a forum of reward. Indeed, as the May planning period that had been devoted to conversation with "the suits" ended and Tim and Sheryl were walking down the hall toward Sheryl's classroom, Tim shared a reward story with Sheryl. He described what he perceived as an important event in the English class he had conducted the day before. Earl, one of the creators of the poster Tim had just displayed, had actually *volunteered* to answer questions about the day's reading in

*Fahrenheit 451.* Moreover, "He had all the right answers!"

This sharing of student success, of rewarding each other, was a familiar common planning period happening. Two examples from November were representative of this tradition. On November 9, Sheryl proudly announced the results of the first test she had given on *Romeo and Juliet*: "I had *no* F's!" After the Thanksgiving break, when Tim had had the opportunity to look at many of the students' family tree projects (an assignment Bernie traditionally gave to world history students), he told his colleagues: "The family trees were *really* good. A lot of work went into them."

While the common planning period was often a forum for rewarding each other with stories of success, it was also a forum for sharing concerns. To be sure, when Sheryl raised her concerns about Jason during the September 14 gathering, her colleagues had offered no response. But in the best of times such shared concerns were met with words and actions that exemplified the third element of the best-of-times personal system cycle: increased commitment to students.

As early as the third week of school, the teachers had become concerned about a few students. About fifteen minutes into the September 10 planning period Bernie asked, "Do you want to talk about kids? It's Friday." Immediately, Sheryl mentioned Mary, a student who already had been absent three times and tardy once. Nodding as Sheryl spoke, Bernie said, "We need to have a conference with her pronto-tonto." Within the next few minutes, Sheryl, Bernie, and Tim had identified several students about whom they were concerned. One girl was doing poorly on tests; a few others, mostly boys, had turned in only one of the five assignments Bernie had already collected. Suddenly, an opportunity came to Bernie's mind. That day an activity period had been scheduled, so Bernie suggested, "We could use the activity period time to talk to these kids." Tim quickly picked up on Bernie's idea: "Maybe we could put together a list [of students behind in their work], and I could take them and work with them." Since the day's plans were centered on Sharon Finch's first art project (designing Connections' logos), Tim's plan was not put into action. But Sheryl, Bernie, and Tim did use the activity time to "visit" selected students and to point out blank places in their grade books.

"Catching students up" remained a concern. On November 19, Sharon Finch presented slides of medieval castle art, Bernie helped supervise those who elected to create stained glass windows, and Dan, while simultaneously grading lab books, monitored students building corrugated cardboard castles. But Tim and Sheryl, in Sheryl's room, were working with twenty students selected by Tim after he had looked through all of the teachers' grade books. Their work was "catching up." Coincidentally, November 19 was the day a conference (not the first) was arranged with Mary's parents for the following Monday.

In the best of times, commitment to students took another form beyond "catching them up." Two incidents, one in late October and one in early December, illustrate. On October 29, Sharon Finch's art project again involved design. For a promotional price, the Crayola company was offering to supply quality T-shirts and transfer the students' crayoned designs to them. While students worked on their designs, Sheryl sat at the teacher desk in the right front corner of room 307 and began drawing. Explaining that this day "I want to be a student," Sheryl planned to create distinctive T-shirts for herself ("Wrestling Mom") and for her son and daughter-in-law, who had just had their second child the week before. For a few minutes that morning, I became "visible," at least to Sheryl. Beckoning me to her desk, Sheryl asked me to stroll nonchalantly around the room and get a look at Betty to see if I thought her make-up covered a black eye. When I returned to Sheryl's desk, she explained her concern: "Normally Betty is upbeat, but she's been depressed the last couple of weeks. One day last week, she cried the whole time. I asked her if she wanted to talk to a counselor or to me. But she said no. I talked to Melissa [Betty's constant companion], but she didn't know anything. Melissa'd talk if she knew." Sheryl's worst fears proved unfounded, but her level of personal concern was reminiscent of several common planning period conversations about the life situations some Connections students faced.

The December incident involved Kyle, the classic nerd in the Connections cohort. On December 8, Kyle was hit by a car and suffered a broken leg. At the December 10 planning session, Tim reported that he had called Kyle the evening before, and "He was thrilled." During the December 14 planning period, it was

Bernie's turn to update Kyle's condition: "I called Kyle last night. I spoke to him in that German schtick he loves." [Kyle was enthralled by Bernie's lapses into a bad German accent, and he loved to copy it.] Not to be outdone in the Kyle department, Sheryl reported that she had been paged for a telephone call that morning at 7:30. When she arrived at the school office and answered the telephone, she found that her caller was Kyle: "He misses me."

The incidents involving Betty and Kyle were more personal expressions of the same commitment to students that had been evidenced in the telephone calls to students that were central in the Renaissance in the Snow Tale. The view of teaching that had been communicated on the first day—that personal connection with students is an integral part of the teaching process—deepened in Connections best of times. More than surface chatter about interests and experiences, personal connection with students, in the best of times, meant commitment and caring.

In the best-of-times personal system cycle, this commitment and caring were related to the element of increased willingness to take pedagogical risks. Within this cyclical element, the first day's dimensions of excitement, teaching as craft, the dignity of risk, and an adventurous, transdisciplinary conception of content all merged. While some of the Connections project ideas had been borrowed from Betsy Grant (the bridge building, the Renaissance Fair) and others had been part of the teachers' former individual practices (the Quest, the Dear Abbess letters, the family tree, the mock trials and simulations), several projects and teaching strategies were creations "new" with Connections. One was the second-semester final project whose grading rubric was a last-minute addition. Another was the twentieth-century time line; there an impromptu bridge between thematic units became a week-long project. Both of these projects included an element of on-the-spot adaptation.

This "tinkerer model" (Huberman, 1993) of the teaching craft was even more visible in many of the day-to-day common planning sessions that were not project related. When Dan arrived at 8:00 on October 19, he asked "What are we doing today?" Sheryl's reply was "We're still working on it." On both November 12 and December 3 Sharon Finch was ill, so the day's plans required last minute compensation for her absence. Sheryl's comment on December 3 was typical: "No problem; we can wing it."

On December 12, the teachers were discussing the next day's field trip to an art museum, a trip undertaken with the dual purposes of preparing for the Renaissance Fair and seeing original examples of artifacts produced by the cultures they had been studying. As the morning PA announcements concluded, Bernie asked Tim, "We gonna organize this field trip, wild man?" In fact, the field trip's organization was fairly complete. But one key task remained. The teachers had decided to group students in clusters related to their chosen Renaissance Fair topics. Some clusters fell in line more naturally than others: putting together kings, queens, and popes; tying together castles, chivalry, and coats of arms; or placing artists with cathedrals. But some were more challenging: Bernie whimsically suggested putting "women's roles" with the Three Musketeers, causing Sheryl to chuckle. Despite his feeling that "this isn't falling in like I thought," Bernie continued working with Tim, attempting to match student interest groups with the chaperones Sheryl had recruited. Finally, Bernie presented the plan and asked, "So do we feel good; do we feel organized?" Dan, looking up from his work of cleaning his room in preparation for his formal evaluation that day, had only one comment—"I want Wendy's"—referring to his choice of interstate interchange restaurants for lunch.

Most especially in this last episode, a consideration of student needs and interests, a creative strategy of linking learning activities (the field trip to the Renaissance Fair), an interdisciplinary perspective on the Renaissance, and a "tinkerer" approach to planning all combined in anticipation of a teaching adventure. As during the planning sessions for the Renaissance Fair and the second semester final project, a distinct air of excitement prevailed. Moreover, the focus of all of this planning was the knowledge students would construct from these learning activities.

The Emma Lazarus, Renaissance in the Snow, and *Romeo and Juliet* Tales converged in a best-of-times personal system that, above all, honored an apparently unitary view of teaching and students. In the *best* of times, the teachers shared a common personal system that mirrored the first day personal system.

*Webs to Other Ecosystems in the Best of Times*

Among the effective strategies that promote the mutual adaptation of an innovative project and its institutional setting are (1) administrative commitment and support; (2) teacher participation in project decisions; and (3) extensive, intensive, and ongoing training assistance.[2] All three were present in Connections' best of times.

During the February 1 meeting with the Connections teachers, comments made by both George Cerny and Mike Davis provided evidence of strong administrative support: George said, "Since day one, it's been your baby," and Mike observed, "Our job is to create an atmosphere for risk." When I interviewed these administrators at the end of the school year, both expanded upon these comments. I asked George what advice he would give a principal of a school about to implement a Connections-like program:

> Make every effort you can for funding and materials. Provide all you can. When you commit to something like this, I think the administration has to have the capacity to step back and let teachers get their feet wet . . . to make mistakes . . . to learn . . . to do some things by trial and error. (April 29, 1994)

When I asked Mike Davis a similar question, he responded in much the same way.

> The secret, I think, to making the program work was empowering the teachers . . . We took cues that said make sure they have joint planning time and time to collaborate over the summer . . . The other advice, I think, is I tried to find a middle ground between administrative intrusiveness and benign neglect. My goal was to stay in touch enough with the team so they knew they had my firm support, but loose enough not to be a watchful eye. (June 9, 1994)

In the best of times the Connections teachers knew they had administrative support, as various incidents within the four tales of triumph illustrated.

The field trips in support of the Renaissance Fair and the Fair itself were cases in point. On September 10, as Sheryl was collecting permission slips for the trip to the Ohio Renaissance Festival, she paused to talk with a boy who had not yet returned his slip. *Sotto voce*, Sheryl told him, "If money is a problem, we have a little slush fund." Sheryl was referring to George Cerny's promise of assistance so that no Connections student would be denied the learning experience of field trips. Administrative support, primarily in terms of logistics, was also necessary for mounting the Fair. Bernie worked closely with the junior high principal to arrange for use of the auditorium and equipment needs. He also relied on the principal to create the schedule of visiting junior high classes. After the first snow day forced rescheduling of the Fair, the teachers met in George Cerny's office to regroup. In a series of telephone calls, George cleared much of the administrative red tape involved in changing the Renaissance Fair date.

There had been other conferences in George's office. When concerns about students surfaced (as, e.g., with Mary's attendance), the teachers turned to their principal for support and remedy. Still more regularly, Frank Barton, in his role as assistant principal, could be counted upon to intervene (as when one student's behavior at the art museum was particularly obnoxious and drew the attention of museum officials).

In large part the administrative support that permitted the Connections teachers great autonomy in instructional and programmatic decisions was possible due to the Nuts and Bolts Tale. Cohen (1988) describes the importance of a school's "social convention about results" (pp. 67–69). The weight that the community, the school, or society attaches to a consensual criterion of results lends legitimacy to teachers' work. The grades, proficiency test results, and attendance rate that were the core of the Nuts and Bolts Tale secured Connections' legitimacy and justified the administrators' support for the program.

The third effective strategy linked to mutual adaptation of a program to its setting, training supports, had a distinctive form in Connections' best of times. Formal training for the Connections teachers had been concentrated during the summer of 1993. During the school year, formal training occupied a lesser role. Sheryl attended a lecture on developing thematic units. All four teachers participated in the regular curriculum-related meetings associated with Cedar City High School. Sheryl met with all of the junior high and high school language arts teachers as they considered whole language issues. Dan and Tim were both members of the district's Instructional Council, a body that held discussions and made recommendations about curriculum proposals. Dan also sat on the district Instructional Technology Council. Bernie had been appointed to a liaison committee composed of teachers and administrators, a forum for discussing concerns raised by either or both parties. But the primary value of these opportunities lay in a dimension other than the professional development that was their sporadic by-product.

The Connections teachers' presence in these forums was part of a larger training scenario. In effect, the Connections teachers were their own goodwill ambassadors to the rest of the Cedar City faculty. The Renaissance Fair was more than a culminating activity for the first semester. It was a Connections showcase. At the Renaissance Fair, junior high teachers, students, and administrators were exposed to and impressed by the Connections program. On two occasions, once at the high school, and once before the district's intermediate-grade teachers, the Connections teachers were asked to present their program. In addition, the Connections teachers' March presentations before the Instructional Council and the board of education were more than progress reports designed to secure the district's official blessing for the program's continuation. A form of training (explaining Connections' curriculum, format, and successes) also occurred—one designed to win significant others to the Connections vision.

These presentations and opportunities for interaction with non-Connections peers made Connections highly visible. The publicity Connections received (in both the local newspaper and the district newsletter) also gave Connections high visibility. Little (1990) points out that "A combination of visibility . . . shared responsibility, and widespread interaction heightens the influence of teachers on one another and on the school as a whole" (p. 170).

Heightening influence, seeking acceptance, and encouraging interest and teacher volunteers for future additional dyads and/or interdisciplinary program options were the hoped-for results of Connections' high visibility. In the *best* of times, it worked. Other teachers (specifically a math teacher, a science teacher, and an art teacher) told Connections teachers they were personally interested in Connections' approach to teaching and curriculum. In the *best* of times, the Connections teachers' Cedar City High School colleagues accepted Connections and shared the teachers' excitement over their successes.

Even so, the influence of their non-Connections teaching peers was not *perceptible* in the four tales of triumph that defined Connections' best of times. As in the first day's ecosystem, in the best of times the larger school and district ecosystem of Cedar City played a supporting, but not determining, role.

### First Impressions Last

In the best of times, the ecology of the first day found renewed expression. The project orientation, flexibility, and family atmosphere of the first day's physical system remained and continued to provide the fundamental condition of opportunity for collegial community. The first day's cultural system of camaraderie, a heterogeneous orientation toward success for all, projects and other active learning strategies, and teacher-student interaction in a family atmosphere became more pronounced yet more woven into a self-sustaining cycle in the best-of-times cultural system. The adventurous learning of the first day's personal system also formed a lasting impression in the best-of-times personal system cycle. "Coming through," "hooking," care and commitment, creative and determined pedagogical risk-taking converged in shared stances about teaching, students and curricular content. The administrative presence and support that were vital within the first day's ecosystem persisted in the best-of-times ecosystem. While the larger influences of grades, attendance, and the state proficiency test were felt in the Nuts and Bolts Tale, and to an extent in the Emma Lazarus Tale, in the best of times the intrusion of the larger ecosystem of Cedar City High School was minimal. In the best of times, Connections was its own world.

In the best of times, all of the systems united to produce a state of equilibrium. Indeed, by definition, the best of times *were* an ecological equilibrium. Equilibrium occurs when systems bear a connectedness to each other. The connectedness within the best-of-times ecology produced such an equilibrium. In the best of times, the saga initiated on the first day was fulfilled.

But the Connections ecology was not always marked by a state of equilibrium. Nor were all of the days in the Connections journey the best of times. It is to those other days that I now turn.

# CHAPTER 6

## The Worst of Times

Problems are our friends because it is only through immersing
ourselves in problems that we can come up with creative
solutions . . . The absence of problems usually indicates that not
much is being attempted.

—Michael Fullan, "Innovation, Reform,
and Restructuring Strategies"

In Homer's epic tale of Ulysses' odyssey, the hero encounters a
series of obstacles that defer and deter his homeward quest.
Ulysses' ultimate triumph comes not because his journey was
without perils and crew loss but rather because, despite the
destructive perils he faced—perhaps in defiance of them—he
steadfastly continued his journey. Throughout their odyssey, the
Connections shipmates would also face their own versions of
tempting siren calls and shipwrecking storms. Ulysses' story and
Fullan's observation on problems (1993, p. 126) suggest that *how*
the Connections teaching team faced the obstacles they encountered would be as significant as the nature of the obstacles themselves. Both the "what" and the "how" of Connections' perilous
moments are visible in the four tales of crisis that follow.

### FOUR TALES OF CRISIS

Less likely to be recounted in milestone meetings, the four tales
of crisis were the subject of many a first-period common planning time session. As with the four tales of triumph, each tale of
crisis focused on a particular event, or a series of events, within
the Connections journey. The first three are closely related and
reflect the development of an issue central to Connections' evolution as a collegial community. The fourth not only reflects
themes within the larger Cedar City High School community but
also provides valuable insights for understanding the first three.

I have entitled these tales the Lab Book Crisis Tale, the Conversion and Backsliding Tale, the Vision Thing Tale, and the Black Cloud Tale.

### The Lab Book Crisis Tale

By the second week of school, Dan had distributed his course syllabus in which his lab book specifications were detailed. Because his requirements were quite specific, Dan offered the students two options. They could find and purchase lab books on their own, or they could "place an order" (advance payment) and Dan would purchase lab books at the university where he was taking graduate courses. Several students took him up on his offer. But, as the events of September 14 revealed, a sizeable minority had neither taken advantage of Dan's offer nor purchased appropriate lab books on their own. Further complicating the matter, Dan would not grade lab reports until they were recorded in an appropriate lab book. Accordingly, a significant number of students were "missing" grades.

Despite planning sessions at which teachers voiced concerns about students who were behind in their work, I heard no planning time discussion of the lab book issue during September. Even during the first midterm week (the week of September 20), the emergent lab book crisis was not a point of discussion among the Connections teachers.

The lab book gridlock *was* a topic, indeed a central topic, on October 1, 1993. As Bernie, Tim, and Dan assembled in room 314 [Sheryl was absent due to illness], Bernie said, "I want to raise an issue for the group to discuss." Speaking of the "ten to fifteen kids we're not reaching all the time," Bernie wanted to create time to help those students who were struggling. Tim nodded, saying, "Most are in Science. They don't have lab books, and they're not following scientific procedure." But Bernie saw a larger issue as well, pointing out that "We have two things to solve, the three of us." He explained, "We need to get closure on the lab books somehow. About ten [students] are starting to go back to an us-them mentality . . . It's starting to frustrate us, make us frustrated with the kids. It's defeating the purpose of what we're trying to do with this class. We need to free up a day and work with kids who are struggling."

As Bernie paused, Dan said, "I agree with you," and Tim piped in, "I'll do it." Bernie continued, "I was thinking about what was going good and what wasn't. The common denominator seemed to be the lack of a science lab book." Dan acknowledged, "Maybe I should have taken up papers, but then I'd grade them twice." Bernie, who had misplaced a set of papers earlier in the week, said, "That's neither here nor there." As the morning announcements interrupted, Dan checked his records. Twenty-two students were still missing lab books. When the discussion resumed, Tim offered to go to a local flea market and "pick up about thirty." Bernie suggested that Tim also "pick up" a few calculators, but "the big thing is lab books, right?" Dan and Tim nodded.

Eventually, all Connections students had lab books, but the crisis remained in memory, in both the short term and the long term. In the long term, it portended other tales of crisis but also—because "This wasn't worth [the hassle]" (Bernie, June 6, 1994)—led to a minor program change: Connections teachers decided to include lab books in the fee schedule for Connections' second year. In the short term, the incident had made Dan the self-acknowledged "bad guy" of the first quarter (October 19, 1993). This was an image that acutely impacted the results of a feedback form Dan asked students to complete at the beginning of November (appendix H). Dan explained that, beginning with his student-teaching experience, providing this opportunity for student feedback had been part of his standard operating procedure. During his portion of a three-class rotation on November 12, Dan devoted almost the entire time to summarizing and responding to the students' feedback.

After telling the students that he appreciated their "not blowing it off," and that Mr. Cerny had seen their feedback forms, Dan read and responded to many of the comments included in the form's last two open-ended questions (what students liked best and least about his class). Regarding the lab books, Dan explained, "I wanted these because the paper can't be torn out easily" and added that it seemed unfair to allow some students to use graph paper when others "were responsible and brought in their money within a week." Issues other than the lab books also surfaced in this November 12 class session. Dan identified one issue, high expectations, as a theme. He told the students, "I expect a lot from myself . . . It's your responsibility to get along with the boss more than the boss's responsibility to get along with you. You might as well get used to that now." Near the end of the period, one of Dan's comments seemed to sum up his thoughts: "Like I said, guys, as the year goes on, things get better." In Connections' worst of times, Dan's statement did not prove accurate.

### The Conversion and Backsliding Tale

After class on the same day that Dan was devoting a period to the student feedback form results, Bernie repeated a comment I had heard before, "I wish Dan was able to plug in better." In interpreting the Connections "charter," Dan's syllabus indicated an emphasis on the provision for "essentially the same [ninth-grade] curricula," while Bernie, Tim, and Sheryl's comments indicated that their interpretation centered on the "different focus on the instruction." Increasingly, Bernie, Tim, and Sheryl expressed their frustration with the team's seeming inability to "connect" science with English and history. Increasingly, they saw Dan as "unplugged" (a Connections term denoting lack of content relation). Their response to this perceived "unplugging" forms the "conversion" portion of this tale.

On December 14, Bernie called a meeting of the Connections teachers for 8:00. He asked that I not sit in on the meeting so that the interaction might be a little "freer." For not quite a half hour, I absented myself from the room. Later that morning Bernie told me, "You could have stayed for this morning's meeting. No blood-letting happened." As Sheryl informed me, "The meeting produced no *great* changes, but we're looking at how we could structure second semester to include science better. We'll each make a list of key things to be covered, then meet to see if thematic groupings suggest themselves." True to their word, Bernie and Sheryl developed the lists they hoped would dovetail with the units within Dan's course outline (see appendix I). Conforming to Connections ritual, the teachers arranged to meet for breakfast at a local restaurant one morning during the Christmas break. But the detailed planning of the Renaissance Fair consumed most of the morning, so the "conversion" meeting continued on January

11, 1994, during the extended time provided in the school's schedule for first-period semester exams.

At the December 28 meeting, Bernie began the discussion of the second semester "conversion": "We need to make an effort to connect better. We need to modify the curriculum for the general kids to have a better chance while enhancing it for honors . . . I'm not sure we're meeting the needs of all our kids . . . Guys, I'm game for anything." What followed Bernie's remark was a two-pronged discussion that carried over into January.

One prong dealt with what to do with those students who, as Tim termed them, "don't like themselves." Bernie asked Tim to develop some ideas to share for the "problem children." Dan, acknowledging that "I don't know much about gifted ed," asked Bernie for ideas. This prong of discussion continued in the January 25 common planning time. Then Dan used the blackboard to outline a possible contract-for-grades schemata. Bernie looked over what Dan had written and said, "I like that; that's good. But let me play devil's advocate." Recounting his experience in attempting implementation of such a contract, Bernie admitted that he found himself "compromising" the standard and "helping" all to at least meet the criteria for a "C." Dan, after pondering the idea of "contracting up or down," asked, "How is this different from what I've been doing all along?"

The second prong of the December discussion dealt with the choice and sequence of the second semester's thematic units. Dan's planned instruction on atomic structure appeared to mesh with Sheryl's planned teaching about grammatic structures. Bernie mulled over his list of key history concepts, and was struck by the idea of combining the "isms" within a Structures unit. Two weeks later, when the teachers again took up the thematic prong, Sheryl had honored what had become a planning ritual—she brought a coffee cake to share. The process of planning took on an air much like that of the summer planning sessions.

SHERYL. I think thematics is the way we should go.

BERNIE. So we're flying by the seat of our pants.

SHERYL. No, we're doing structures first, right?

DAN. Structures?

SHERYL. Like atoms.

BERNIE. What do you think?

SHERYL. Let's go thematic.

DAN. I thought that's what we've been doing all along.

BERNIE. I've been more sequenced, topical but chronological.

From the Structures unit the teachers moved on to the next logical topic within the remaining units on Dan's syllabus: chemical change. Sheryl had planned to begin *To Kill a Mockingbird* after the grammar and research paper focuses of Structures, and Bernie knew that the themes of the Harper Lee novel would fit well with the themes of justice and human rights he planned to stress as students studied World War II. Neither Sheryl nor Bernie was sure how that content would accommodate a thematic emphasis on "change." In the discussion that followed, "change" became Reactions, a theme that both Bernie and Sheryl felt would add a new and exciting dimension to their chosen content. For the year's last unit, the teachers agreed upon Future, a unit that would allow tie-ins among history (the United Nations, third-world issues, a global economy), English (*Fahrenheit 451* and the genre of science fiction), and science (technological advances). (See appendix J.)

The new plan had promise. But on January 11 occurred another event, one that was a partial catalyst for the "backsliding" portion of this tale. Dan had been assigned a student teacher, Jim Pelfrey, for the second semester. Jim's assignment had been unanticipated. The result of a last-minute decision, Jim's presence was largely based on his roommate's student teaching assignment with another Cedar City High School science teacher; the roommates could car pool.

After the Renaissance Fair and exam week, Jim settled in for an initial time of observation and what the Connections teachers termed "lackey" work—photocopying, grading papers, and the like. Two weeks into Jim's Connections sojourn, I asked Dan for his first impressions of his student teacher. "His roommate is a real go-getter; Jim is more introverted." Perhaps because Jim did not seize the conversational initiative in the team's daily meetings, he was rarely called upon to contribute to Connections activities other than the science portion of any day's rotation scheme.

One such occasion came in late April, two weeks before Jim's sixteen-week Connections sojourn ended. The April 25 planning period was devoted to the search for an activity that would serve as a powerful introduction to the Future unit. The next day, as I interviewed Jim, he offered his version of the session: "Yesterday, they kind of assigned me to come up with an idea for introducing the futuristic unit. When my response wasn't immediate, Dan and Sheryl immediately turned their attention away."

Sheryl's account was different: "And then *Jim* [in a tone of surprise] came up with a neat idea." The idea involved showing a montage of science fiction movie clips. Two days later, Sheryl's enthusiasm for Jim's idea had not waned, but she talked of having a "back-up" plan if "Jim doesn't come through." The day after the big screening, Dan described Jim's efforts as "Okay, I guess. I don't know; it was kind of mixed." Sheryl's reaction was less ambiguous: "We had the good and the bad. There were some good choices. [But] he chose a clip from *Back to the Future* that featured profanity. We were just disgusted . . . It's not a nice thing to say, but I won't be sad to see Jim go." Sheryl's feelings were clear, even if they were never voiced in the public forum of the planning period. Tim and Bernie generally remained mute about their impressions of Jim. But, on April 26 when I asked Jim "To what extent did you feel a part of the Connections teaching team," his response was, "I *still* don't feel part of the team."

Slow to insinuate himself into common planning period conversations and never quite accepted as a teaching team member, Jim was also launched into Connections teaching slowly. February 22 marked Jim's first "full load" teaching day. On that day, and for the next few weeks, Dan began the science classes much as he had on September 14—with attendance, returning graded work, and announcements. Then Dan turned to Jim, saying "All right, Mr. Pelfrey, please begin." Whether by retaining his role in the class-beginning ritual or remaining in the classroom to grade papers or work at his computer, Dan continued to be an active presence in Connections science classes several weeks after Jim had "taken over" primary teaching responsibilities.

If Dan remained an active presence in his classroom during Jim's sojourn, his presence during common planning periods became more distanced. A combination of factors appeared to be at work in this distancing. Having a student teacher who assumed (or was perceived as expected to assume) primary planning and teaching duties was one factor. Another factor lay in Dan's role as senior class advisor. As March turned into April, Dan became ever more preoccupied with all of the details associated with the junior-senior prom. Often busily engaged at his computer, creating or adding to his prom data bank, Dan often missed part, or even most, of many planning period meetings.

But Dan's more apparent disengagement and Jim's uncertain Connections role were not the only changes the second semester brought. Two such changes were significant, and both were also part of the "backsliding" portion of this tale. With the semester change, the teachers had decided to rearrange color group membership. Some students' associations needed to be dissolved. Moreover, as Sheryl planned her Structures unit around grammar, Connections' heterogeneity posed a problem. Within Cedar City Schools, tracking mechanisms became pronounced at the junior high level. Consequently, the Connections students' backgrounds in grammar varied with their tracking designation. So it came to be that for the several weeks that grammar was Connections' English focus, the basis for rotation among the teachers changed. Rather than color groups, the designations of honors, academic, and general became the grouping mechanism.

A second significant change lay in the disappearance of the daily gathering time in room 307. After several instances when Connections relinquished room 307 to other pressing needs for the room (dissemination and interpretation of proficiency test results, conducting a career interest survey), the teachers implemented an idea that had originated in the students' midyear thoughts about Connections. Rather than being informed each morning of the schedule for the day, the students indicated that they wanted a weekly schedule in advance. Tim took charge of putting together the next week's schedule each Friday and seeing to it that all students received a copy. The new mode shifted ten minutes of precious time from gathering-in to instructional time, a change seen by the teachers as advantageous.

These two changes, like Jim's unanticipated presence as Dan's student teacher, had a profound impact on the second semester.

That these events occurred during the second semester does not mean that the second semester as a whole represented "the worst of times." Far from it. The "conversion" portion of the tale was not so much a worst-of-times narrative as the story of the teachers' response to a problem which had been openly acknowledged: a level of connectedness among their subject areas which did not meet their first impression hopes and expectations. The "backsliding" portion of the tale recounts words, actions, and events which affected the teachers' ability to implement their second semester "conversion" plan. "Conversion" and "backsliding" converged on February 28 when the Reactions unit was introduced.

As the Structures unit was drawing to a close, the need for a "major thing" that would both announce the new reactions theme and "tie it together" became a topic of planning time conversation. Both Bernie and Sheryl hoped a science-oriented activity could serve such a transition/integration function. During the planning period on February 22, Dan announced that Jim had come up with an idea. Jim proposed conducting a science demonstration of a chemical reaction and then giving a writing assignment that would require students to apply the concept of reaction to an area of English or history. Consideration of the form such a writing assignment (or any follow-up to the science demonstration) might take intensified as the week passed. By Thursday, the teachers had decided that after the science demonstration, one with (as Sheryl put it) "lots of smoke or noise, something really visual," each color group would develop a skit depicting reactions to certain scenarios and present the skits to the full group. Bernie, concerned about "how heavy you want to get," suggested scenarios such as a soldier leaving for war or a parent losing his or her job. Tim suggested cases involving legislation requiring year-round school or raising the driving age to eighteen. Dan offered the circumstance of being unjustly accused of a crime. With time passing quickly, Sheryl tendered the idea that each teacher develop a "case" for his or her group.

The plan, one in which each teacher had a part, reflected the interdisciplinary connections the conversion to thematic units had envisioned. But on February 28, all did not go according to plan. Jim had not developed a science demonstration ("Nothing worked"), nor had he devised a scenario for the green group. Dan did not come to Jim's rescue, and Tim was occupied with IEP meetings for LD students at the county vocational school. So Sheryl and Bernie improvised. In the hallway outside room 307, they enlisted three students to participate in staging a little "drama." After allowing the buzz of student talk to continue for a few minutes past the bell, the drama's theatrics called for Bernie to launch into a five-minute tirade, including name-calling directed at the three student confederates. The unBernie-like tempest certainly provoked the reactions among the Connections students which Bernie and Sheryl had anticipated, reactions primarily of disbelief. Quickly confessing that the tirade had been an act, Bernie revealed the reactions theme and explained the color advisory group skit plan. After the skits had been presented, Sheryl announced a writing assignment. Students would identify not only the reactions they had witnessed but also coping skills alternatives to problem situations. Later in the unit, Sheryl would ask students to recall these reactions and coping skills as the problems of *To Kill a Mockingbird*'s plot unfolded. Similarly, Bernie would couch the events of the 1930s and 1940s in terms of reactions, or "the ways nations deal with each other, how they react to each other and events." In such ways, both Sheryl and Bernie made explicit the academic connections envisioned in the conversion shift to thematic units.

During the second semester, best-of-times moments (including the Reactions drama and skits) continued to reflect the promise of Connections' first impressions. Yet "backsliding" events (like Jim's default) kept that promise from being fully realized. Ultimately, "backsliding" led to the third tale of a related trilogy, the Vision Thing Tale.

## The Vision Thing Tale

By the year's end, the seeds of difference within the teaching team that, in retrospect, had been at least somewhat apparent on September 14 had become deeply rooted. In the Lab Crisis Tale and the Conversion and Backsliding Tale, the teachers had begun the work of acknowledging their differences and reconciling those differences with the first impression vision that held fast in the best of times. But their work was not totally successful, as this tale reveals.

When the four Connections teachers responded to my year-end "Reflecting on Connections" questions (appendix K), their words revealed differences that remained as the year drew to a close.

> TIM. The "connection" with the team members was very solid in the English and world history areas and at times in the science area. For the most part, the area of science did not "connect" as all of us would have liked . . . The area of science not only was difficult for them [students] academically, but it also became a personality conflict between student and teacher.

> SHERYL. My advice to a new group would be to try to be "like-minded" in the area of levels or tracking . . . I liked the comradeship among the other teachers and the "team" feeling. I was often disgusted that only two of us were on time for our A.M. meetings. I think another drawback was not making a science connection on a regular basis.

> BERNIE. [Advice to new Connections-like teachers]
> 1. Communicate
> 2. Plan over summer
> 3. Go thematic units
> 4. Make program accessible to all *but* then follow thru
> 5. Ensure success
> [If you had it all to do over again]
> We have to delineate science to make it accessible for all—more projects.

> DAN. [Advice to new Connections-like teachers]
> Get together on certain things like tardies, discipline, late policies. Put together a syllabus or contract for the kids and parents explaining what the course is about and what is *expected*.
> [How did your teaching change?]
> Very little actually—which may or may not be good. We pretty much just put together existing courses—not really the way we (I) originally envisioned Connections.

What had been November's need to "do something about Dan" and the subject of December's off-the-record meeting and spring's private conversations became a quasi-open topic during the plan-

ning time of June 3, 1994. Shortly after 9:00, while waiting for
Dan to return from running an errand, Bernie, Tim, and Sheryl
began to discuss plans for Connections' second year.

> BERNIE. What's the agenda? Want to talk about potential projects,
> themes?
>
> SHERYL. We need to talk about Dan, about whether he'll buy into
> this.
>
> BERNIE. I'll do that. [Pause] Solo?
>
> SHERYL AND TIM. Yeah.
>
> BERNIE. I think the way to approach it is from a philosophical basis.
> We need to make science accessible to all students . . . If you don't
> want to make the commitment, then let's bail out now and find
> someone else.
>
> SHERYL. It's not like abandoning ship. It's the vision thing.

The next Monday, June 6, was the "teacher work day" that
marked the official end of the school year. That morning, before
they spent the afternoon tending their individual rooms and
before summer plans would limit their opportunities to meet, the
Connections teachers gathered one last time. After some discussion of next year's fees (which *would* include lab books) and
thoughts about changes in texts and novels (e.g., replacing
*Fahrenheit 451* with *The Martian Chronicles*), Dan was called to
the office. With Dan out of the room, Sheryl asked Bernie about
his "solo" conversation with Dan. Offering no details, Bernie told
Sheryl and Tim that he had talked to Dan for "about an hour."
Bernie also revealed that he had talked to George Cerny about the
situation and that George planned to call Dan later in the week
to "check about next year's teaching assignment." As I left the
halls of Cedar City High School on that last day of the Connections year, Dan's future and the future of the Connections community had come down to "the vision thing."

## The Black Cloud Tale

During the course of the 1993–94 school year at Cedar City High
School, problems arose not only within Connections but without.
Two such problems became particularly visible, like black clouds
looming, and they affected the Connections community both

directly and indirectly. The first was a gathering cloud that became most visible in November. The second became a storm cloud during the spring.

On November 9, 1993, an ON-TASC survey (in an envelope, with balloons attached) was delivered to each Cedar City High School teacher. The survey's questions focused on such issues as "feeling appreciated," interaction among departments, teacher isolation, and various factors and resources that might be an impediment to teacher effectiveness (e.g., lack of materials, student apathy, community pressures). The teachers were instructed to return their completed surveys by November 11 so that results could be available for a December staff meeting. Later that month, the ON-TASC acronym and its significance to Cedar City High School were explained to the community in a local newspaper article:

> [Cedar City High School] recently received a $27,000 grant from the Ohio network for training and assistance for schools and communities (ON TASC). The grant is for a three year program with two objectives, to combat alcohol and drug problems among teens *and to improve school climate by improving communications between teachers and administrators.* (Emphasis added)

Many of the school's teachers, including all four Connections teachers, had seen a gathering cloud surrounding school climate long before the ON-TASC survey appeared. Snippets of conversation and pointed comments during the first months of school had indicated that the relationship between staff and administration was hardly ideal.

As early as August 31, when the Connections teachers were preparing permission slips for the Renaissance Festival field trip, one such comment surfaced. When the issue of "families who can't pay for the trip" was raised, Sheryl said that George Cerny had promised funds to meet that contingency. Dan commented, "We'll take him at his word, for now." This expression of a lack of trust echoed in other anecdotes and remarks throughout the year.

While Sheryl was completing her ON-TASC survey, she expressed her feelings, ones she identified as shared by others. In

Sheryl's view, many faculty members saw Martin Young, the superintendent who had come to Cedar City in 1990, as "removed," as someone who was "not going to be around here very long." (In point of fact, Martin Young announced his July 31, 1995 retirement at the January 1995 board of education meeting.) She also offered her opinion of the principal, George Cerny: "He doesn't know his staff." Sheryl's opinion was understandable.

The circumstances of George's coming to Cedar City the year before had not been auspicious. The previous principal, Jeff Edwards, had been at CCHS for a number of years. After Martin Young's arrival in 1990 and Mike Davis's arrival the following year, two administrative shifts were made. One involved the exchange of principals between two elementary buildings. The other involved moving Jeff Edwards to the junior high as assistant principal and bringing in George Cerny from another town in Ohio. As Mike Davis explained in our May 11, 1993, meeting, "My first year here, we needed to make some administrative changes. I knew George would support alternatives [like Connections]." Clearly, the administrative changes had *not* been random; they *were* unsettling to the Cedar City High School faculty.

Sheryl did not confine her critique to unfamiliarity with the staff. She also viewed George as unreliable and told a story from the previous year to illustrate her point. At one school dance, a student was hurt and the teacher-chaperones were unable to locate George in the building. Apparently, he had driven two students home, but the teachers were unaware of his action. Missed communication was not confined to this incident.

Another occurred with the arrival on September 17, 1993 of Terri Gabriel as a student field observer assigned to Sheryl. George escorted Terri to room 314 and told Sheryl that Terri would be coming each Friday for most of the first semester. Terri's arrival had come as a surprise, and Sheryl did not appreciate the lack of notice. Missed communication was again evident in Dan's November 9 explanation for missing much of the previous day's planning time: "I had an appointment to see George yesterday. I went back three times, but he wasn't there."

In addition to unsettling change and missed communication, staff fragmentation was also a theme in the talk about school climate and teacher-administration relations. During the fall, each time a summons to the office for a telephone call came over the PA system, Sheryl had the same reaction, "We need a phone in here, guys!" While Dan, Bernie, and Tim usually just nodded their assent, on November 16 Tim had more to say. At the last staff meeting, "I stuck my neck out" and raised the idea of reinstalling a telephone in the teacher workroom. "But I got no support from the teachers. They're afraid of George since he just moved it."

George, from his perspective as principal, also saw fragmentation among the high school staff, but his view was somewhat different: "This school is highly fragmented . . . It has evolved over the years. There are turf wars . . . Our biggest problem to school climate is the fierce unionism in this building . . . People start gathering in hallways and buzzing" (Interview, April 29, 1994).

Mike Davis was also aware of fragmentation at the high school: "In the high school, we have a culture problem—there's not enough trust yet. Part of staff development is developing that trust. George got that started with ON-TASC. The second thing is the turf issue, a manifestation of the competitive culture we've built into schools. One of the things we can effect, that the Connections teachers will communicate, is that you can give up turf and still have a rewarding experience" (Interview, June 9, 1994).

Bernie viewed the rift between faculty and administration and staff fragmentation from a wider perspective. Holding forth on community politics at the March 22 planning session, Bernie questioned the number of central office administrators: "Certainly one less would be okay." From his point of view, Bernie saw Martin Young as "without vision" and Mike Davis as having a vision but "not bringing along others in the education community to promote that vision and take action." Recently, Bernie had discussed staff morale in a conversation with one member of the board of education. As Bernie related his portion of that conversation, "You can't blame the teachers for being hacked off at the Central Office when [at the December staff meeting] Young said there'd be no [reductions in force], and then there are six or seven." The context of Bernie's assessment lay in the second black cloud.

The March 9, 1994, edition of the local newspaper announced the district's plan to cut $300,000 from the budget, a reduction that would be effected regardless of the outcome of the tax levy to be placed on the May 3 ballot. When the board met on March 21, they not only heard the presentation by the Connections teachers and Mrs. Archer about the program's success, they also heard the superintendent's recommendation for a reduction in force. Despite pleas from four attendees (heard after the vote because they had not requested to speak prior to the agenda's formation), the board accepted the recommendation and voted to suspend contracts for six and one-half positions. For the next six weeks, talk of the cuts and of the needed levy's chances for passage dominated teacher talk at Cedar City High School.

In such an atmosphere, it was not surprising that some would look askance at the Connections teachers' extra common planning period (in effect, a half position). But the cuts only exacerbated an already eroding support for Connections among Cedar City faculty. When the teachers had presented their program at a February 7 after-school staff meeting, Tim's impression was that the presentation had gone well, even though it was after 3:00 when it began and "by then they were ready to go home." But Tim had noted that "*Some* were unhappy about the extra plan period." As George Cerny considered this reaction during an interview in late April, he acknowledged: "The most important thing we did *not* do was bring the entire staff along from the beginning . . . [Referring to the extra plan period] People sort of resented that a little bit—and rightly so." Not bringing the staff along also "hurt us in developing a second year." At the February 1 gathering of Connections teachers with George and Mike, George had reported receiving several inquiries from parents anxious for the addition of a tenth-grade Connections option. But, as Sheryl informed me, when the issue was raised at an English departmental meeting, there were no takers. Both that paucity of English volunteers and the traditional tenth-grade curriculum affected the tentative plans for a tenth-grade version of Connections proposed during the first week of March. The proposal called for combining math, geography, and business/economics. However, budget cuts and staff changes ultimately intervened, and no second Connections program was implemented.

This distinct lack of enthusiasm was not confined to the high school. On March 16, Tim and Sheryl described Connections to a meeting of the district's fourth- and fifth-grade teachers. With the construction of a new school building, the fourth and fifth grades would form a separate school during the following year, and curriculum innovations were being considered. The day before the meeting Tim told Sheryl that his wife, Peg (a fifth grade teacher), had told him, "No fourth- or fifth-grade teachers are interested." Sheryl, upon hearing this, asked, "Then we have to be cheerleaders?" Evidently the "cheerleading" met with a more pressing concern among the intermediate teachers. As Sheryl reported the next day, "They were more concerned about moving to a new building."

However, throughout the latter part of March and all of April, expressed planning time concerns about the erosion of support from their peers took a back seat to the black cloud of hard financial times. The levy's passage was not a sure thing. On April 7, before buses bearing students arrived, two members of the board of education came to the high school to distribute doughnuts and levy support buttons to the teachers. The week before the election, teachers (including Sheryl, Tim, and Bernie) who were also Cedar City residents staffed telephones, making calls to elicit community support for the levy. During this period, both the local newspaper and planning period discussions pointed to the absolute need for the levy and the dire consequences if it failed.

The May 3 levy did fail. And despite the board of education's decision to try again in August, the financial black cloud loomed ever larger over Cedar City High School as the school year ended.

*Four Tales = One Trilogy + Its Context*

The Lab Book Crisis Tale, the Conversion and Backsliding Tale, and the Vision Thing Tale were but different phases of a continuing story of difference. Differences became apparent. Their reconciliation was attempted. Unanticipated events, changes, and unresolved stances converged in a worst-of-times backsliding. Finally, one central difference, the vision thing, remained. The Black Cloud Tale, with its twin clouds of school climate and financial woes, revealed that the larger school environment could not be counted upon as a problem-solving resource when the Connections teachers faced their worst of times. Clearly, the four tales of crisis intersected and overlapped. How they interwove can be seen even more clearly in the ecology these tales reflected.

## THE WORST-OF-TIMES ECOSYSTEM

Within the systems that compose the worst-of-times ecology, the dimensions of the obstacles along the Connections odyssey can be seen. More importantly, the dynamics of how those problems were met can also be seen. For McLaughlin (1993), the essential hallmark of a collegial environment lies in a professional community's capacity for problem solving. Such a capacity, McLaughlin explains, is marked by explicit problem-solving structures and norms, by a sense of mutual support and mutual obligation, and by democratic decision-making. Insofar as that sort of problem-solving capacity was inherent in the four tales of crisis, the Connections teachers, like Ulysses, would be able to continue steadfastly on their journey despite and in defiance of the obstacles they encountered.

### Worst-of-Times Physical System

By the beginning of February, the new science classrooms at Cedar City High School were ready for occupancy. In a "grand move" the school's science teachers moved from what had been the "science wing," and new uses were found for some of the rooms they vacated. On February 15, a sign above the door to room 208 appeared, designating the room as "Club Twenty-8." As part of the ON-TASC effort, the room had been transformed into a teachers' lounge. Room 312 became the room in which the spring's DARE program was held. So also room 314 changed owners. As Dan moved his materials and equipment from room 314 to his new room, Tim moved in with his posters, calendars, and teaching resources. While some aspects of Connections' physical world remained constant (the coffee maker and each day's common planning period remained in room 314), the "grand move" signaled a change in Connections' physical system that was paralleled in the worst of times cultural and personal systems.

In the worst of times, separation, rather than unity, marked Connections' physical system. Early in October, when a conference with a parent had consumed most of one Thursday's usual common planning period and decisions about the schedule had not been confirmed, the Connections teachers reverted to a three-class rotation "because it's easiest" (Sheryl, October 5, 1993). During the second semester especially, schedule conflicts and catching up on content after snow days seemed to make necessary that which was also easiest. During the week of March 7, the second round of proficiency testing (one test section each day for those who had not passed that test in October) precluded use of room 307 for gathering or projects and made three-class rotations the most practical Connections schedule. For the first two weeks of April, the DARE program's schedule of classes also necessitated a three-class rotation schedule on most days. So on April 5, as a belated weekly schedule was distributed to students, it was not surprising to hear one student, as he commiserated with two others, say, "Three-class rotation, three-class rotation, three-class rotation every day this week!"

In their discussion of the social realities of teaching, Lieberman and Miller (1990) affirm one of the tacit "rules of thumb" that govern the dailiness of teaching: "Be practical." In the worst of times, "being practical" and "doing what's easiest" translated into the changes associated with the backsliding portion of the Conversion and Backsliding Tale. It seemed more practical to distribute a weekly schedule rather than consume several minutes each day with a gathering time. It seemed practical to change the composition of color advisory groups. It seemed practical to follow a three-class rotation schedule when the Connections block was interrupted with DARE and proficiency testing.

Practicality also underlies the concept of strategic individualism. When room 314, the room where the Connections teachers gathered each morning, was no longer Dan's, practicality and the physical system converged. On September 14, and many other days during the first semester, Dan had been present at common planning time if only because the meeting was held in his room. As the other three teachers talked, Dan could prepare lab equipment, write notes on the blackboard, or work at his computer and still overhear and/or join the conversation. But after the early February "grand move," combining the practical individual work that needed doing in his room with the collective work of the common planning period was more difficult.

Dan was not the only Connections teacher who faced this physical/practical dilemma. March 3 found Bernie leaving the gathering early to set up his room for the day's computer simulation game on imperialism/colonialism. February 17 found Sheryl departing room 314 for a meeting with a "fund-raiser person" in conjunction with her role as a class advisor. But far more common was the physical/practical conflict that made Bernie's attendance at the March 1 session sporadic. He had been late in arriving due to another teacher's extended use of the photocopier, and he left after about ten minutes to check on the machine's availability.

The convergence of practicality and the worst-of times physical system had its effects on Connections' problem-solving capacity. In the worst of times, the forum of the common planning period had suffered attrition. As the explicit problem-solving structure of Connections' physical system, the common planning period was central to the teaching team's capacity for democratic decision-making. In the worst of times, Connections' physical system diminished, rather than enhanced, any opportunities for reflection, feedback, and problem solving. In other words, in the worst of times, the physical system failed to provide that which it *did* provide in the best of times.

With the Connections teachers' individual classrooms even more widely scattered throughout the building, with pressing practicalities that made strategic individualism a more frequent response, with room 307 no longer just across the hall from one of the three-class rotation sites, and with room 307 fading and then disappearing from use as a daily gathering place, Connections' physical world lost the unity of time and place that had been so prominent in the first day's physical system. Sarason (1971) notes that "Characteristics of individuals are always, to some extent, a reflection of the setting in which these characteristics are manifested" (p. 171). In the worst of times, then, a physical system marked by separation would be mirrored by separation in other systems.

## Worst-of-Times Cultural System

In telling the tales of Connections' worst of times, I deliberately entitled them tales of crisis, for crisis was a theme that crossed all four narratives. At the March board of education meeting when the reduction in staff was enacted, one person in the audience raised the question that had been circulating throughout the community ever since the local press had reported the impending budget cuts. The questioner wondered why the district's declining balance had not been addressed earlier so that such drastic cuts would not have been necessary. In considering the crises embedded in the worst-of-times tales, the same question begs for an answer: why were problems permitted to attain crisis proportions before problem-solving actions were initiated?

The answer, I believe, can be seen within the tales themselves. On December 14, when the Connections teachers met to deal with the problem of academic nonconnectedness with science, Bernie asked that I not attend. On June 3, when Sheryl wanted to "talk about Dan," she waited until he was not present. Further, both she and Tim were content (in fact relieved) that Bernie would talk to Dan "solo." Moreover, as Bernie contemplated the approach he would take in initiating his solo conversation with Dan, he decided that a "philosophical basis" would be best; and Sheryl, as she concurred with Bernie, was quick to point out that "It's not like abandoning ship." Clearly, the teachers were complying with the widespread school cultural norm of avoidance of controversy.[1]

In adhering to this cultural norm, questioning is relegated to the private, rather than the public, sphere. Long before the December 14 meeting that led to the second-semester shift to thematics, Bernie had privately bemoaned the lack of connectedness with science, and Sheryl and Tim had talked together after class about the need to "do something" about Dan. If the best-of-times culture had included the common planning time norm of sharing success stories, the worst-of-times culture included a far more private and separate norm of communication. Public communication would violate the tacit understanding that conflict and/or controversy were to be avoided.

Avoidance of controversy allows teachers to sidestep situations where performance adequacy might be questioned—to engage in a self-protective strategy of isolation or disengagement. In serving as a buttress against uncertainty and potential threats to self-esteem, this pattern of avoidance, or what Little (1990) calls a norm of "mutual noninterference," stands as a powerful norm, one that is not easily set aside. To do so requires the creation of yet more potent norms.

One such norm involves what Little has termed "professional reciprocity." Under this collaborative norm, teacher talk would concentrate on practices and consequences rather than people and competence. Clearly, it is this norm that is evident in the ways in which Bernie framed the issues on October 1 and June 3. Bernie's manner of approaching these problems served to reduce the threat inherent in confronting Connections' worst of times. Yet Bernie's approach involved more than facework.[2]

Another, still more powerful, norm was at work. Despite the potential threat to self-esteem and despite the norm of mutual noninterference, *eventually* the Connections teachers *did* engage in problem-solving dialogue. On October 1, when Bernie raised the lab book issue, he did so in the context of larger concerns for "kids we're not reaching all the time" and what he perceived as an emerging "us-them mentality" that was "defeating the purpose of what we're trying to do with this class." Similarly, Bernie's call for the meeting of December 14 arose out of a concern about Connections' eroding degree of subject matter connectedness. In both instances, Bernie was voicing what he believed was a shared sense of dissatisfaction about the status quo. Articulating concerns in order to get the group "back on track" resonates with the notion of loyalty.[3]

When problems threatened the best-of-times cultural norms of "hooking," ensuring success for all, and meaningful interaction with their students, *that* was when the Connections teachers confronted and dealt with their worst of times. Tacit norms that recognized each teacher's autonomy within his or her classroom and honored mutual noninterference (norms that, as will be seen in a later section, were part of the larger school ecosystem) were suspended when the core cultural values of the best of times were endangered. They became endangered when the Connections' teachers' individual cultural and personal systems clashed.

In the worst of times, difference, autonomy, mutual noninterference, the avoidance of controversy, and separation held sway in Connections' cultural system. But when those worst of times reached crisis proportions, the work of reconciling differences, engaging in mutual support, acknowledging conflict, and seeking consensus began. In large part, that work involved coming to an understanding of the worst-of-times personal system.

### Worst-of-Times Personal System

In the worst of times, the differences among the four Connections teachers' personal systems that had been apparent on September 14 became the basis for the Lab Book Crisis/Conversion and Backsliding/Vision Thing trilogy of tales. Those differences, dormant and unacknowledged on September 14, were clearly recognized during the seminal meetings of October 1, December 14, and June 3. In the worst of times, and especially in the Lab Book Crisis Tale, the personal system cycle that had been so evident in the best of times was disrupted. In the worst of times, the self-sustaining cycle of coming through → teacher rewards → commitment to students → willingness to undertake adventurous teaching ruptured in more than one phase.

Dan clearly attributed the rupture to the failure of students to come through. As he explained to the students on November 12, the problem arose when many of them failed to be "responsible" and order a lab book within the window of opportunity. In the commentary that followed, Dan compared the students' meeting his high expectations with their certain future responsibility to "get along with the boss." Again, only far more explicitly than on September 14, Dan communicated a personal stance in which the workplace was a metaphor for school. From this work-orientation perspective, ensuring student success was something only students could do. A codicil to the October 8 discussion of Billy (p. 215) illustrated this perspective. After the teachers had agreed that Billy would be "out" if he did not improve, Tim talked about offering Billy some after-school help. Dan responded, "He's got to bring *himself* out of this. We'll help, but we can't coddle him."

Dan's distinction between "help" and "coddling" pointed to yet another phase of the best-of-times cycle that had ruptured. In early January, Dan prepared students for their science semester exam while Sheryl reviewed for the "mini-exam" she would give to supplement the Renaissance Fair project. In essence, Sheryl's review was a collective effort in generating a master "crib sheet" from which students could select items to include in fashioning individual notes to be used during the mini-exam. Dan's version of the crib-sheet strategy was slightly different: each individual student would generate his or her own exam notes based on clues Dan gave as to what items would be important. Both strategies permitted students to use notes, but Dan's version placed the onus of responsibility for success on each individual student while Sheryl's relied upon the teacher's and students' shared commitment to success for all.

The difference was subtle, but important. A similar subtle but important difference became apparent during the February 1 milestone meeting of Connections teachers and administrators when George asked the teachers for their recommendations for Connections' second year:

> SHERYL. We need to work out something about levels for science.
>
> DAN. Having general and academic physical science has been a little bit of a problem.
>
> GEORGE. Can you do this like Sheryl does with the tracks now?
>
> DAN. That would be another prep. I thought the original idea was for all one science.

Dan's interpretation of what constituted a unitary curriculum obviously differed from Sheryl's. As he explained during the March 3 common planning period, "I thought the program was about all students getting the same curriculum. And then we have Tim to help LD and other students who need it." For Dan, "the same curriculum" meant something quite different than it meant to Sheryl, Tim, or Bernie. For Dan, "same" involved primarily one adaptation: allowing students more time to work in class. For Sheryl, Bernie, and Tim—as the discussion of their September 14 personal systems indicated—"same" implied devising many adaptations and hooking strategies to ensure student success.

Twice in the Conversion and Backsliding Tale, Dan voiced perplexity when he asked, "How is this different from what I've been doing all along?" and said, "I thought that's what we've been doing all along." Dan clearly did not understand that the second-semester shift to thematics represented more than an effort toward curriculum integration. Curriculum integration and curriculum coherence are distinctly different.[4] Curriculum *inte-*

*gration* involves thematic connections. Curriculum *coherence* resides in shared ideological beliefs, a shared personal system. As the Vision Thing Tale revealed, for Tim, Sheryl, and Bernie, ultimately conversion was not so much about curriculum integration as it was about curriculum coherence. Although thematic connectedness was clearly an important part of the Connections vision as it emerged and evolved, sharing a personal system that encompassed commitment both to success for all students and to the risk and adventure of a pedagogy dedicated to that success was clearly the core value of "the vision thing."

In the worst of times, Dan's work-oriented personal system remained incompatible with and unreconciled with Bernie's relational teaching, Sheryl's responsive teaching, and Tim's caring/ensuring success stance. Conversion efforts intersected with the cultural dimensions of threatened self-esteem and noninterference. As the talk about grading schemes illustrated, the Connections teachers carefully skirted the unequal power arrangement implicit in advice giving as they engaged in discussion to realign the second semester in a thematic plan. Conversion efforts also intersected with the physical system, for teachers' stances about the nature of their work—how it should be done, what constitutes success—are guided by a construction of meaning that cannot help but be influenced by the structure of their daily activity. In a worst-of-times ecology, with a physical system marked by separation, a cultural system characterized by avoidance of controversy, and a personal system troubled by differences, the reconciliation of those differences remained elusive. The interdependence that is fundamental to collegial community was not present during Connections' worst of times.

*Webs to Other Ecosystems in the Worst of Times*

The separation and avoidance of controversy that marked Connections' worst-of-times physical and cultural systems could also be seen in the larger school ecosystem. Within the Black Cloud Tale, two themes paralleled themes within the Lab Book/Conversion and Backsliding/Vision Thing trilogy.

Just as private conversations displaced public discussion of problems in the Connections common planning period, the cloud surrounding faculty-administrator relations at Cedar City High School was largely a topic of what George Cerny had termed "buzzing in the halls." On December 3, Sheryl informed me of the latest topic of private hallway conversation. George had taken the Monday after Thanksgiving as a vacation day to go deer hunting. For Sheryl, and all whose voices she had heard buzzing, "That's a no-no. We've had people docked [in pay] who did that. If you don't think *that* didn't make some folks hot!" But no one complained publicly.

If teachers did not communicate their complaints and frustrations with the administration directly, neither did administrators always engage teachers in a direct dialogue. During the time between Martin Young's declaration of no reduction in force at the December staff meeting and the March announcement of budget cuts, rumors floated, but no reports of faculty-administration conversations about the nature and extent of the impending cuts circulated in the halls of Cedar City High School.

The ON-TASC initiative began its work of improving school climate with efforts Bolman and Deal (1991) would view as symbolic: the creation of "Club Twenty-8" in mid-February, for example. The "grand opening" of the new teachers' lounge was marked by a party for a teacher who was leaving Cedar City and moving south. Similarly, on April 7 two members of the board of education enlisted teacher support for the upcoming levy's passage as they distributed doughnuts and levy support buttons in the new teachers' lounge. More formally, faculty-administration communication was the purpose of the liaison committee, a representative body at whose meetings issues of concern were discussed. Both Bernie and Tim were representatives on this committee, so as the December 7 common planning period was ending, they talked about the agenda for a committee meeting that had been scheduled for the next week. Bernie wanted to limit the agenda ("none of this forty-two-item stuff") and focus on two items he had been approached about: a promised photocopying aide and the issue of internal substituting. As Bernie and Tim conversed, their frustrations with the minutiae and slow pace of the committee's problem solving were expressed, but privately.

Separation was a second theme common to both the Black Cloud Tale and the Connections worst-of-times trilogy. Among the Connections teachers, separation had taken both a physical and a personal form. Between the Cedar City High School faculty and administrators, particularly Central Office administrators, the theme of separation assumed a different form. On March 23, an article in the local newspaper had offered explanations by the school system's central office personnel for the recently enacted budget cuts. The next morning Bernie and Tim discussed the article. Martin Young had been quoted as saying that while he could not make promises, "I see all but two teachers [of those whose contracts had been suspended] coming back next year" if the May levy passed. But other "leaks" from the central office had indicated that the reduction in staff would stay in place regardless of the levy's outcome. Tim concluded that at the central office "they don't know what others are doing." Bernie noted that the March 21 board meeting had devoted considerably more time to a discussion of technology (computer acquisition and donations) than to "other issues." Bernie's parting comment, like Tim's conclusion, pointed to the separation theme: "And then they wonder why staff morale is so shitty."

The Black Cloud Tale reveals that, like the Connections teachers, Cedar City High School had come to recognize that problems existed. But also like Connections, Cedar City High School's problems reached crisis proportions before problem solving began. If separation, private conversation, and the avoidance of open conflict were part of the Cedar City High School environment, it is not surprising that they would also be part of Connections' worst-of-times ecology. If effective implementation requires *mutual* adaptation, then the school and district settings (including school climate) must support and foster that process. In the worst of times, with the twin black clouds of financial problems and school climate problems looming, Cedar City High School did not offer such support.

## AN ODYSSEY OF OBSTACLES AND TRIUMPHS

The previous chapter began with Mike Davis's year-end thought that "knowing the best of times only happens when you know the worst of times." Certainly Connections knew both. Even more certainly, despite their widely different ecologies, the best of times and the worst of times were bound together. Just as the narrative of the first day marked the initiation of the Connections saga, the four tales of triumph within the best of times marked that saga's fulfillment. The complete saga, including the first day and best-of-times ecologies, evolved during the Connections year to form a Connections "vision."

In a sense, as the Connections vision emerged, the values of the first day and the best of times took on the qualities of what Purpel (1989) calls an "overarching mythos," a commitment to a sacred set of values that gives moral meaning to and energizes a culture. Purpel's overarching mythos, and what Sheryl called "the vision thing," is what Fullan (1993) terms a "shared vision." Fullan's words concerning shared vision make clear the relationship between the best of times and the worst of times:

> Visions come later because the process of merging personal and shared vision takes time . . . Deep ownership comes through the learning that arises from engagement in solving problems. In this sense, ownership is stronger in the middle of a successful change process than at the beginning, and stronger still at the end than at the middle or beginning. (p. 127)

In the Vision Thing Tale, Sheryl spoke of vision and Bernie spoke of commitment. Consistent with Fullan's observation, the Connections vision was most clear at the end of the year. That vision required a commitment to ensuring success, a commitment to students, and a commitment to an adventurous pedagogy. As the Connections year came to an end, Bernie, Tim, and Sheryl were ready for a second year that would honor that vision and those commitments. The only question that remained was whether Dan would join them.

# CHAPTER 7

# *June 1994:*
# *The Odyssey's Epilogue?*

If I had to do it all over again, with these three, I'd do it again.
—Bernie Lyons, February 1, 1994

When Homer's Ulysses finally reached Ithaca after his seafaring odyssey, he found a less than welcoming environment. Obstacles, in the form of Penelope's suitors, remained to be conquered before a heroic homecoming could be celebrated. As the 1993–94 school year drew to a close, the Connections teachers' odyssey paralleled that of their metaphorical counterpart.

## THE COUNCILS OF JUNE

*June 3, 1994*

Connections' first year ended much as it had begun. The last "official" day for teachers found the four Connections teachers again in room 314, again making plans for the year to come. The gathering that day was, of necessity, short: there were makeup exams to administer, classroom inventories to complete, and grade sheets to mark. Before surrendering to the day's deadlines, several topics merited a mention, and one warranted more extensive conversation. Sheryl noted that $150 in grant funds remained to be spent, so she asked her teammates to "look over supplies and see what may need to be ordered" to supplement or replenish both texts and such consumables as markers, poster board, and the like. While they munched on the apple cake Sheryl had brought and waited for Bernie to arrive from proctoring an exam, Dan (mindful of the limits his internship with an area technology consortium would impose on his availability for summer planning sessions) pointed out that "We need to look at times [for meeting together] for the summer." Accommodating Tim's basketball camp commitment, Dan, Sheryl, and Tim set aside the morning of the following Monday, June 6. Before Tim left to administer math exams to two LD students, Sheryl had another announcement to make—both she and Bernie had been assigned student teachers for next year's first semester.

Half an hour later, when Tim had returned and Bernie had assented to the plan to meet the next Monday morning and Dan had not yet returned to the room, the "vision thing" and Dan's continuing status on the Connections teaching team became the focus of conversation.[1] The "vision thing" conversation, while centering on Dan's "buying into" the Connections vision, was not limited to a shared concern about Dan personally or alone. Bernie wondered aloud about Connections' viability as a three-subject-based program: "Sometimes I wish it would have been done . . . [as] two dyads [English/history, science/math]." Sheryl's "vision thing" anxiety extended to the coming fall's student teachers— "We need to get their names and contact them now." Just as the three teachers agreed that Bernie would talk with Dan that afternoon, they also agreed that "We'll lay that stuff [Dan and the student teachers] on George," and that, if necessary, they could get another science teacher "on board" on Monday. Having reached that consensus, the meeting dispersed to the pressing tasks awaiting each of the Connections teachers.

*June 6, 1994*

The day following the Cedar City High School graduation ceremony was a muggy day—one that dictated the casual apparel of shorts. Promptly at 9:00, Sheryl arrived in Tim's classroom carrying several school supply catalogs and a pile of tissues (necessitated by allergic sneezes). She found Tim and Bernie planning a summer fishing trip together. While Dan finished his grading chores, Bernie turned the conversation to the issue of which items among those to be ordered for Connections' second year should be included in departmental orders and which should be incorporated in a Connections fee schedule. In sharing his planning thoughts, Bernie sought reactions to a change of history text, to one that was arranged topically and might be better suited to thematic units. But, Bernie noted, the text's readings, while only of a few pages in length for each topic, would be at a challenging level for many of next year's Connections students—a group of predominantly "general" students. Sheryl's response posed two questions: were there visual elements such as charts and illustrations that would help with understanding, and would Bernie have available a class set of supplemental texts at a lower reading level if needed. Those considerations noted, and Tim's assistance with any remediation assured, talk proceeded to a text change Sheryl proposed. Rather than *Fahrenheit 451*, Sheryl suggested *The Martian Chronicles* as the literature base for next year's Futures unit: "It can be chunked better." If the change were to be made, Sheryl assured Tim, an audiotape of the Ray Bradbury novel was available and would be ordered. A quick check with Tim verified that "we're okay" with *Romeo and Juliet* and *To Kill a Mockingbird*. The lab notebooks arose as the next concern. Voicing his judgment that "This [the lab book crisis] wasn't worth it," Bernie suggested "It's best to go direct with this" and order a lab notebook for each Connections student. Only a few minutes of discussion were required to, as Bernie said, "put closure on fees." Sheryl and Bernie would include their new books in their department's orders, and Dan would list lab notebooks as a Connections fee item.

For the remainder of the morning, the subjects of discussion wove back and forth between matters of temporal and spatial organization and matters of curriculum. To Sheryl's question "Do we know anything about the room setup for next year," Bernie replied that George had indicated Connections teachers could plan on having the same rooms. But, as they would discover in a later conversation with George, the school's proposed 1994–95 master schedule did offer some changes. While the first period common planning time would be preserved, rather than directly following that planning time, the Connections block would occupy periods three, four, and five. In addition, financial and staffing considerations meant that both Sheryl and Tim would no longer have a second individual planning period during the second semester. Neither piece of information was welcomed. Discussing scheduling issues, Dan asked if Sheryl, Tim, and Bernie wished him to continue to develop a monthly Connections calendar (as he had in May). Because doing so would "force us to plan monthly" (Bernie) and would be "good for research projects" (Sheryl), Dan's offer not only gained ready acceptance, but also was a conversational segue to the topic of curriculum planning.

Bernie observed, "We need a big thing at the beginning of each unit. It got the kids into it—gave it a focus." Sheryl concurred, "That's where the tie-in has to be." With the last week's Connections blocks still fresh in her mind, she added, "The best was at the end with the final projects and all of us grading together. We need more of that." A digression or two later (a possible speaker Bernie had discovered for Connections' study of World War II and increased staffing needs in science and English), the conversation returned to the need to make curricular connections.

> DAN. For each unit, each one of us [should] talk about stuff . . . plant the seeds for the connections there.
>
> SHERYL. Like the use of key words in tests.
>
> DAN. Key words that get said over and over.

With the morning's swift passage, the work of finding those key words and of (in Tim's words) "setting up units with projects" would have to wait for another time. As Bernie said, just before the meeting ended, "That's the really big thing we have to do this summer."

## CONNECTIONS' "ITHACA"

At the conclusion of the May 17, 1994, visit from several area curriculum directors, Bernie reiterated the statement he had made on February 1 as he told the visitors, "If I had to do this again, I'd do it in a minute." Tim echoed Bernie's thoughts: "I agree with Bernie. I'd do it again in a minute—not so much for myself, but for the kids." As the two councils of June revealed, being willing to "do it again" involved two correlates of commitment. One commitment entailed efforts to expand and elaborate the elements of opportunity and interdependence that had characterized Connections' best of times. The corollary commitment resolved to preserve and defend those elements from the perils of Connections' worst of times. Honoring both commitments called upon the Connections teachers to attend to all of the systems that composed the Connections ecosystem.

*Physical Systems*

The provisions for summer planning, the designation of a common planning period, the allocation of room 307, and a three-period Connections block offered opportunities for collegiality that had been part of Connections from its inception. As significant as these physical dimensions had been to their odyssey, it is no wonder that the Connections teachers regarded the preservation of each of these elements as important. Each had afforded the Connections teaching team a window of opportunity in which community-building connections might be forged. These connections took three forms: (1) those that nurtured a mutuality of practice, (2) those that strengthened personal relationships, and (3) those that shared information and served as a resource to practice.[2]

Mutuality of practice is more than the coordination of parallel, but separate, practices. To be sure, there were times—during the subject-by-subject summer sessions and, most notably, on occasions like September 14 when last-minute schedule changes were necessary—when practicality demanded that the primary work of a planning gathering involve the coordination and accommodation of the instructional needs of each subject area. Whenever the white board appeared, and it appeared less frequently as the year passed, the temptation arose to render the process of planning a process of filling in who was going to do what on which days and with what time requirements. But the teachers eagerly abandoned this pattern of coordination whenever inter- or cross-disciplinary possibilities existed. As Sheryl commented about the final project, "We need more of this."

"This" meant working together, sharing and overlapping subject areas, and bearing joint responsibility for instruction and assessment. "This" meant mutuality of practice. Certainly, such mutuality of practice required time for planning together. But, as many an episode from the best of times suggested, the availability of room 307 and the flexibility of the three-period Connections block were significant as well. That significance went beyond providing the time and facilities to mount projects. During the first two weeks of school, when a full-cohort, full-block schedule was the rule rather than the exception, the Connections teachers first had the opportunity to observe what few secondary teachers witness: their colleagues engaged in teaching. Throughout the year, each time this schedule option was repeated or one teacher became another teacher's "lackey," the Connections teachers again made their teaching practices visible to each other. In a very close-up and direct way, Sheryl, Bernie, Dan, and Tim removed the traditional barriers of individual classrooms, risked exposure, and came to know each other's style and art of teaching.

The second type of connection, personal relationships, involved openness and revelation as opposed to disengagement and privacy. On any given morning, before getting down to the business of the common planning period or after the day's business was done, either Sheryl, Tim, or Bernie was likely to initiate a conversation about their most recent life experiences. Dan did so less often, perhaps because he was more reticent and private by nature. Collectively, the teachers shared personal upheavals (parent deaths, moving to a new home), personal joys (family, vacation plans), personal frustrations (home repairs, family problems), and personal interests (sports, gardening, movies, music). The personal connections that had begun with the summer meetings in their homes continued to be forged during each day's common planning period. As a result, Tim and Bernie, especially, developed a friendship that extended beyond school hours and walls.

The third type of connection, sharing information as a resource for practice, wound throughout the councils of June. Bernie's mentioning the Normandy invasion veteran as a classroom speaker, his contemplation of a textbook change, and Sheryl's consideration of an alternative science fiction novel were a recurrence of the pattern evident on September 14 as Tim showed Sheryl the workbook about ancient Greece. This type of information sharing—making colleagues aware of resources such as relevant books, videos, CD-ROM data bases, and persons willing to visit and speak to classes—was a valued but relatively minor form of Connections information sharing. More often, indeed almost daily, the Connections teachers shared information about students.

In the best of times, the information the Connections teachers shared about their students was often good news. Sharing this kind of information (as Sheryl did in repeating Mrs. Archer's *Romeo and Juliet* Tale) made the common planning period a celebration of success. At other times, especially in the worst of times, talk about students focused on their misbehavior or apathy in what I call "conversations of commiseration." In the Connections context, these conversations of commiseration were more like affirmation-seeking queries. A statement like "Rob is missing five assignments for me," was consistently preceded or followed by a question like, "What's he doing for you?" The question clearly implied the unvoiced thought, "It's not just me, is it?" The problem with such conversations of commiseration is that no action issues from them. Like Sheryl's unanswered query about Jason on September 14, even affirming responses do not remove the concern; they tend only to shift the burden for remedy from the teacher to the student. Shifting the burden *does*, however, remove any questions about teacher competence. In the best of times, teacher competence was beside the point; conversations about students focused on actions the teachers might take to revive those whose performance caused concern.

The opportunities for community-building connections inherent in Connections' physical systems—the summer meetings, the common planning period, room 307, and the Connections block—did not ensure that the Connections teachers would use these opportunities to forge ties of collegiality. When those opportunities were hollow structures and participation was minimal to nonexistent, connections were more forgeries than forged. When the common planning period was marked by strategic individualism and room 307 and flexible scheduling were largely displaced by three-class rotations, Connections suffered the worst of times. Yet in the best of times, when those elements of the physical system did become the vehicles for making community-building connections, then collegial community was achieved. So while the mere presence of a common planning period, a three-period block, room 307, and summer planning meetings could not *guar-*

*antee* the best of times, in the councils of June the Connections teachers were adamant that these components of Connections' physical system be preserved.

## Cultural Systems

If the councils of June revealed the Connections teachers' commitment to preserving the opportunities for connectedness within Connections' physical systems, the teachers also made plain their commitment to build upon and refine components of Connections' best-of-times cultural system. The storms and sirens of the worst of times had assailed the cultural norms of ensuring student success and cross-disciplinary connections, in particular. In their June gatherings, the teaching team sought to begin the work of shoring up and strengthening those norms.

A central concern in the "vision thing" conversation had been the need to, as Bernie said, "make science accessible to all students." That concern found partial expression in the deliberations about ordering lab notebooks for the next year's Connections students. That they would be ordered was beyond discussion; the only question remaining lay in which budgetary list they would be placed. Yet not only science and lab notebooks needed to be accessible in order to ensure student success. Sheryl's questions about the history text Bernie had proposed registered a parallel concern. Accommodating learning needs so that the text's content would be understandable to all of Connections' heterogeneous students was a prime criterion for text adoption. That criterion had also been paramount in Sheryl's proposed substitution of *The Martian Chronicles* for *Fahrenheit 451*. Sheryl considered the change only because the Bradbury novel "chunked better" and was also available on audiotape.

Recognizing that backsliding had followed the conversion to thematics attempt of the second semester, the Connections teachers remained undaunted in their pursuit of connectedness among Connections' three subject areas. Indeed, as Bernie declared, forging curricular connections would be "the really big thing we have to do this summer." The teaching team clearly viewed that effort as involving far more than the selection of themes. For Bernie, it would include choosing a history text whose format was more compatible with thematic pedagogy. For Dan, curriculum integration would begin with each of the teachers more explicitly planting the seeds for connection through use of "key words that get said over and over." Making curricular connections more explicit was also the purpose of Bernie's call for a focusing event, "a big thing," to introduce each unit. More than beginning units with an explicit articulation of the unit's theme, thematic coherence would, as Tim counseled, be enhanced by "setting up units with projects." The project orientation that had been a hallmark of the Connections culture in the best of times needed to be even more pronounced *all* of the time. Moreover, as Sheryl's comment about the final project urged, the "best" projects would involve "all of us grading together." Doing that would require that the Connections teachers be, in Sheryl's words, "more like minded."

*Personal Systems*

As the Connections teachers discovered, forging connections is not necessarily or always the agreeable experience of the summer of 1993. When something is forged, heat and a hammer are the shaping tools. Odden (1991) describes the heat and hammer of implementation as "bargaining and transformation" (p. 191). This bargaining and transformation attempts to resolve the tensions between individual and group practicality and ideology, ambiguity and certainty, control and loss of control, plans and unanticipated events. In other words, creating a collegial community involves a process of mutual adaptation of formerly individual practices with a new collective practice. Being adaptable, being willing and able to bargain and transform, was no simple matter. But it was a matter each of the Connections teachers dealt with during their odyssey together.

At the end of the first week of school, Dan handed each of his colleagues a copy of the science course syllabus the Connections students were about to receive (appendix E). Despite the endnote advising students that "this syllabus is subject to change," Dan's syllabus did not substantially change during the course of the year. Apparently, the sequence of course content was a science curriculum item not considered negotiable in the team planning process.

Sheryl and Bernie also wrestled with the limits to which they would bargain their subject area content. On February 1, Bernie described the negotiating that had been part of both his Connections and American studies dyad experience. "The hard part has been jettisoning materials; [but] I've found out I wouldn't kill for them." The hardest decision for Bernie came with the Structures unit. Substituting a thematic perspective on the "isms" for his usual chronological flow of cause and effect represented a real sacrifice on Bernie's part. But that decision as well as the decisions to jettison projects like the trial of Galileo had unanticipated benefits. The flexible schedule allowed Bernie to complete simulations and mock trials in a single session rather than consuming almost a week of regular class sessions. Consequently, Bernie felt the projects had more coherence and meaning for students.

Sheryl, ever mindful of the school's language arts sequence of courses and the content expectations students would face in future courses, also struggled with the bargaining limits of her discipline's content. Retaining essential elements of the literary canon as well as the grammar lessons and research paper project which she felt could not be jettisoned, Sheryl surrendered the poetry and short stories included in the traditional anthology. But more than bargaining content, Sheryl transformed her pedagogical approach to that content. Consciously and conscientiously, Sheryl infused Connections themes in her teaching. Consequently, the interpretive focus for *Romeo and Juliet* was on "change" manifested in characters, and the study of *To Kill a Mockingbird* centered on "reactions" the characters Jem and Scout had to the novel's events.

But the greatest adaptation Sheryl made during the Connections year related to the heterogeneous nature of the Connections student cohort. At the beginning of the year, Sheryl voiced her concern about providing for diverse student needs and abilities "in the least noticeable manner" so that no "elitist" mentality would develop (September 14, 1993). Her previous experience with class sections of general students had made Sheryl dubious about how well they would adapt to the more challenging English content of the Connections curriculum. In her past experience, "the LD and general kids, they feed off each other. Everything has to be a joke." But in the mix of Connections, Sheryl observed "when their [LD and general students'] opinion was as valid as any others, they were more willing to take the risk" (June 3, 1994). Early on, as several general students "came through" on assignments (with imaginative myths and artistic logos, for example), the best-of-times personal cycle took hold in Sheryl's practice. As a result, Sheryl's commitment to a flexible pedagogy for success was greatly enhanced by her Connections experience. At the year's end, as she wrote about how her teaching had changed, Sheryl noted: "I like the project approach we're using in Connections. I've incorporated that into my afternoon classes. But I don't think it's as effective without the input of the other two subjects."

Bernie's experience was similar to Sheryl's. Like Sheryl, the best-of-times personal system cycle began for Bernie with early experiences of students "coming through." Bernie's repertoire of simulations and mock trials assumed a prominence they had not previously enjoyed in his practice. When Bernie wrote about how his teaching had changed during the Connections year, his characteristic staccato blips of thought listed "more student centered, more interactive, less tests, more writing."

Tim, in his experience as a learning disabilities teacher, had always viewed himself as flexible—the very nature of his work demanded flexibility. Yet, at year's end, Tim saw himself as being even more flexible. As he explained, the increased flexibility lay in the Connections experiences of teaching "other subject matter as well as other students." George Cerny also noticed the change in Tim. At the end of the May 17 meeting with visitors, when a question was raised about Tim's "floating" among subjects and teachers, George looked at Tim and said, "I'd say more than anyone else you've been revived." Tim agreed.

For Tim, Bernie, and Sheryl, the process of adapting their individual practices to their new collective Connections practice magnified personal stances that had been dormant or less developed. No great ideological shift or transformation was required for these teachers to blend their responsive (Sheryl), relational (Bernie), and caring (Tim) personal systems. Moreover, all three, and especially Sheryl, had an extensive pedagogical repertoire developed over years of practice upon which to draw. For Dan, the adaptation seemed more difficult. At the year's end, when asked how his teaching had changed, Dan wrote, "Very little actually—which may or may not be good."

Rosenholtz (1989) points out that "Shared goals about teaching should develop most readily when the daily patterns of activities in which teachers engage, and their interpretations of their engagement in those activities are congruent with a unitary definition of teaching" (p. 6). As the September 14 three-class rotation and the worst-of-times trilogy indicated, the Connections teachers did not always share a unitary definition of teaching. Conflicting personal systems had been the foundation for the worst-of-times crises. How such conflict might be averted in the formation of teaching teams remained a question implicit in Sheryl's year-end advice to anyone contemplating implementation of a Connections-like program. From her perspective, being "like-minded" was important—so important that personal systems compatibility should have been an essential component in the initial formation of the teaching team. For Connections, it had not. So, in the conversations of June 3 and 6, one central concern lay with questions of personal systems compatibility—would Dan "buy into" the Connections vision of teaching and learning, and remain a part of the teaching team? Would the coming fall's student teachers also share that vision?

*Webs to Other Ecosystems*

During the councils of June, as throughout the Connections odyssey, influences of the surrounding ecosystems of Cedar City High School and the Cedar City school district were perceptible. Pressing demands from those ecosystems encroached on the teachers' meeting time—this time in the form of year-end paperwork deadlines. The ramifications of the district's financial status impinged on the teachers' planning, this time in terms of the availability of planning time. Departmental structures also exerted their influence, this time in the form of the channels for ordering instructional materials. The administrative support that had been visible throughout the Connections year remained evident in the teachers' year-end consultations with George Cerny. Yet administrative support did not change the physical, cultural, and historical systems within the school's or district's ecosystems. Among the salient features of that ecosystem, departmental and tracking structures, financial concerns, and communication issues influenced the Connections ecosystem as it emerged.

At Cedar City High School, as at most high schools, departments were the primary organizational source of teachers' identity and community. [3] As the primary "up close community" at Cedar City High School, departments could either support or not support examination of practice, changes in practice, and constructive challenges to stances about subject matter and students (McLaughlin, 1992). When the Connections teachers introduced themselves to audiences or visitors, they always followed their names with their department affiliation (e.g., "I'm Sheryl Hart. I teach English at the high school"). But more than identity, departments at Cedar City High School influenced the Connections teachers in very practical ways. Course content in the Connections program was expected to conform to the scope and sequence of each department's adopted curriculum. Moreover, insofar as each department's curriculum reflected certain section and course designations as more appropriate to students with certain ability levels, the tracking system also influenced the Connections program. Not only did these practical considerations influence the Connections teachers' curricular choices, they also influenced each teacher's previous teaching experience. Consequently, each teacher's stance toward both students and classroom subject matter had been shaped by the department and tracking structures that were so clearly evident at Cedar City High School. As was the case with the secondary schools McLaughlin (1993) studied, departments at Cedar City High School were historically the professional communities of greatest significance to teachers' norms of practice, conception of task, and attitudes toward teaching and students.

The influence of departments was also felt in the extent of their support for Connections. In the spring, as administrators and department chairs laid plans for a possible tenth-grade version of Connections, no English teachers volunteered to join the effort. At least two math teachers expressed interest, but the tracking system made the inclusion of math difficult. After all, which course would contribute the math component was problematic when tenth grade students customarily enrolled in as many as three different math courses. The social studies department faced a somewhat similar dilemma since the current Connections students were enrolled in world history, a traditional sophomore course. That enrollment had not caused the Connections students to "miss" any course (the curriculum did not designate a ninth-grade history course). Yet taking world history as freshmen did limit their tenth-grade social studies options. The Connections teachers witnessed this departmental scramble to assemble components for a tenth-grade Connections program at the very same time that their presentation to intermediate grade teachers was met by a response that was less than enthusiastic. Also within the same time frame, the district's financial status took on black cloud proportions.

With May's levy passage far from certain and the March announcement of a reduction in staff, the once enviable position of the Connections teachers became a target for resentment. According to George Cerny, the funding for Connections materials, albeit from grant funds, consumed almost 20 percent of the school's total budget for materials (April 29, 1994). When I asked Mike Davis for his perceptions about the impact Connections had on the rest of the staff, he replied thus: "One of my concerns from the beginning was the resentment that might come with the attention given to Connections. I saw very little of that. There was some attrition to that [support] as the year wore on—the squeeze of finances for example" (June 9, 1994). In the April common planning period meetings, talk of the financial crisis and its implications for Connections' future, of local politics, and of the state of faculty-administration relations dominated. The forum designed to facilitate collaboration became the grounds for grousing.

Of all the school and district influences the Connections teachers felt, none had more impact than the state of the school's and district's lines of communication. Two important communications issues directly affected the Connections teachers. The first centered on feedback mechanisms. Feedback mechanisms provide opportunities for teachers to inform administrators about their difficulties openly and frankly in an invitational atmosphere (Gross et al., 1971). In Cedar City Schools those mechanisms were clogged. When I asked Mike Davis to identify what he thought were Connections' worst of times, he responded by saying, "I haven't built enough trust that they [the Connections teachers] would share the worst of times with me" (June 9, 1994). If informal feedback mechanisms failed to provide an open door, then the formal feedback mechanism of evaluation shut the door between administrators and teachers quite firmly. For Dan, especially, evaluation seemed to be more a threatening inspection than an opportunity to air difficulties and seek assistance. Instead of meeting with his colleagues, Dan spent one December morning cleaning his room in preparation for the formal observation scheduled for that day. Sheryl, too, was annoyed by an evaluation system that seemed more an intrusion than a mode of instructional leadership. In the highly fragmented (and from George's perspective, highly unionized) high school, evaluation served to place teachers and administrators in an adversarial relationship. The channels for feedback at Cedar City High School were not open lines of communication.

A second communication issue also profoundly affected Connections. True to Sarason's (1971) general observation about school culture, Cedar City High School's cultural system did not encourage vehicles of discussion, communication, or observation that would allow for substantive questioning, debate, encouragement, or support for either change or professional growth. With teacher lounge talk that increasingly expressed dissatisfaction, with staff meetings dominated by day-to-day concerns and clouded by teachers' mistrust of administrative promises, and with a liaison committee preoccupied with issues such as photocopying aides, the opportunities for dialogue about practice were rare exceptions within the school's culture. Consequently, the Connections teachers had little, if any, experience with the kind of democratic dialogue that defines a collegial community. When differences among the Connections teachers could no longer be ignored, the traditional school norm of mutual noninterference held sway until differences became crises. Only then, and haltingly, did the Connections teachers make of their common planning periods a forum for democratic dialogue and discussion.

In the best of times, the school and district environment supported the Connections teachers' creation of a distinct Connections ecosystem. In the worst of times, the larger school and district environment failed to equip the Connections teachers for problem solving.

## THE CONNECTIONS SHIP: A FRAGILE ECOSYSTEM

In the spring of 1993, the four Connections teachers embarked on a journey. The work of the Connections journey, in large part, was to define its own space along the continuums of autonomy to collaboration, isolation to collegiality, and individual practice to shared practice so as to create and sustain a collegial community. In a journey with many obstacles and detours as well as many triumphs, how far the Connections teachers journeyed depended on the seaworthiness of their ship. Being able to sail swiftly with favorable breezes and also ride out storms required a sturdy craft indeed. The Connections odyssey suggests that such sturdiness comes only as all of the systems within the vessel's ecosystem contribute to the progress of the journey.

On August 19, 1993, at the Connections parent meeting, Dan placed a transparency on the overhead projector. Flashed on the screen was the Connections vision statement. With that brief flash on the screen, the vision statement vanished. A tentative provisional vision, it had marked the beginning of the Connections journey. By the end of the year, three elements of the vanished vision of Connections' beginnings had become the cultural icons of Connections' best of times. Building on student interests and curiosity translated into hooking strategies. Accommodating learning styles translated into ensuring student success. Integrating subject areas became the project orientation that encouraged students to come through. The vision had been refined during the Connections year.

For the Connections teachers, that refinement process revealed their progress in building an ecosystem that could create and sustain collegial community. In the best of times, the common planning period did become a vehicle for democratic discussion and decisionmaking. In the best of times, the Connections physical system supplied opportunity. In the best of times, shared values and purposes marked the collective personal and cultural systems. In the best of times, joint teaching and close collaboration manifested mutuality. In essence, in the best of times, all of the systems within Connections' ecosystem contributed to a state of equilibrium. Such a state of equilibrium betokened a functional, healthy, and productive teaching team relationship. In other words, collegial community had been created.

Sustaining collegial community was another matter. Sustaining the collegial community that emerged during the best of times proved difficult. The overriding practicalities of daily teaching reduced discussions and decision making to coordination and accommodation and often caused a retreat to strategic individualism. How to displace the practical demands reflected in strategic individualism with interdependence *without* going through crises remained a problem. It was unsolved in the Connections experience. Certainly, sustaining the opportunity of the physical system's common planning period was not easy. Sustaining shared personal and cultural systems was even more difficult. In looking for community in structured occasions of shared projects, the Connections teachers neglected the more subtle, but more potent, features of interdependence—the way persons act or do not act in or outside of the presence of others.

Collegial community exists when there is a reciprocal relationship between the community and its individual members, when each promotes the growth of the other. For Sheryl, Tim, and Bernie, that reciprocity was present. For Dan, it was uneven. On many occasions, Dan's practical assistance was an enabling force for community endeavors. Yet the failed conversion effort and Dan's admission that his teaching had not changed during the year indicated that the community had not been as successful in promoting Dan's growth. Along the continuum from autonomy to interdependence, Dan's progress differed from that of his colleagues. At the end of the year, several unresolved issues remained. At what point do the best of times outweigh the worst of times and allow a teaching team to be considered a collegial community? Can a teaching team be considered a collegial community when profound differences in personal stances toward students and teaching separate one member from the others? Would the dynamics of creating and sustaining a collegial community have been different if the polarity of personal systems had been different—if three teachers had shared a work orientation while one adhered to a relational pedagogy, or if two had had a work orientation and two a relational stance? How would the processes of community building have been different or the same if Connections had been implemented schoolwide?

How far did the Connections teachers' odyssey take them in their journey toward collegial community? In discovering the fragility of ecosystems, the Connections teachers found that collegial community does not come easily or cheaply. Yet, as the Connections journey so clearly evidenced, the rewarding power of student success, of the best of times, was and is great indeed— so powerful that the teachers were willing to tackle that which was neither simple nor easy. Community is a process, not an event. The Connections shipmates endured obstacles and shared triumphs. They recognized their differences and attempted to reconcile them. From these shared trials and triumphs, a vision emerged. Three teachers were committed to that vision and to continuing the journey; they asked the fourth to join them.[4]

The central lesson to be learned from the Connections journey can be stated simply: above all, building a collegial community requires time. The Connections teachers' greatest fear was that their pilot program would endure a year or two and then be canceled due to financial concerns. That was what had happened to Betsy Grant's Connections-like program. Time is necessary for trust to develop, for courage to grow, for communication to become open, for commitment to develop, and for vision to emerge. A year is not time enough. For the four Connections teachers, after a year together the journey toward collegial community had just begun.

# APPENDIX A

## [CEDAR CITY] SCHOOLS VISION STATEMENT, ADOPTED 1992
## A LEARNING COMMUNITY SHAPING THE FUTURE

We believe every child can and will learn and must be actively involved in the learning process.

Recognizing that every child is unique with special talents and gifts, we pledge to respect and nurture these individual differences.

We strive to encourage curiosity, creativity and enthusiasm for learning in all students.

## [CEDAR CITY] HIGH SCHOOL VISION STATEMENT, ADOPTED 1993

We believe every child can and will learn and must be actively involved in the learning process.

We are committed to providing varied learning environments so that students can learn in an atmosphere designed to stimulate participation. These delivery systems will include cooperative and active learning techniques that develop critical thinking skills.

Recognizing that every child is unique with special talents and gifts, we pledge to respect and nurture these individual differences. We will provide a broad spectrum of classes responsive to diverse needs. Students will be encouraged to explore many fields of study from creative and artistic performance to analytic research. In all classes communication skills will be developed through frequent writing and speaking opportunities.

We strive to encourage curiousity, creativity and enthusiasm for learning in all students.

We will implement course structures that meet the curricular requirements of students including innovative scheduling such as the Connections Program, dyads, and double blocked classes. In addition to forging links between academic disciplines, our goal is to develop inquiring, responsive minds.

# APPENDIX B

## CEDAR CITY HIGH SCHOOL SCHEDULE

| Periods | Time |
|---------|------|
|  | 7:20—Building open to students |
|  | 7:30—Warning bell |
| 1 | 7:35–8:37 |
| 2 | 8:42–9:32 |
| 3 | 9:37–10:27 |
| 4 | 10:32–11:22 |
| 5 | 11:27–12:52 (Class/Lunch or Lunch/Class format) |
| 6 | 12:52—1:42 |
| 7 | 1:47—2:37 |

*Activity Schedule*

On an as-needed basis, the schedule would be altered to accommodate an "activity period" of thirty minutes between periods three and four, shortening each of the day's seven periods by five minutes. Activity period time was used for extracurricular organization meetings, class meetings, and the like. Students who did not have a meeting to attend remained in their third period classroom and used the activity time as a study period.

*Other Schedule Options*

A "Plan B" schedule provided for a one-hour delay (usually due to inclement weather) by shortening class periods to forty minutes each.

A "Pep Assembly" schedule shortened class time for periods three through seven to create fifteen minutes for a pep assembly at the end of the day.

# APPENDIX C:
# PROPOSAL LETTER

April 29, 1993

Dear [Mrs. Hart, Mr. Centers, Mr. Schwartz, and Mr. Lyons],

I am very interested in the Connections program and your work implementing it. Because Connections involves interdisciplinary study, teacher collaboration, elements of alternative assessment, and a heterogeneous mix of students, the program represents a change I would very much like to study.

Since many aspects of Connections are more about process than content in curriculum, a standard research design of pretest/posttest would not lend itself to understanding the change the students and you, as teachers, will experience. A qualitative research focus might better inform my potential research questions. My goal is not to judge Connections, but to understand how it works. I bring no preconceived theories or assumptions to such a study. While the following questions are part of my thinking, depending on how the study emerges my research focus may change direction depending on what happens on site:

Essentially, how does Connections work?

What teaching strategies are part of the Connections world?

How is collaboration worked out among you?

What administrative/curricular structures become barriers to implementing Connections?

Which are helpful?

What preservice/continuing/consultative education needs do Connections teachers come to see as important for programs like Connections?

How do students adapt to Connections?

These kinds of questions are best answered by regularly observing you and the students in your classrooms and common planning time as you go about making Connections work. The goal of such observation is to become "invisible" at [Cedar City] High School. I would also want to observe your work and study as you prepare for Connections over the summer and to look at Connections' "paper trail."

I would not want to study Connections if you were uncomfortable with my presence, and in no way do I want to disrupt or distract from the Connections process. If you have questions or concerns, I invite (indeed, welcome) your calls. I appreciate your willingness to consider my research interests.

Sincerely,

# APPENDIX D:
# PRE-TRIAL SURVEY

Your name _____

Directions: Circle SA, if you strongly agree; A, if you agree; NO, if you have no opinion; D, if you disagree; SD, if you strongly disagree.

1. Teachers should be judged by the success and failures of their students.

   SA   A   NO   D   SD

2. Young people should be taught to question authority.

   SA   A   NO   D   SD

3. The best way to learn is by example.

   SA   A   NO   D   SD

4. A wise person is someone who recognizes that he or she knows nothing.

   SA   A   NO   D   SD

5. The rights of an individual are not as important as the rights of society as a whole.

   SA   A   NO   D   SD

6. The best decisions are usually made by majority rule,

   SA   A   NO   D   SD

7. Freedom of speech should not include the right to undermine democracy.

   SA   A   NO   D   SD

8. A government has the right to impose the death penalty on serious offenders.

   SA   A   NO   D   SD

# APPENDIX E:
# SCIENCE CONNECTIONS
# SYLLABUS

SCIENCE CONNECTIONS

NAME _____ PER._____

Welcome to Science Connections! In this area of the Connections class we will engage in discovering things about the scientific world around us. Much of our time will be spent in the laboratory working through experiments thus providing us with the skills we need for solving problems. A list of the science topics we will be investigating has been provided.

There are a few items we will need for Science Connections and it is necessary for you to bring them to class everyday. The first item is a lab notebook. The lab notebook will be used for recording data based on your observations in lab, constructing tables and graphs, and answering questions at the end of each lab. Lab notebooks must be *bound* and contain graph paper. The second item is a scientific calculator. A scientific calculator is different from a standard calculator in that it has additional functions such as exponential notation, square roots and statistical functions, to name but a few. We will gain expertise in the use of scientific calculators. The third item is a pair of safety goggles which protect your eyes when working with certain chemicals or equipment in the lab. Last but not least is a pencil with eraser or an erasable pen. It is mandatory that you bring an erasable writing utensil and paper to class every day! No excuses will be accepted.

THE LAB REPORT: Lab reports will be required for each lab we complete in Science Connections. The basic lab report will consist of an INTRODUCTION, a brief outline of the PROCEDURE, a MATERIALS section including all lab materials and apparatus used, a DATA section where observations and data tables will be recorded and graphs will be constructed, and finally an ANALYSIS section where lab questions will be answered and conclusions will be drawn.

TEXTBOOK: A text book will be provided you although it is not necessary for you to bring it to class each day. The text will serve mainly as a resource for you and should be kept at home. Required reading assignments will be given periodically and it is important that you complete them on time.

HOMEWORK ASSIGNMENTS: Homework questions and problems will be assigned at the beginning of each science unit and a due date will be given. These assignments should be completed at home (or in school as time permits), using your text as a reference. The homework will consist of vocabulary words and terms, questions (to be answered in complete sentences), and problems to be worked out.

FORMAT FOR LAB REPORTS: All lab reports should include the following sections:

INTRODUCTION—a brief statement of the objective of the lab. Any hypotheses will be included here.

PROCEDURE—an outline of the procedure including all necessary steps.

MATERIALS—a list of all lab materials and lab apparatus used in the experiment.

DATA—a record of all observations made in the experiment—may include tables & graphs.

ANALYSIS—a statement of the outcome of the experiment. Your conclusion(s) will be recorded here. Also, any lab questions that were assigned will be answered here in complete sentences.

## SCIENCE TOPICS FOR CONNECTIONS CLASS:

### 1. WHAT IS SCIENCE?
The Nature of Science
the scientific method
sources of error & error analysis
use of the scientific calculator; powers of ten
introduction to graphing
instruments of science: laboratory apparatus

2. MEASURÉMENT
   SI units (the metric system)
      linear, surface area, volume
      mass, weight, & density
      units; unit conversion
      further adventures in graphing
      problem solving; set-up and solution
      scalar & vector quantities; scaling

3. FORCE, WORK AND ENERGY
   force as a vector
   gravity, weight, and inertia
   potential energy, kinetic energy, conservation of energy
   friction; work & efficiency of simple machines
   graphing; interpolation, extrapolation; "best" curve; error
      analysis
   Archimedes' principle (buoyancy); pressure & Pascal's
      principle

4. MOTION
   distance vs. displacement
   motion: speed, velocity, acceleration & momentum
   kinematics & projectile motion
   graphing motion; interpretation of motion graphs
   Newton's laws of motion

5. TEMPERATURE & HEAT
   physical states of matter
   change of state

6. ATOMS & ELEMENTS
   models of the atom
   atomic structure & electrical nature of atoms
   the periodic table
   carbon
   isotopes, radioisotopes
   nuclear forces, reactions & energy

7. CHEMICAL REACTIONS
   types of chemical bonds
   mixtures, solutions, alloys; compounds

types of chemical reactions
reaction rates and determining factors
acids, bases & salts

## 8. ELECTRICITY & MAGNETISM
charge: electric forces & fields
measurement of elec. potential, current & resistance
simple circuit design and analysis
batteries, fuses, circuit breakers, transformers & capacitors
magnetic forces & fields; magnetic domains
permanent magnets and electromagnets
electromagnetic induction; motors & generators
computer disks: floppy & hard drive

## 9. LIGHT & SOUND
waves; transverse, longitudinal, surface
    –frequency, wavelength, amplitude
found; pitch and the Doppler effect
    –A look inside the ear: How we detect and perceive
    sound
light; color and the electromagnetic spectrum
    –A look inside the eye: How we detect and perceive light
optics: reflection, refraction, mirrors, & lenses
illumination and the inverse square law
optical disc technology: audio CD, CD-ROM, & laser discs.

Note: This syllabus is subject to change.

# APPENDIX F:
# RENAISSANCE FAIR

This year in Connections we will be doing a Renaissance Fair for our exam grade in history, English, and perhaps science. The fair will be the first week back to school in January. All the logistics have not been worked out yet but it appears that we will do it at the Junior High during the afternoon and probably in the evening for our parents. You may work in teams of 1–3 people. You need to agree on a topic from either pre-Elizabethan times or the Renaissance (1300–1700). The topics are on a first-come, first-serve basis, so get your choices in early.

You may choose a person, event, idea, etc. You need to become a mini-expert on your particular topic.

Requirements: 1) You need to have visual aids and be costumed in authentic time period outfits
2) It needs to be dynamic, not static. In other words, your project must come to life, or have something that works, or involves participation, etc.
3) It must show cause and effect.
4) You must include a TYPED ANNOTATED BIBLIOGRAPHY. The general classes must use a minimum of three sources, academic must use a minimum of four sources, and honors must use a minimum of six sources. Only ONE of these sources must be an encyclopedia.

Here are some possible ideas:
[A list of fifty-three possible topics]

NEEDLESS TO SAY, THERE ARE MANY POSSIBILITIES. IF YOU NEED HELP, SEE ONE OF US FOR DIRECTION. GOOD LUCK.

# APPENDIX G:
# FINAL PROJECT
# CONNECTIONS

*Modern Technology Project*

Choose a recent technological advance (1940–present) and address the following questions:

1. What scientific research, developments, or previous technologies made this advance possible?
2. How was its use originally envisioned?
3. How is this technology used today? What are some of the experts' predictions of its future application?
4. How do you envision it being used in the future?
5. What discoveries or advances are needed to make better use of this technology?

*Problem Identification and Analysis*

Choose a problem affecting some area of [Cedar] County. Address the following criteria:

1. Define the problem and how it affects the population. That is, why is it a problem? Who does it affect? How wide-spread is the problem?
2. Research: Problem must be supported with data. Sources may include public library, "experts" (city manager, police, county offices, etc.)
3. Data: Must be presented in a clear, informative, visually oriented format.
4. Explore solutions: What is being done? What are the results? What could be done? What are the stumbling blocks?

*Invention!*

Must solve a problem.

Must present a working model or mock-up of your invention.

Must include the accepted theory(s) behind the concept of your invention.

Research: may include library, scientific texts and journals, "experts", etc.

Bibliography: May include books, magazines, journals, "expert" testimonials . . .

**All projects must follow these guidelines:**

1. Due: Monday of exam week. This grade will count as your semester 2 exam.
2. Paper: minimum 750 words typed.
3. Groups can be no larger than 3 students. Each student must identify his/her major contribution to the project.
4. Presentation:
   Oral, video, simulation, etc. in front of large group.
   Must use visually oriented materials such as posters, charts, graphs, overhead transparencies, video, drawings, etc.
   Bibliography: based on research paper style, minimum 3 to 5 sources.

# APPENDIX H:
# STUDENT FEEDBACK
# FORM — DAN CENTERS

This student feedback form is designed to assist Mr. [Centers] in determining how well he is meeting his goals in teaching this class and will help him make improvements in the future. Please circle the response that most closely matches your feelings. Do not put your name on this form. Please write any suggestions you may have on the back of this sheet. Thank you.

1. Mr. [Centers's] presentations to the class are clear and to the point.
    a. always
    b. most of the time
    c. sometimes
    d. hardly ever

2. Does Mr. [Centers] seem to know the subject matter that he is teaching to your class?
    a. knows subject matter very well
    b. knows subject matter pretty well
    c. doesn't know subject very well
    d. doesn't know subject well at all

3. I feel comfortable asking Mr. [Centers] to help me with a question or problem in class.
    a. yes
    b. pretty much so
    c. not really
    d. definitely not

4. Mr. [Centers] is helpful when assisting you personally with a question or problem.
    a. always
    b. most of the time

c. sometimes
d. hardly ever
e. can't say

5. Do you feel Mr. [Centers] communicates effectively?
    a. always
    b. most of the time
    c. sometimes
    d. hardly ever

6. Does Mr. [Centers] seem friendly?
    a. always
    b. most of the time
    c. sometimes
    d. hardly ever

7. Is Mr. [Centers] helpful when conducting a lab or assisting in the lab area?
    a. always
    b. most of the time
    c. sometimes
    d. hardly ever

8. Do you feel that Mr. [Centers] has graded your homework and test papers fairly?
    a. always
    b. most of the time
    c. sometimes
    d. hardly ever

9. The thing I like *best* about having Mr. [Centers] teach our class is:

_____

_____

_____

10. The thing I like *least* about having Mr. [Centers] teach our class is:

_____

_____

_____

# APPENDIX I

## SECOND SEMESTER KEY CONCEPTS
## IN HISTORY AND ENGLISH

Key Concepts—History
Colonialism
Imperialism
Nationalism
Capitalism
Communism
Totalitarianism
20th Century Conflicts—WWI, WWII, Future flashpoints
Dictatorships—Hitler, Stalin
Individual civil rights—Holocaust
Taxation
Industrialization
Technology
World Standard of Living Levels—1st, 2nd, 3rd world; poverty;
    world hunger
Development in Third World
Global Economy
Republics (Representative Democracy)
World Geography—maps for countries, etc.
Important people can be integrated into each unit
The question is—event driven, concept driven, or chronology
    driven—or thematic driven?

English
Concepts for 2nd semester:
human rights—equality—discrimination > Literature
    *To Kill a Mockingbird*
    Composition

research paper
(works cited)
Grammar basics—sent[ence]. structure, n v pattern,
    modifiers, gerunds, infinitives,
    participles—relate to writing process
Literature: extension of human rights, esp. related to censorship
    and freedom of choice > *Fahrenheit 451*

# APPENDIX J

A Chronology of Connections Instructional Units

| Time Frame | Unit | Activities |
|---|---|---|
| August | Bridges | Bridge building<br>Introduction to texts, highlighting, assignment notebooks |
| September–October | Beginnings | Art: Visual language/logos; pyramids, parthenons, Egyptian masks<br>Field trip: Renaissance Festival<br>Science: Measurement, graphing, lab report format (units 1 and 2)<br>English: Greek myths, *The Odyssey*, Quest project<br>History: Civilization simulation, Greeks, Trial of Socrates, Roman government, family tree project beginnings, fall of Rome—feudalism, the Middle Ages |
| October | Proficiency Test | Science: Math review<br>English: Writing practice<br>History: Citizenship review<br>Art: T-shirt project |
| November–Early January | Change Renaissance | Art: Stained glass, castles, coats of arms<br>Field trip: Art museum<br>Science: levers, torque, force, friction, simple machines (units 3 and 4)<br>English: *Romeo and Juliet*, Dear Abbess letters |

| *Time Frame* | *Unit* | *Activities* |
|---|---|---|
| | | History: Exploration (the Columbian exchange), Reformation, scientific revolution, Enlightenment (political spectrum, French Revolution, Louis XVI trial) Cross-disciplinary: Invention database/inventor report; family tree project; the Renaissance Fair. |
| Late January– February | Structures | Introduction: Envision ideal Connections structures Science: Physical/chemical properties; atomic structure, periodic table, adopt-an-element project (units 5 and 6) English: Parts of speech in sentence structures, diagrams; research paper format History: Economic, governmental, and religious structures; colonialism simulation; nationalism, alliances, and World War I |
| March–April | Reactions | Introduction: Reactions "drama," skits Field trip: County court house Science: Chemical equations (reactants and products), types of reactions, chemical bonds (unit 7) English: *To Kill a Mockingbird* (project: visual/dramatic depiction of event and reactions); research paper project (personal position on an issue) continued History: Reactions (Depression, dictators, phases of the Holocaust); Nuremberg Trial |

| Time Frame | Unit | Activities |
|---|---|---|
| May–June | Futures | Introduction: Futuristic film montage |
| | | Science: Electricity, circuits, magnetism (unit 8) |
| | | English: Science fiction short stories (elements of the genre), *Fahrenheit 451* |
| | | History: Present/future issues (genocide, quality of life, nuclear proliferation, and the first, second, and third worlds), mock United Nations |
| | | Cross-disciplinary: two-week mini-unit (twentieth-century people, events, and technology by decades); Connections final projects |

*Note:* Second-semester art projects conducted by Sharon Finch have not been included since they were not observed.

# APPENDIX K

## REFLECTING ON CONNECTIONS

Recognizing the demands on your time, please jot down your thoughts in the next couple of weeks. Then we can chat about your reflections as we have the opportunity.

If you were playing a Betsy Grant role and visiting a new Connections-like group of teachers preparing to start a program like Connections in a school like "Cedar City High School," what advice would you offer?

Still in the Betsy Grant role, and assured of confidentiality, what advice would you give to the administrators about their work with these teachers?

In looking back on the last twelve months, what would you identify as the significant moments (which may or may not be the same as the highlights)?

In being part of Connections, how did your teaching change? Think about both what you teach and how you teach.

Were there any changes in your perspective of students compared to your pre-Connections views?

What about "Cedar City High School" impacted you as a Connections teacher? Did any events, ways of doing things, or other staff members help or hinder your work in Connections?

If you had it all to do over again, or in planning for next year, what will you do the same and what will you do differently?

How well and in what ways were you able to "connect" with each other? With students? With parents?

# NOTES

## WELCOME TO CONNECTIONS

1. The school district and its administrators, teachers, and students are all identified by pseudonyms throughout this study. To further assure confidentiality, local sources which might reveal identities will also incorporate pseudonyms (e.g., Cedar City School's Annual Report). All quotations in the text that are not referenced derive from interviews or observations. If the date and/or place for these citations is significant, that information will be included parenthetically.

2. The ecological framework against which the Connections stories will be told is an adaptation of Yinger and Hendricks-Lee's (1993a, 1993b) ecological intelligence.

## CHAPTER 1

1. The "Chiefs" is the school logo and team name for the Cedar City Schools.

2. In Ohio, local school taxes can be raised only if approved by the public in a referendum called a "levy." A levy may take different forms: a bond issue, a permanent improvement levy, or an operating levy.

3. The five buildings include three elementary schools for grades K–4, an intermediate (grades 5 and 6) and junior high (grades 7 and 8) housed in the same building, and the high school.

4. Ohio requires that students pass a test, usually referred to as the ninth-grade proficiency test, in order to receive a high school diploma. Four areas compose the test: reading, writing, math, and citizenship.

5. Channel One is a daily news program produced by Whittle Communications. In exchange for classroom television sets, Cedar City High School and Junior High had subscribed to this service for three years.

## CHAPTER 2

1. Prominent among the books in George Cerny's office were copies of *Horace's Compromise* and *Horace's School* by Theodore Sizer.

2. At Cedar City High, a student fee schedule was developed each year to include consumable supplies and materials associated with specific courses.

3. As I was unable to attend this second meeting with Betsy, this information is derived from a telephone conversation with Sheryl two days later.

4. Orientation and preparation are the first two of eight levels of use Hall and Loucks (1982) have noted accompany implementation of an innovation. For discussion of the significance of time in supporting innovation, see, for example, Little 1990 and Wilson, Miller, and Yerkes 1993.

5. Cupach and Metts (1994) identify "affinity seeking" as a strategy of "facework" necessary to the development of loyalty in a relationship.

6. This understanding of personal systems is adapted from Ann Haley-Oliphant's (1994) consideration of ecological intelligence, including personal systems, within classroom settings.

7. The rotating designation of "chair" devised by the Connections team is illustrative of Judith Warren Little's (1990) observation that most school-based teams tend to be equal-status groups in which leadership roles are rarely assigned.

8. Both Odden (1991) and Louis (1991), for example, draw attention to the requirement that teachers have sufficient material resources to carry out their work.

9. The uncertainty of teacher's work is well-documented in such works as Cohen 1988, Jackson 1986, and especially Rosenholtz 1989.

10. The reference here to personal and management concerns is to the stages of concern described by Hall and Loucks (1982). Their observations are especially significant since they posit that a stage of collaboration can be reached only after the concerns of earlier stages within the Concerns Based Adoption Model—including personal and management—have been met.

## CHAPTER 3

1. The tracking system at Cedar City High School included the designations of honors (often associated with advanced placement or weighted courses), academic (or college preparatory), and general.

2. See Cohen, 1988; Hemmings & Metz, 1990; Lieberman & Miller, 1990; and especially McLaughlin, 1993).

3. An organizational saga is "a unified set of publicly expressed beliefs about the formal group that is rooted in history, claims unique

accomplishment, and is held with sentiment by the group." (Clark, 1972, p. 178–79)

4. See Fiedler & Garcia, 1987; Cohen, 1988; Jackson, 1986; and especially Rosenholtz, 1989.

# CHAPTER 4

1. Orange textbooks were given to academic and honors students; white textbooks to general students. *The Odyssey* was included in both. The white volume provided an abridged or digest version for many of the epic's books.

2. As Bowers and Flinders (1990) point out, this differentiation in social spacing patterns, or proxemics, is a form of communication that often unconsciously conveys cultural and personal messages.

3. On September 14, the white board encapsulated Sheryl's teaching as "Library," "Formal Essay," "Quest Assignment," and "Test." Bernie's plans were labeled "Intro to Greeks," "Socrates Trial," and "Library." Dan's science work bore the nondescript descriptors of "Lab on Force," "Lab prep," "Lab," and "Go over Lab." Tim's role for the week was noted by "Architecture" for Wednesday and by "and Tim" in Dan's column on Monday and in Bernie's column on Tuesday and Friday.

4. Flinders (1988) has noted that in the tension between collegiality and the task demands of instruction, teachers attach value to collegial interaction in terms of its potential for immediate positive impact on their ability to complete instructional tasks.

5. Relational teaching here refers to the dialogic process described by Marcia Baxter-Magolda (1995). In this process the teacher introduces his/her knowledge in the context of students' perspectives rather than imposing that knowledge unilaterally.

6. These conceptions are consistent with Jackson's (1986) metaphor of "knowledge transformation" and Bowers and Flinders' (1990) "responsive teaching."

7. Such studies have noted that high school teachers belong to distinct subject subcultures characterized by differing beliefs, norms, and practices. Grossman and Stodolsky (1995), for example, contrast the perceptions of math teachers and those of other content areas as to the sequentiality, degree of definition, and static character of their discipline. They conclude that reform efforts such as detracking and interdisciplinary curriculum will meet resistance stemming from such differences.

8. In coining this term, Bowers and Flinders (1990) explain that "responsive" denotes the teacher's both being aware of and responding to the total classroom environment in educationally constructive ways.

This conception of teaching echoes Huberman's (1993) "tinkerer model."

9. In Ohio, tenure is linked to both years of teaching experience in a district *and* level of certification in a tiered system of licensure. Consequently, despite their years of teaching experience in Cedar City schools, Dan, Sheryl, and Tim did not hold the "professional" level certification required to earn tenure.

10. Cedar City High School was applying for a grant from the Ohio Network for Training and Assistance for Schools and Communities (ON-TASC). A follow-up ON-TASC survey figures in the narrative in chapter 6.

11. My intent is *not* to portray Dan in an unflattering light. Rather, the point is that differences in pedagogy and philosophy existed between Dan and the other members of the Connections teaching team, and those differences mattered in the team's odyssey toward community, collaboration, and collegiality.

## CHAPTER 5

1. During the fifth week of each quarter Cedar City teachers issued "midterms." Midterms were progress reports sent to parents of students whose academic status was of concern.

2. See McLaughlin 1991 and Odden 1991.

## CHAPTER 6

1. Seymour Sarason offers an elegant description of this norm in *The Culture of the School and the Problem of Change* (1971).

2. Facework, as conceptualized by Goffman (1967) and Cupach & Metts (1994), is a tacit cooperative principle operating in social relationships whereby people support each other in maintaining "face." Facework *can* take the form of avoidance or disengagement *or* it may be seen in "positive tone"—a process of sense-making without casting blame. For a more thorough analysis of facework in Connections worst of times, see Dorsch (1996).

3. Here I am using the term *loyalty* in the same sense as Hirschman 1970, where loyalty is a preference or judgment to attempt the uncertainty of improvement (rather than exit) in the face of a deterioration in the quality of the service provided by an organization.

4. Gloria Ladson-Billings's (1995) discussion of the distinction between curriculum integration and curriculum coherence is particularly illuminating.

CHAPTER 7

1. This conversation among Sheryl, Tim, and Bernie is recounted in "The Vision Thing Tale" in the preceding chapter, and so is not repeated here.

2. This typology of connections is adapted from McLaughlin 1993.

3. The influence of departments is noted by Johnson (1990), Little (1992), and McLaughlin (1992).

4. Dan *did* continue the journey as part of the Connections teaching team for the program's second year.

# BIBLIOGRAPHY

Astuto, T. A., & Clark, D. L. (1991). Challenging the limits of school restructuring and reform. In A. Lieberman (Ed.), *The changing contexts of teaching* (pp. 90–109). Chicago: University of Chicago Press.

Baxter-Magolda, M. B. (1995, April). *Connecting teaching to students' lived experience: Relational pedagogy.* Paper presented at the annual meeting of the American Educational Research Association, San Francisco.

Bellah, R. N., Madsen, R., Sullivan, W. M., Swidler, A., & Tipton, S. M. (1985). *Habits of the heart: Individualism and commitment in American life.* Berkeley: University of California Press.

Bolman, L. G., & Deal, T. E. (1991). *Reframing organizations: Artistry, choice, and leadership.* San Francisco: Jossey Bass.

Bowers, C. A., & Flinders, D. J. (1990). *Responsive teaching: An ecological approach to classroom patterns of language, culture, and thought.* New York: Teachers College Press.

Brown, J. (1993). Leadership for school improvement. *Emergency Librarian, 20*(3), 8–20.

Bruner, J. (1986). *Actual minds, possible worlds.* Cambridge: Harvard University Press.

[Cedar City] High School. (1993). *[Cedar City] High School student handbook 1993–1994.* [Cedar City,] OH: Author.

[Cedar City] Schools. (1993). *Annual Report 1992–1993.* [Cedar City,] OH: Author.

[Cedar] County Convention & Visitors Bureau. (1994). *Visitors Guide.* [Cedar City,] OH: Author.

Clark, B. R. (1972). The organizational saga in higher education. *Administrative Science Quarterly, 17*(2), 178–84.

Cohen, D. K. (1988). Teaching practice: Plus que ca change . . . In P. W. Jackson (Ed.), *Contributing to educational change* (pp. 27–84). Berkeley: McCutchan.

Cohen, M. (1987). Improving school effectiveness: Lessons from research. In V. Richardson-Koehler (Ed.), *Educators' handbook: A research perspective* (pp.474–90). New York: Longman.

"Connections" make [Cedar City] freshmen smile, laugh, listen, learn (September 15, 1993). [*Cedar City weekly newspaper*], 8–B.

*Connections newsletter* (1993, August).

Cupach, W. R., & Metts, S. (1994). *Facework*. Thousand Oaks, CA: Sage.

Denzin, N. K. (1989). *Interpretive interactionism*. Newbury Park, CA: Sage.

Dewey, J. (1966). *Democracy and education*. New York: Free Press. (Original work published 1916)

The district keeps growing, and growing, and growing . . . (1994, January) *[Cedar City] School Slate*, p. 4.

Dorsch, N. G. (1996, April). *Conflict and collegiality: A dialectic of community-building in an interdisciplinary teaching team's first year.* Paper presented at the annual meeting of the American Educational Research Association, New York City.

Drake, S. M. (1993). *Planning integrated curriculum: The call to adventure*. Alexandria, VA: Association for Supervision and Curriculum Development.

Eisner, E. W. (1988). The ecology of school improvement: Some lessons we have learned. *Educational Leadership, 45*(5), 24–29.

Fiedler, F. E., & Chemers, M. M. (1984). *Improving leadership effectiveness: The leader match concept* (2nd ed.). New York: John Wiley & Sons.

Fiedler, F. E., & Garcia, J. E. (1987). *New approaches to effective leadership: Cognitive resources and organizational performance*. New York: John Wiley & Sons.

Flinders, D. J. (1988). Teacher isolation and the new reform. *Journal of Curriculum and Supervision, 4*(1), 17–29.

Freire, P. (1983). The importance of the act of reading. *Journal of Education, 165*(1), 5–11.

Fullan M. G. (1990). Change processes in secondary schools: Toward a more fundamental agenda. In M. W. Mclaughlin, J. E. Talbert, & N. Bascia (Eds.), *The contexts of teaching in secondary schools: Teachers' realities* (pp. 224–55). New York: Teachers College Press.

Fullan, M. (1993). Innovation, reform, and restructuring strategies. In G. Cawelti (Ed.), *Challenges and achievements of American education: 1993 yearbook of the Association for Supervision and Curriculum Development* (pp. 116–33). Alexandria, VA: Association for Supervision and Curriculum Development.

Goffman, E. (1967). *Interaction ritual: Essays on face-to-face behavior*. New York: Pantheon.

Goodlad, J. (1994). *What schools are for* (2nd ed.). Bloomington, IN: Phi Delta Kappan Educational Foundation.

Gross, N., Giacquinta, J. B., & Bernstein, M. (1971). *Implementing organizational innovations: A sociological analysis of planned educational change*. New York: Basic Books.

Grossman, P. L., & Stodolsky, S. S. (1995). Content as context: The role of school subjects in secondary school teaching. *Educational Researcher, 24*(8), 5–11, 23.

Haley-Oliphant, A. E. (1994, March). *Exploring the teaching of math and science in an urban setting: Emergent conversations regarding the ecological systems in a healthy classroom.* Paper presented at the annual convention of the National Association of Research in Science Teaching, Anaheim, CA.

Haley-Oliphant, A. E., & Yinger, R. J. (1993). *A metaphorical analysis of science lessons in a middle school classroom: Making meaning in the margins of instruction.* Paper presented at the annual convention of the National Association of Research in Science Teaching, Atlanta, GA.

Hall, G. E., & Loucks, S. F. (1982). Bridging the gap: Policy research rooted in practice. In A. Lieberman & M. W. Mclaughlin (Eds.), *Policy making in education: Eighty-first yearbook of the National Society for the Study of Education* (pp. 133–58). Chicago: University of Chicago Press.

Hargreaves, A. (1993). Individualism and inidviduality: Reinterpreting the teacher culture. In J. W. Little & M. W. McLaughlin (Eds.), *Teachers' work* (pp. 51–76). New York: Teachers College Press.

Hemmings, A., & Metz, M. H. (1990). Real teaching: How high school teachers negotiate societal, local, community, and student pressures when they define their work. In R. Page & L. Valli (Eds.), *Curriculum differentiation* (pp. 91–111). Albany: State University of New York Press.

High school prepares for interdisciplinary learning (March 13, 1993). [*Cedar City weekly newspaper*], 2-A.

Hirschman, A. O. (1970). *Exit, voice, and loyalty: Responses to decline in firms, organizations, and states.* Cambridge: Harvard University Press.

Huberman, M. (1993). The model of the independent artisan in teachers' professional relations. In J. W. Little & M. W. McLaughlin (Eds.), *Teachers' work* (pp. 11–50). New York: Teachers College Press.

Jackson, P. W. (1986). *The practice of teaching.* New York: Teachers College Press.

Johnson, S. M. (1990). The primacy and potential of high school departments. In M. W. McLaughlin, J. E. Talbert, & N. Bascia (Eds.), *The contexts of teaching in secondary schools: Teachers' realities* (pp. 167–84). New York: Teachers College Press.

Joyce, B., Wolf, J., & Calhoun, E. (1993). *The self-renewing school.* Alexandria, VA: Association for Supervision and Curriculum Development.

Kahne, J. (1994). Democratic communities, equity, and excellence: A Deweyan reframing of educational policy analysis. *Educational Evaluation and Policy Analysis, 16*(3), 233–48.

Ladson-Billings, G. (1995). A coherent curriculum in an incoherent society? Pedagogical perspectives on curriculum reform. In J. A. Beane (Ed.), *Toward a coherent curriculum: 1995 yearbook of the Association for Supervision and Curriculum Development* (pp. 158–69). Alexandria, VA: Association for Supervision and Curriculum Development.

Lieberman, A. (1982). Practice makes policy: The tensions of school improvement. In A. Lieberman & M. W. Mclaughlin (Eds.), *Policy making in education: Eighty-first yearbook of the National Society for the Study of Education* (pp. 249–69). Chicago: University of Chicago Press.

Lieberman, A., & Miller, A. (1990). The social realities of teaching. In A. Lieberman (Ed.), *Schools as collaborative cultures* (pp. 153–63). New York: Falmer Press.

Little, J. W. (1990). Teachers as colleagues. In A. Lieberman (Ed.), *Schools as collaborative cultures* (pp. 165–93). New York, Falmer Press.

Little, J. W. (1991). Opening the black box of professional community. In A. Lieberman (Ed.), *The changing contexts of teaching* (pp. 157–78). Chicago: University of Chicago Press.

Little, J. W., & McLaughlin, M. W. (1993). Conclusion. In J. W. Little & M. W. McLaughlin (Eds.), *Teachers' work* (pp. 185–90). New York: Teachers College Press.

Louis, K. S. (1991). Restructuring and the problem of teachers' work. In A. Lieberman (Ed.) *The changing contexts of teaching* (pp. 138–56). Chicago: University of Chicago Press.

Marshall, H. H. (1988). Worker learning: Implications of classroom metaphors. *Educational Researcher, 17*(9), 9–16.

Marshall, H. H. (1990). Beyond the workplace metaphor: The classroom as a learning setting. *Theory into Practice, 29*(2), 94–101.

McLaughlin, M. W. (1991). The Rand change agent study: Ten years later. In A. R. Odden (Ed.), *Education policy implementation* (pp. 143–55). Albany, NY: State University of New York Press.

McLaughlin, M. W. (1992). How district communities do and do not foster teacher pride. *Educational Leadership, 50*(1), 33–35.

McLaughlin, M. W. (1993). What matters most in teachers' workplace context? In J. W. Little & M. W. McLaughlin (Eds.), *Teachers' work* (pp. 79–103). New York: Teachers College Press.

Morgan, G. (1986). *Images of organization.* Newbury Park, CA: Sage Publications.

National Commission on Excellence in Education. (1983). *A nation at risk*. Washington, DC: Author.

Odden, A. R. (Ed.). (1991). *Education policy implementation*. Albany, NY: State University of New York Press.

Ohio Department of Education. (1990). *Ohio speaks: Working together to shape the future of special education*. Worthington: Author.

Ohio School Boards Association. (1990). *An analysis of S.B. 140 the Omnibus Education Reform Act of 1989*. Columbus: Author.

Palmer, P. (1987, September/October). Community, conflict, and ways of knowing: Ways to deepen our educational agenda. *Change*, pp. 20–25.

Pauly, E. (1991). *The classroom crucible: What really works, what doesn't, and why*. New York: Basic Books.

Peck, M. S. (1987). *The different drum*. New York: Simon & Schuster.

Pellegrin, R. J. (1976). Schools as work settings. In R. Dubin (Ed.), *Handbook of work, organizations, and society*. Skokie, IL: Rand McNally.

Purpel, D. E. (1989). *The moral and spiritual crisis in education: A curriculum for justice and compassion in education*. New York: Bergin & Garvey.

Rosenholtz, S. J. (1989). *Teachers' workplace: The social organization of schools*. New York: Longman.

Sarason, S. B. (1971). *The culture of the school and the problem of change*. Boston: Allyn and Bacon.

Sergiovanni, T. J. (1992). *Moral leadership: Getting to the heart of school improvement*. San Francisco: Jossey-Bass.

Skrtic, T. M. (1991). The special education paradox: Equity as the way to excellence. *Harvard Educational Review*, 61(2), 148–95.

Staff profile. (1993, October). *[Cedar City] School Slate*, p. 3.

Teachers speak out. (May 4, 1994). [Cedar City weekly newspaper], 9-C.

What is "Connections"? (1993, March). *[Cedar City] School Slate*, p. 4.

Wilson, S. M., Miller, C., & Yerkes, C. (1993). Deeply rooted change: A tale of learning to teach adventurously. In D. K. Cohen, M. W. Mclaughlin, & T. E. Talbert (Eds.), *Teaching for understanding: Challenges for policy and practice* (pp. 84–129). San Francisco: Jossey-Bass.

Yinger, R. J., & Hendricks-Lee, M. (1993a). Working knowledge in teaching. In C. Day, J. Calderhead, & P. Denicolo (Eds.), *Research on teacher thinking: Understanding professional development* (pp. 100–23). Washington, DC: Falmer Press.

Yinger, R. J., & Hendricks-Lee, M. S. (1993b). An ecological conception of teaching. *Learning and Individual Differences*, 5(4), 269–81.

# INDEX